# ASSESSING STUDENTS' DIGITAL READING PERFORMANCE

This book provides a systematic study of the Programme for International Student Assessment (PISA) based on big data analysis, aiming to examine the contextual factors relevant to students' digital reading performance.

The author first introduces the research landscape of educational data mining (EDM) and reviews the PISA framework since its launch and how it has become an important metric to assess the knowledge and skills of students from across the globe. With a focus on methodology and its applications, the book explores extant scholarship on the dynamic model of educational effectiveness, multi-level factors of digital reading performance, and the application of EDM approaches. The core chapter on the methodology examines machine learning algorithms, hierarchical linear modeling, mediation analysis, and data extraction and processing for the PISA dataset. The findings give insights into the influencing factors of students' digital reading performance, allowing for further investigations on improving students' digital reading literacy and more attention to the advancement of education effectiveness.

The book will appeal to scholars, professionals, and policymakers interested in reading education, educational data mining, educational technology, and PISA, as well as students learning how to utilize machine learning algorithms in examining the mass global database.

**Jie HU** is Professor of the Department of Linguistics at the School of International Studies at Zhejiang University, China. Her research interests include PISA/PIRLS Reading Test, Digital Reading, and Educational Technology.

# ASSESSING STUDENTS' DIGITAL READING PERFORMANCE

An Educational Data Mining Approach

*Jie HU*

LONDON AND NEW YORK

Designed cover image: © Getty Images

This book is supported by the National Social Science Fund of China, "Construction and Research on the Multidimensional Evaluation of the Database of Chinese Second Language Students' Reading Literacy" [Grant Number: 21BYY024].

First published in English 2023
by Routledge
4 Park Square, Milton Park, Abingdon, Oxon OX14 4RN

and by Routledge
605 Third Avenue, New York, NY 10158

*Routledge is an imprint of the Taylor & Francis Group, an informa business*

© 2023 Jie HU

The right of Jie HU to be identified as author of this work has been asserted in accordance with sections 77 and 78 of the Copyright, Designs and Patents Act 1988.

All rights reserved. No part of this book may be reprinted or reproduced or utilised in any form or by any electronic, mechanical, or other means, now known or hereafter invented, including photocopying and recording, or in any information storage or retrieval system, without permission in writing from the publishers.

*Trademark notice*: Product or corporate names may be trademarks or registered trademarks, and are used only for identification and explanation without intent to infringe.

English version by permission of Zhejiang University Press

*British Library Cataloguing-in-Publication Data*
A catalogue record for this book is available from the British Library

ISBN: 978-1-032-39730-6 (hbk)
ISBN: 978-1-032-40315-1 (pbk)
ISBN: 978-1-003-35110-8 (ebk)

DOI: 10.4324/9781003351108

Typeset in Bembo
by codeMantra

# CONTENTS

*List of figures* vii
*List of tables* ix
*List of abbreviations* xi

1　Introduction　1

2　Literature review　48

3　Methodology　58

4　Results　165

5　Discussion　170

6　Conclusion and limitation　178

*Appendix: The detailed description of the original 146 variables/factors*　181
*Index*　221

# FIGURES

| | | |
|---|---|---|
| 1.1 | The main domains related to EDM | 2 |
| 1.2 | The framework of PISA 2018 | 9 |
| 2.1 | The dynamic model of educational effectiveness | 50 |
| 3.1 | The classification of machine learning algorithms | 59 |
| 3.2 | The AI process loop | 59 |
| 3.3 | An illustrative example of DT binary classification about high performers and low performers in the study | 60 |
| 3.4 | An illustrative example of RF binary classification of high performers and low performers in reading | 62 |
| 3.5 | An illustrative example of XGBoost classification of good readers and poor readers | 63 |
| 3.6 | An illustrative example of Bayesian network about the determinants of the quality of recommendation letter | 63 |
| 3.7 | The structure of ANNs | 64 |
| 3.8 | The structure of PISA data | 65 |
| 3.9 | Various hyperplanes that could divide the training data into two groups | 66 |
| 3.10 | The basic model of SVM | 67 |
| 3.11 | The graphic illustration of ten-fold cross-validation | 70 |
| 3.12 | The different types of classification results | 72 |
| 3.13 | A conceptual diagram of a simple mediation model with a single mediator variable M causally located between $X$ and $Y$ | 116 |
| 3.14 | A statistical diagram of simple mediation model with a single mediator variable $M$ causally located between $X$ and $Y$ | 119 |

| | | |
|---|---|---:|
| 3.15 | A conceptual diagram of a simple mediation model with statistical controls | 127 |
| 3.16 | A statistical diagram representing a parallel multiple mediator model with $k$ mediators | 132 |
| 3.17 | A serial multiple mediator models in statistical diagram form with two mediators | 134 |
| 3.18 | A statistical diagram of the simple mediation model with a multicategorical antecedent $X$ with g categories | 137 |
| 3.19 | The 38 OECD countries selected in this study | 152 |
| 4.1 | The five-fold cross-validation for the SVM model | 166 |

# TABLES

| | | |
|---|---|---|
| 1.1 | The patterns and algorithms used in EDM | 3 |
| 3.1 | The confusion matrix | 72 |
| 3.2 | Demographic information of samples | 153 |
| 4.1 | The classification performance of the two SVM models | 165 |
| 4.2 | The ranking and detailed description of the top 20 factors | 167 |
| 5.1 | The ranking of the student-level factors | 171 |
| 5.2 | The ranking of the classroom-level factors | 173 |
| 5.3 | The ranking of the school-level factors | 175 |

# LIST OF ABBREVIATIONS

| | |
|---|---|
| ACC | accuracy score |
| AI | artificial intelligence |
| ANCOVA | analysis of covariance |
| ANOVA | analysis of variance |
| ANN | artificial neural network |
| AUC | area under curve |
| CFA | confirmatory factor analysis |
| CFI | comparative fit index |
| CI | confidence interval |
| CV | cross validation |
| DM | data mining |
| DT | decision tree |
| EDM | educational data mining |
| EER | educational effectiveness research |
| EFA | exploratory factor analysis |
| EM | expectation maximization |
| ESCS | economic socio-cultural status |
| ESEM | exploratory structural equation model |
| FML | full information maximum likelihood |
| FRL | free and reduced lunch |
| GDP | gross domestic product |
| GEE | generalized estimation equations |
| GFI | goodness of fit index |
| GLS | generalized least squares |
| HLM | hierarchical linear models |
| IALS | International Adult Literacy Survey |
| ICC | intra-class correlation co efficient |

| | |
|---|---|
| ICT | information and communications technology |
| IDI | information development index |
| IEA | International Association for the Evaluation of Educational Achievement |
| IFI | incremental fit index |
| IQ | intelligence quotient |
| IRT | Item Response Theory |
| KNN | K-Nearest Neighbor |
| LA | learning analytics |
| LR | logistic regression |
| MBA | master of business administration |
| MCC | Matthews correlation coefficient |
| MI | imputation with several variables |
| ML | maximum likelihood |
| MLM | multi-level modeling |
| NAEP | National Assessment of Educational Progress |
| NB | naive Bayes |
| NN | neural network |
| NNFI | non-normed fit index |
| OECD | Organization for Economic Cooperation and Development |
| OLS | ordinary least squares |
| PA | path analysis |
| PIRLS | Progress in International Reading Literacy Study |
| PISA | Programme for International Student Assessment |
| Q & A | question and answer |
| RAM | McDonald Network Motion Model |
| RF | random forest |
| RML | restricted maximum likelihood |
| RMSEA | root mean square error of approximation |
| ROC | receiver operating characteristic |
| SEM | structural equation model |
| SEN | sensitivity score |
| SER | school effectiveness research |
| SES | students' socioeconomic status |
| SPE | specificity score |
| SPSS | statistical product service solutions |
| SR | structural equation models |
| SRL | self-regulated learning |
| SRMR | standardized root mean square residual |
| SVC | support vector classification |
| SVM | support vector machine |
| SVM–RFE | support vector machine-recursive feature elimination |
| SVM-RFE-CV | support vector machine-recursive feature elimination-cross-validation |

| | |
|---|---|
| TER | teacher effectiveness research |
| TIMSS | Trends in International Mathematics and Science Study |
| TLI | Tucker–Lewis index |
| USA | United States of America |
| WABA | Within Analysis Between Analysis |
| WEKA | Waikato Environment for Knowledge Analysis |
| XGBoost | extreme gradient boosting |

# 1
# INTRODUCTION

## 1.1 Educational data mining (EDM): A promising field

### 1.1.1 The definition of EDM

In the era of information explosion, huge amounts of data entail advanced techniques to examine the hidden and nontrivial relationships between different variables (Alonso-Fernández et al., 2019). Data mining (DM) is defined as a computer-based information system (Vlahos, et al., 2004) applicable to scan large datasets and discover latent knowledge (Alejandro, 2014). It could help discover the patterns and rules behind the dazzling data ocean and identify the complex relationship between various parameters (Križanić, 2020). Penetrating all fields, it can be recognized as an effective tool for building knowledge management systems (Gantasala et al., 2009).

Large repositories of educational data have been produced by a series of technology-enhanced learning applications, including learning software, online/blended education, and large educational large-scale dataset built by states or organizations, to name a few (Romero & Ventura, 2017, 2020). Effective tools to automatically analyze this kind of data are thus urgently needed because of all this information provides a goldmine that can be explored and exploited (Baker, 2015). By collecting and analyzing some metrics such as individual student engagement data, test scores, and the number or length of video views, EDM helps teachers optimize their teaching programs and support students in adjusting their learning strategies, improving engagement and learning performance, thus helping teachers improve teaching efficiency and allowing students to have a more personalized learning experience (Figure 1.1).

Assessment underpinning by big data could be reliable and effective to evaluate the performance of the students, ascertain their drawbacks and merits and shed

DOI: 10.4324/9781003351108-1

**2** Introduction

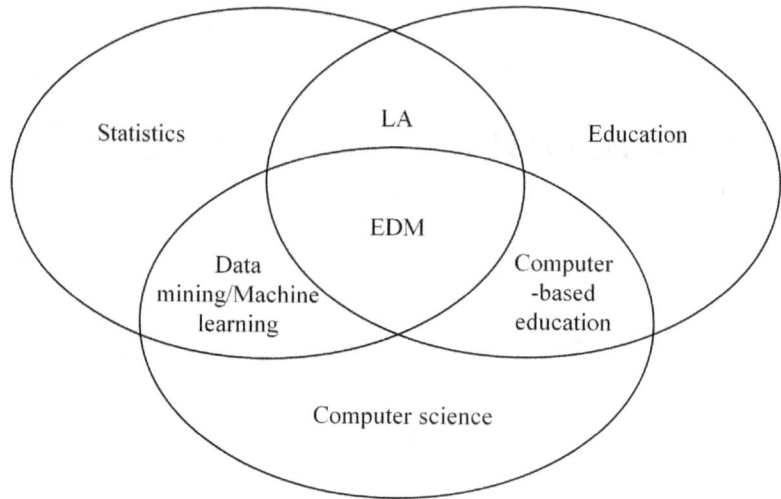

**FIGURE 1.1** The main domains related to EDM.

light on their future development. In addition, with the help of DM approaches, researchers could better clarify what specific competencies are required and are becoming gradually essential for students. In this way, EDM could conduce to leveraging data for improving student performance, providing insights for policymakers around the globe to make education-related decisions, and calling for growing attention to education amelioration (Table 1.1).

### 1.1.2 Major approach patterns and research topics of EDM

### 1.1.3 The impact of EDM on educational factors

Educational data mining (EDM) provides teaching decision-making and learning support services. These powerful and effective technologies could help educators improve teaching quality and conduce to the self-diagnosis of the students. The two interact with learning resources in both directions, optimizing the allocation of learning resources, and education managers regulate and control according to the actual situation. The innate complexities of education indicate that it is a group of factors that interact and collectively promote effective teaching. The purpose of EDM is to predict the development trend of learners, promote effective learning, and make the educational ecosystem operate better.

#### 1.1.3.1 The impact on students

Students are the subject of learning and the main source of educational data. The data generated are mainly divided into the following four types: learners' own

**TABLE 1.1** The patterns and algorithms used in EDM

| Methods | Mechanism | Algorithms | Application to EDM |
| --- | --- | --- | --- |
| Classification & regression | Prediction of the category of data object (discrete variable) or its value (continuous variable) | Decision tree, Bayesian network, support vector machine, logistic regression | Student achievement prediction, learning style prediction, judging whether students drop out of school, etc. |
| Clustering | The process of dividing a set of data objects into classes composed of similar objects | K-means, fuzzy c means, etc. | Keywords cluster analysis, student grouping, etc. |
| Association rules | Discovery of associations or dependencies between data objects | Apriori algorithm, FP Tree frequency set algorithm | Course recommendation, correlation analysis, etc. |
| Recommendation system | Recommend resources that may be preferred to users | Collaborative filtering, content-based recommendation, hybrid recommendation, etc. | Recommendation of Personalized learning resources such as test questions and learning methods |

learning situation data, learning behavior process data, learning evaluation stage result data, and learning feedback stage data. First, through the cleaning and mining of learning situation analysis data, EDM technology comprehensively analyzes the basic situation of the students learning style, learning motivation, and learning ability, so as to make a learner portrait of the students' early comprehensive ability (e.g., HU et al., 2021). Second, as one of the key technologies of EDM, time series analysis technology can track, collect, process, and analyze learners' behavior data and phased learning evaluation data for a long time and evaluate the learners' learning status and learning efficiency, so as to generate personalized learning performance reports at different stages, which is helpful for parents, teachers, and students themselves to monitor their learning status. Third, for the problems in the learning process, the real-time data feedback system can carry out real-time regulation according to the results of DM analysis and provide learning analysis and diagnosis reports to help students make periodic adjustments. Fourth, student performance prediction helps to forecast students' future learning performance through existing data, which is one of the earliest and most popular applications of EDM (Romero & Ventura, 2010). Based on the preliminary data results, EDM technology deeply excavates the preliminary results of DM again, explores the learning law of the educated, integrates various factors, speculates the development trend of the educated, explores its potential, and assists the educated in objective and comprehensive self-cognition (Abu, 2016).

### 1.1.3.2 The impact on instructors

The factors of the educational environment do not exist independently. They are interrelated and work together. The two-way interaction between educators and students is a crucial link. Therefore, educators' teaching activities are mostly based on students' data results.

EDM technology provides learners' portrait models in the early stage of students. On the basis of machine-intelligent judgment, educators integrate their own understanding of the reality of the students and carry out auxiliary portraits to make the result more reliable. At the teaching preparation stage, educators inevitably and actively interact with learning resources, using a large number of teaching resource databases to generate a personal teaching resource database. With the help of EDM technology, the educators could quickly generate a reasonable teaching plan and adjust it according to the different conditions of the educated and the factors such as teaching cycle, teaching purpose, and teaching object. At the same time, students are comprehensively analyzed according to their phased evaluation results, discussion data of the learning process, and final data of course evaluation. The standard of educational evaluation is not limited to achievement, but comprehensive evaluation in combination with various dimensions; students' learning style, learning attitude, learning interest points, and other aspects of the educated change dynamically. Therefore, the process of EDM continuously provides comprehensive learning situation data for the educated, and the educators adjust the teaching strategies to improve and adapt to teaching (Guleria et al., 2013).

### 1.1.3.3 The impact on educational policymakers

Educational institutions are increasingly being held accountable for the academic success of their students. The system framework of intelligent education management mainly includes four systems: educational visual management and control, educational intelligent decision support, educational security early warning, and educational remote supervision. The progress of education big data collection and mining technology makes up for the lack of unified and standardized data storage in the past, the low intelligence and practical value of data processing results, the untimely feedback of education data results, and the difficulties in real-time regulation. EDM technology presents the data results in the educational management system in the form of charts, videos, modeling, etc., and it is much easier for the human brain to process visual information than written information such as words. Therefore, educational managers can quickly and deeply understand the information behind the data in multiple dimensions, and timely and scientifically regulate the problems and general direction. The traditional decision support system needs people's participation, uses various quantitative models to manipulate data, and only provides support for semi-structured, structured, and clear process decision-making problems. In the process of intelligent education management, the program of data operation is complex and the data model is diverse, so some complex decision-making problems are given directional decision-making opinions through EDM technology combined with the data generated by previous human processing experience and their own prediction results; The important role of education management is to find out the problems existing in the education system and take measures to solve the problems, so as to prevent them and avoid them. The intelligent education management system uses the prediction function of education DM to analyze the development trend and small problems of the education system in the process of teaching and learning, and give warnings and reminders in time to escort the healthy operation of the education system; Education managers macro-control the operation of the whole education system from the perspective of managers, and the circulation, processing, analysis, and application of data are under supervision. Therefore, correct supervision is indispensable. The correct management of education managers promotes the flow of data, and the data flow promotes the correct and efficient guidance and supervision of Education managers, which is a virtuous circle.

### 1.1.3.4 The impact on educational resources

An educational resource is the only objective thing among the four elements, which is not mixed with subjective emotion, so it can better reflect the role of EDM. Education development is increasingly showing a personalized and accurate trend, which is also the result of paying attention to "small data" in big data. What needs to be positioned is not only the trend of the overall environment of the whole education system but also the growth and development of every educator and student. As a kind of big data, educational resources are processed through a series of technologies such as data cleaning, data integration, data reduction, and data transformation. Their own resources are a preliminary data screening, leaving some high-quality resources. Therefore, the circulation and sharing of resources is an important link. The model of "educational resources + educators + students" can promote the reproduction of educational resources. Therefore, the establishment of an educational resource-sharing platform is very important. The development of "small" data (or targeted data) is also indispensable to the overall trend. Educators and students interact dynamically with educational resources in the teaching process. After their interests, types, and frequency of using resources are continuously recorded, it can be targeted to form a personalized learning resource database to meet individual needs. The main audience of educational resources is still the students: most of the high-quality educational resources produced by educators are to facilitate the students to master and deeply understand knowledge in the learning process. After the students' access data to the materials are converted and calculated, combined with their learning hobbies, learning interests, and other dimensions, the system intelligently recommends appropriate educational resources that can arouse their interest in learning to the students so as to improve their learning efficiency.

### 1.1.4 The advantages of EDM

Compared with the traditional way of processing educational data, EDM technology makes the value of data further explored, makes data increasingly transformed into data assets, and truly facilitates the development of education with the help of intelligent means. The specific advantages are mainly reflected in four aspects, namely, the depth of data processing, the personalization of data analysis, the visualization of analysis results, and the high efficiency of data utilization.

The program logic of data processing is becoming increasingly rigorous. Deep learning is the further development of neural network algorithm. Multi-layer feature extraction is carried out on the input data to obtain a feature set more suitable for classification, so that the machine can better learn the laws between data, to improve the accuracy of prediction or classification of new samples. Deep learning at the technical level promotes the in-depth development of participants in the process of teaching and learning. The learning of data statistics, educational psychology, and other knowledge are becoming more and more popular, and the improvement of people's own skills is indispensable. The data results of machine in-depth processing are processed manually to make the data results closer to the reality of life and better used by participants in the process of education.

In the big data environment, learning support services such as learning resources, learning behavior analysis, and learning assistance are not only realized on the basis of "big" data but also tend to systematically match the individual student and adapt to the development of the students. In the era of big data, data analysis results are no longer confined to the static and single form of traditional charts. New visual presentation methods are dynamic and interactive, such as three-dimensional modeling, video, data visualization, and dynamic charts. Dynamic visualization enables multi-dimensional data to be presented and deepens users' understanding of data processing results. The results of DM are more visual, intuitive, easy to use, and indirectly improve the utilization efficiency of data.

The improvement of data processing technology, the easy understanding and dynamic visualization of data presentation, and the more intelligent data support services make the data utilization rate continuously improve. Education big data is applied to education management, education decision-making, teacher teaching, smart campus, online classroom, and other aspects, while traditional data applications only provide analysis results. At this stage, DM technology provides real-time intervention after analyzing data, supplemented by an efficient support service system, so as to significantly improve the efficiency of dealing with affairs and improving teaching.

## 1.2 An overview of PISA 2018 and its reading assessment

The Programme for International Student Assessment (PISA) of the Organization for Economic Cooperation and Development (OECD) has begun its seventh phase, with the purpose of establishing the most important things that people should know and be able to achieve. Our ability to assess whether or not 15-year-old youngsters have learned the information and abilities necessary for full participation in modern society can be determined by using the PISA. In addition to the core subjects of reading, mathematics, and science, the triennial assessment analyzes a variety of additional aspects of the school's operation. Students will also be evaluated on their ability to innovate in a range of circumstances and settings, in addition to their academic performance. Several factors must be considered when evaluating a student's capacity to duplicate knowledge. It is also important to evaluate the student's ability to infer from what has been learned and apply it to fresh scenarios both within and outside of the classroom setting. The reality that individuals are paid not for what they know, but rather for what they can do with their knowledge, is reflected in modern economics. Student abilities to replicate knowledge are measured by PISA, but it also measures their ability to infer from what they have learned and apply that knowledge to new situations, which is measured by the PISA. A strong emphasis is placed on mastery of the process, understanding of concepts, and the ability to perform in a range of contexts and circumstances.

Students across the world and student groups within each country participate in the PISA, which is a continuing endeavor that tracks trends in knowledge and skills acquired by students around the world and by student groups within each country. On average, a detailed test on a key subject takes up almost half of the time in each cycle of the PISA. For the third consecutive year, reading remains the most important field, as it was in 2000 and 2009. Mathematics was the dominant subject in 2003 and 2012, whereas science was the dominant subject in 2006 and 2015.

In addition to distributing surveys to students and teachers as well as targeted questionnaires to parents and instructors, PISA gathers information about students' family backgrounds, learning styles, and learning environments through a variety of methods. An in-depth review of achievements in the three core areas is offered every nine years with varying configurations in the major areas; a trend analysis is provided every three years. Combining information acquired through a large number of questionnaires, PISA evaluations offer three types of outcomes that are useful for policymakers: (1) indicators from the questionnaire survey, demonstrating the relationship between these skills and various demographics, social, economic, and educational variables; (2) indicators from the questionnaire survey, demonstrating the relationship between these skills and various demographic, social, economic, and educational variables; (3) indicators from the questionnaire survey, demonstrating the relationship between these skills and various demographics, social, economic, and educational variables; (4) at the student, school, and system levels, the indicators reflect the trend and distribution of results, as well as the context in which they are occurring. The relationship that exists between variables and outcomes.

Results from PISA are used by decision-makers around the world to assess students' knowledge and skills within their own country or economy and in other participating countries or economies, to set benchmarks for improving education and/or learning outcomes, and to understand the comparative advantages and disadvantages of their educational systems.

There were computer-based examinations that lasted two hours for each student as part of the evaluation procedure. On the test, there are multiple-choice questions as well as ones that require students to come up with their own solutions to the problems. All of these things are organized into categories based on articles that describe the current state of affairs. The exam items took approximately 930 minutes to complete, and students utilized a variety of strategies to complete them. It took the students 35 minutes to complete the background check as well. Those who took part in the poll were asked about their educational experiences, their families, their schools, and other factors. The principal answered questions regarding the school's structure and learning environment in a questionnaire that was distributed to students. For the purpose of gathering more information, some countries/economies decided to distribute a questionnaire to teachers, asking them questions about their training and professional progress, teaching practice, and work satisfaction. Several countries/economies were chosen to participate in the survey, and parents were asked to provide information about their children's school, their support for family learning, and their own involvement in reading and other cultures.

Aside from the mandatory questionnaires, countries/economies can choose from three optional student questionnaires (see Figure 1.1): one asks about students' familiarity with and use of information and communications technology (ICT); another asks about students' education so far, including whether there have been any interruptions in their studies and whether and how they prepare for their future careers; and a third questionnaire, which was first published in the International Student Assessment Program (PISA 2018), focuses on students' well-being and life satisfaction. As part of the review process, questionnaires on financial literacy are delivered to nations and economies that have been identified as needing additional attention (Figure 1.2).

A comprehensive and rigorous worldwide program for assessing student performance and obtaining data on student, family, and institutional characteristics that might help explain performance gaps, PISA is the most comprehensive and rigorous international study available. Key experts from participating countries make decisions on the scope and type of the assessment, as well as the background

# Introduction 9

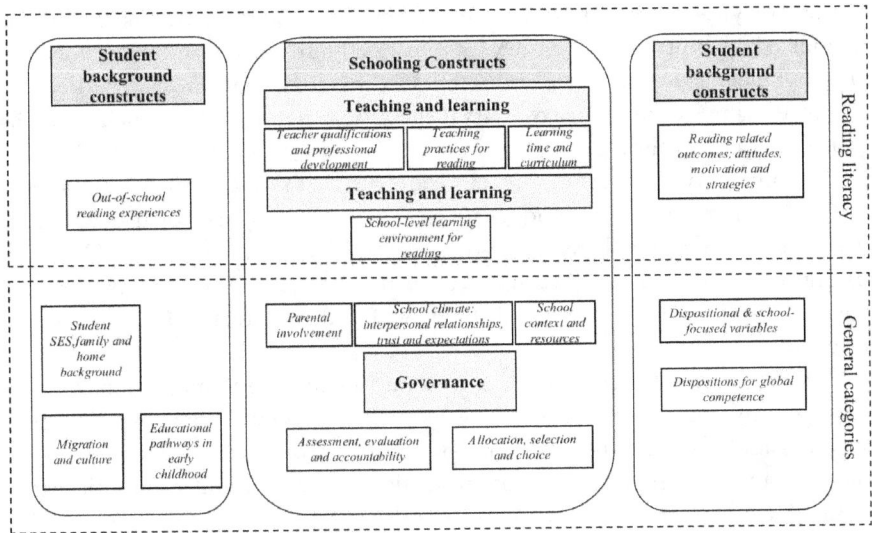

**FIGURE 1.2** The framework of PISA 2018.

material that will be collected, and governments are guided by common, policy-driven objectives throughout the process. For this reason, we invested a significant amount of time and effort in ensuring that the assessment materials were broad and balanced in terms of culture and language. Quality assurance methods are in place for translation, sampling, and data collection, and they are rigorously followed. This has resulted in the PISA findings being extremely valid and dependable.

## 1.2.1 An introduction to PISA 2018

The PISA evaluation in 2018 was mostly conducted using a computer, and the procedure was first utilized in 2015, according to the results. Provision of paper-based assessment tools for nations that opt not to participate in or pass the online exam; nevertheless, paper evaluation is restricted to topics related to reading, mathematics, and scientific trends (i.e., items used in previous paper evaluations). The new project will only be utilized for computer assessment, and nothing else.

The computer assessment for 2018 is intended to be a two-hour exercise. Each essay that is delivered to pupils has four exam materials that last 30 minutes each. Six clusters from the domains of mathematics and science are included in the test design to assess trends. It was decided to construct 15 sets of 30-minute materials for the primary reading area. Due to the adaptive nature of the 2018 PISA reading exam, materials are structured into units rather than groups, and students are assigned to units depending on their performance in prior units of the assessment. Aside from that, four sets of global capacity projects have been prepared for nations who desire to take part in the evaluation.

Various types of testing are used in various countries that are taking part in the global capability assessment. A total of one hour is spent on reading evaluation (which includes the core level followed by two more or less challenging stages), and another one or two hours is spent on other disciplines such as math, science, or general ability.

To evaluate student performance in countries that selected paper distribution as their primary survey method, a 30-page paper-and-pencil form comprising three core PISA regional trend questions was utilized to collect data. All of the reading projects on this page are based on the 2009 Reading Literacy Framework; no projects based on the 2018 New Reading Literacy Framework are included.

Students from a sufficient number of countries and economies complete each test form, allowing us to estimate the number of students from each country/economy and the relevant subgroups of students from each country/economy (such as boys and girls, or students from different social and economic backgrounds) who are proficient in all projects.

The approach for financial literacy evaluation is the same as that used in PISA 2012–2015 and is available as an option in PISA 2018. The financial literacy exam was administered at schools that participated in the PISA study to a subset of pupils who were not included in the main sample. Apart from the one-hour financial literacy exam, students are required to complete a one-hour reading assessment and a one-hour math assessment.

Practical knowledge and skills are emphasized in all three categories specified by the 2018 PISA evaluation, which allow individuals to engage fully in society. To engage in decision-making, it is not only necessary to have the capacity to complete externally imposed responsibilities, such as those assigned by the employer, but it is also necessary for the ability to participate in decision-making. Instead of providing a single perfect response to a question, the more challenging activities in PISA demand students to reflect on and assess the information rather than providing a single correct answer.

### 1.2.1.1 Reading literacy

As defined by the National Council on Literacy, reading literacy is the capacity of students to comprehend, utilize, analyze, reflect on, and engage in texts to attain their objectives. The capacity to comprehend and utilize texts to attain objectives, develop knowledge and potential, and engage in society is shown by individuals' understanding, usage, evaluation, reflection, and participation in texts.

When evaluating pupils' reading abilities, the PISA program employs questions. These are some of the questions: (1) the process (or a feature of it): We do not evaluate kids on the basis of their most fundamental reading abilities since we feel that the majority of 15-year-old youngsters already possess these abilities. Locating information, which includes obtaining and retrieving information from the text as well as searching and selecting related text; understanding text, which includes obtaining the literal representation of the text as well as constructing the overall representation of the text; and analyzing text. It is important to note that the text's assessment and reflection include the evaluation of the text's quality and credibility, as well as the reflection on the text's substance and form. Secondly, the text format is used in PISA. Single-source text is used. Multi-source texts, static and dynamic texts, continuous text (sentences and paragraphs), discontinuous text (such as lists, tables, charts, and diagrams), and mixed text are used as well. (3) Context: The use in the article defines the settings in which the terms are used. Novels, personal letters, and biographies, for example, are written for the personal enjoyment of the reader; official papers or announcements are written for the general public; this manual or report is written for professionals; and textbooks or worksheets are created for educational objectives. Because some students may score better in one reading context than in another, the exam provides a number of different reading settings for students to choose from.

Since the most recent revision in 2009, new reading forms, particularly digital reading, have continued to develop and become more popular. Reading materials in both printed and digital versions have grown more diverse, and this has been reflected in the redesigned 2018 PISA reading framework, which has been updated to reflect this.

### 1.2.1.2 Mathematics literacy

When students propose, articulate, solve, and explain solutions to mathematical issues in a variety of circumstances, mathematical literacy refers to their capacity to successfully evaluate, reason, and communicate ideas with one another. Mathematical competence is a skill. The capacity to articulate, apply, and explain mathematics in a variety of contexts, incorporating mathematical reasoning, as well as the application of mathematical ideas, techniques, facts, and instruments to describe, explain, and forecast events is referred to as mathematical reasoning.

Student mathematical performance is assessed using the PISA test, which asks the following questions: (1) the procedure: according to PISA, there are three processes: defining circumstances using mathematics; applying mathematical ideas and facts; performing mathematical procedures; and understanding, applying, and evaluating mathematical findings. They explain how students make the connection between the subject's historical context and the mathematics needed in addressing the difficulty. Three fundamental mathematical skills are required for each process: communication; mathematics; representation; reasoning and argumentation; formulation of problem-solving strategies; use of symbology; formalization of formalized technical language and operations; and use of mathematical tools. Everything about a problem solver's talents is dependent on his or her deep mathematical understanding of a specific subject area. There are four main ideas (quantity, space and form, change and relationship, and uncertainty and data) that are related to conventional number, algebra, and geometry courses in overlapping and complicated ways. (2) Structure: The course is divided into four sections. (3) Situations: These are issues that arise in the student community. The framework distinguishes between four types of backgrounds: personal, educational, societal, and scientific backgrounds.

### 1.2.1.3 Science literacy

As defined by the International Science Literacy Association, scientific literacy is the capacity to reflect on citizens' engagement in science-related problems and scientific thinking. Participants in the rational debate of science and technology who have scientific literacy must be able to explain phenomena scientifically, assess and plan scientific research scientifically, as well as analyze data and evidence in a scientifically sound manner.

Through the use of the following questions, the PISA science assessment program assesses students' ability in science: (1) contextual information: Among the topics covered are personal, local/national, and global difficulties, as well as current and historical challenges that need a working knowledge of science and technology. (2) Scientific knowledge is comprised of the comprehension of the fundamental facts, ideas, and interpretive theories that constitute scientific understanding. In addition to knowing how to develop ideas (program knowledge), this knowledge encompasses knowing the natural world and technological artifacts. It also includes knowing how to use these programs and understanding the fundamental principles of how they work and why they are used (scientific knowledge). The capacity to scientifically explain events, assess and plan scientific projects, as well as scientifically analyze data and evidence, are all examples of scientific competence.

### 1.2.1.4 The context questionnaires

Background questionnaires for PISA 2018 have been largely adapted from those used in past PISA cycles, allowing for the tracking of trends in student, school, and system-level elements that may be linked to student results. Student background constructs, schooling constructs, and non-cognitive/metacognitive constructs are among the constructs explored. As part of the PISA study procedure, children and their teachers are issued questionnaires to obtain background information. These jobs took 35 minutes and 45 minutes to complete, respectively. The questionnaire responses are compared with the assessment findings, resulting in a more accurate and trustworthy picture of students, schools, and system performance.

The questionnaire covers the following topics: (1) students and their families' backgrounds, including economic, social, and cultural capital; (2) all aspects of student life, including learning attitudes, living habits, and family environment, among other things; (3) the questionnaire's results are shared with the participants; (4) the school's human and material resources, public and private administration, financing, and so on, as well as its decision-making process, staffing methods, school curriculum goals, and extracurricular activities offered; (5) teaching experience, including organizational structure and styles, as well as classrooms and students scale, classroom and school spirit, reading activities in the classroom, and so on; and (6) student learning, including organizational structure and styles, as well as classroom and school spirit, classroom and school spirit, etc.

PISA 2018 includes five new surveys that may be selected as options: (1) a computer familiarity questionnaire, which examines the availability and usage of information and communication technology (ICT) as well as the mobility of students' information and communication devices. In PISA 2018, two new projects were introduced: (1) the computer use questionnaire, which measures students' attitudes toward computer use and (2) a happiness questionnaire, which measures students' perceptions of their own health, life satisfaction, social relationships, and activities both inside and outside of school. Encourage the acquisition of new languages. Student, school, and optional questionnaires were used to obtain background information; however, this information represents only a tiny portion of the information accessible in PISA. On a regular basis, the OECD develops and applies descriptions of the overall structure of the education system (its demographic and economic background indicators such as cost and enrollment, characteristics of schools and teachers, and the process of certain classes), as well as its impact on labor market outcomes (e.g., in the annual publication of the OECD, Education Overview).

### 1.2.2 PISA reading framework

The International Student Assessment Program's primary assessment area for 2018 is reading comprehension (PISA). As defined in this chapter, reading ability is a measure of cognitive ability used by the 2018 International Student Assessment Program. Reading aptitude in PISA activities is assessed using a variety of techniques and situations, as described in this section of the manual. Also included is a description of how the nature of reading ability has evolved over the last two decades, particularly in light of the rising prevalence of digital material. Also covered in this chapter are the methods by which PISA assesses the difficulty and efficiency of students' reading, as well as the methods by which it assesses different metacognitive components of students' reading activities. After that, talk about ways to evaluate and report on pupils' reading abilities. At the conclusion of this chapter, you will see examples of projects for different reading evaluations.

#### 1.2.2.1 Evolving of the reading framework

For the third time, reading has been identified as a priority area in the PISA 2018 assessment, and it is also the second time that the reading literacy framework has been substantially updated. It is necessary for these updates to take into account changes in the concept of reading literacy as well as the environment in which reading is used in civic life. So the present updated framework is based on a complete theory of modern reading literacy and takes into consideration how students access and utilize information in a variety of contexts.

There is a tremendous increase in the number and diversity of written materials, and people want them to be utilized in new and more complicated ways. It is now widely acknowledged that our concept of reading ability evolves in tandem with the changing nature of society and culture. Compared to now, the reading literacy abilities necessary for personal development, educational achievement, economic involvement, and citizenship were quite different 20 years ago. These skills are expected to alter much more in the next 20 years.

The goal of education is to move beyond information collection and memory to a more comprehensive concept of knowledge development: "For technical personnel and professionals who can communicate, share, and use information to solve complex problems, the ability to adapt and innovate is critical to their success". As a result of revised specifications as well as the constantly changing environment, "to harness the power of amplifier technology to generate new information, extend human capacities, and increase original production" (Binkley et al., 2011). Individuals must have the capacity to discover, access, comprehend, and reflect on information if they are to fully participate in our knowledge-based society. Reading literacy is not only a precondition for success in other subjects within the educational system, but it is also a requirement for involvement in the majority of adult activities as well (e.g., Cunningham & Stanovich, 1997; OECD, 2013a). The PISA framework for evaluating students' reading ability should therefore be focused on reading skills at the end of compulsory education, including the discovery of textual information related to situations outside the classroom as well as selection, interpretation, integration, and evaluation of all textual information related to those situations.

In the past, the capacity to comprehend, evaluate, and reflect on specific texts was the primary goal in measuring pupils' reading abilities. These abilities are still necessary, but with more emphasis placed on the integration of information technology into citizens' society and work life, an update and expansion of the concept of reading literacy will be required. It must take into account the comprehensive renewal of skills connected to the literacy duties necessary in the 21st century, among other things. This necessitates a broader interpretation of what constitutes reading competence.

In tandem with changes in the nature of reading literacy, changes have occurred in the structure that supports it. First and foremost, reading ability is the focus of the PISA 2009 testing (OECD, 2000). It was the first major topic to be re-examined in the fourth PISA cycle (OECD, 2009), necessitating a full assessment of its structure as well as the creation of new tools to depict the results of the study. The framework was altered one further for the seventh cycle of PISA 2018, which took place in 2018.

The first PISA reading literacy framework, designed for the PISA 2009 cycle via an expert consensus-building process, was developed for the PISA 2009 cycle. The International Reading Literacy Research and the International Adult Literacy Survey (IALS) contributed to the development of the concept of reading literacy in part. Furthermore, reading theory, which is still popular today, has an impact on it.

The majority of the material from the PISA 2012 framework has been carried over to the PISA 2009 framework, ensuring that one of the basic aims of PISA is maintained: the collection and reporting of information on student performance patterns. Since the year 2000, the understanding of reading has evolved. The concept of reading literacy has been broadened to include both the motivation and behavioral qualities of reading as well as the cognitive characteristics of reading, according to recent research. At the conclusion of the first PISA Reading Framework's "Other Issues" section, a short reference is made of reading participation and metacognition—understanding and comprehension of how to grasp text and use reading strategies—as well as the use of reading techniques (OECD, 2000). In a recent study, it has been discovered that reading participation and metacognition have a more important role in the PISA reading framework in 2009 and 2015, and that these features may be fostered and nurtured as part of the process of developing reading literacy.

The addition of digital text in the PISA 2009 survey was a significant change from the PISA 2000 survey, which recognized the increasingly important role that digital text plays in personal development and active involvement in society. This modification was made in connection with the introduction of a new computer-based assessment format, and as a result, text was shown on the computer screen throughout the process. PISA 2009 is the first large-scale worldwide research to measure electronic text reading, and it was conducted by the United Nations Development Programme.

According to the PISA 2015 test, reading ability is a secondary component, while the PISA 2009 test kept both the description and description of reading ability. PISA 2015, on the other hand, has introduced significant modifications to the examination management process, some of which need the revision of the language of the reading frame.

The Reading Literacy Framework for PISA 2018 preserves the portions of the 2009/2015 framework that are relevant to PISA 2018. Although there have been some changes, the framework has been improved and altered in the following areas: (1) The framework integrates conventional reading with new reading modes that have evolved in recent decades and are continuing to emerge with the increasing use of digital devices and digital texts. (2) The frame comprises the structural elements that are engaged in the fundamental reading process. They are essential for processing multiple texts with complex or specific purposes. If students are unable to perform advanced text processing functions as a result of difficulties with these foundational skills, educators must determine whether the failure is due to difficulties with these foundational skills or a combination of these skills. (3) The framework re-examined the way the field organizes the reading process, including aspects such as judging text correctness, locating information, reading from various sources, and integrating/synthesizing information from numerous sources, among other things. With the new version, the relevance of various reading processes is more evenly distributed to better represent the global importance of different structures, while maintaining a relationship with the prior framework to track performance changes. (3) The updated version explores how to employ new technological alternatives and programs, such as printed and digital texts, to provide a more realistic reading assessment that is compatible with the texts that are now in use throughout the globe.

### *1.2.2.2 Defining reading in PISA 2018*

With the passage of time, the concept of reading and reading literacy has evolved to reflect changes in social, economic, cultural, and technical circumstances. Unlike in the past, reading is no longer believed to be a skill that can only be learned in school throughout early childhood. Individuals develop knowledge, skills, and tactics with their peers and the larger community in a variety of living contexts, and this collection of information, skills, and strategies is always increasing. As a result, reading must take into account the many different ways in which individuals engage with text-based items as well as their function in lifelong learning.

According to the definition of reading literacy in 2018, reading literacy includes the ability to comprehend, use, evaluate, reflect on, and engage in texts to attain personal objectives, develop one's own knowledge and potential, and participate in society.

It is preferred to use the word "reading literacy" rather than the phrase "reading" since it is more accurate in conveying the substance of survey measures to non-expert audiences. Reading is often perceived as basic decoding (e.g., translating written text into sound) or even reading aloud; nevertheless, the evaluation tries to test a more comprehensive and encompassing structure. Reading literacy encompasses a wide range of cognitive and language skills, ranging from basic decoding to knowledge of required words, grammar, and larger language and text structure, as well as the ability to combine meaning with an understanding of the world. It also includes the ability to combine meaning with an understanding of the world. Metacognitive talents are also included: being aware of and capable of using suitable techniques while processing text. A reader's metacognition is triggered when he or she considers, monitors, and adjusts their reading actions to achieve certain objectives. However, although the word "literacy" is often used in the context of a person's understanding of a certain topic or sector, it is most closely associated with an individual's capacity to study, utilize, communicate, and share written and printed information. It seems that this definition is fairly similar to the meaning of the word "reading literacy" in this framework: the active, deliberate, and functional use of reading in diverse circumstances and for varied purposes (see definition above). PISA assesses a large number of different pupils. Some of these students will continue their education at a university, maybe to pursue an academic or professional career; others will continue their education to prepare for work; and yet others will join the job market immediately after finishing their secondary school program. Students' capacity to read, regardless of their academic or professional goals, is required in order for them to engage fully in their communal, economic, and personal lives…comprehend, apply, analyze, and reflect…. It is simple to compare the term "understanding" with the generally known term "reading comprehension". Reading, according to this idea, includes integrating textual material with the reader's prior knowledge to some degree. Even in the earliest stages of reading, readers must rely on their prior understanding of symbols (such as letters) to comprehend the text, and they must rely on their prior knowledge of words to construct meaning. The integration process, on the other hand, might be more generalized, including, for example, the construction of mental models of how the text connects to the outside world. The notion of application and function is conveyed by the term "use", which means to put what we have learned to use in a practical way. The word "assessment" introduces the notion that reading is often done with a purpose in PISA 2018, and readers must consider variables such as the correctness of text parameters, the author's perspectives, and reader objectives connected to the text to pass the test. "Thinking" and "understanding" are combined with the words "usage" and "assessment" to stress the fact that reading is an interactive process in which readers learn from their own thoughts and experiences while reading texts. Every act of reading requires some level of contemplation. For readers to understand the information in the text, they must evaluate it and make a link between it and information from outside the text. During the course of their reading journey, readers regularly assess what they've read against their existing knowledge, as well as constantly reviewing and revising their comprehension of the material. The process of reflecting on a text might entail evaluating the author's assertions, analyzing their use of rhetoric and other discourse techniques, and inferring the author's viewpoints from the text. At the same time, readers' reflections on the book may cause their worldview to shift gradually or even slightly as a result. Readers may also be required to evaluate the substance of the text, to draw on their existing knowledge or understanding, or to consider the structure or form of the text as part of the reflection process. The skills included in the definition, including "understanding", "applying", "evaluation", and "reflection", are all essential, but they are not sufficient, for good reading performance.

A well-educated individual not only has reading abilities and information but also places a high value on reading and employs it for a variety of reasons. Because of this, the purpose of education is not just to develop reading abilities, but also to develop reading abilities that are more significant than just reading abilities. Participation in this context refers to the motivation for reading, which includes a variety of emotional and behavioral characteristics such as reading interest and pleasure, a sense of control over reading content, social participation aspects of reading, a variety of reading genres, and regular practice.

The word "text" refers to any language that is represented graphically, whether it is handwritten, printed, or shown on a screen. For the sake of this definition, we omit goods that use just aural language, such as records, movies, television, animated graphics, and photos that are not accompanied by a written text. The text comprises visual displays such as schematics, photographs, maps, tables, diagrams, and comic books, as well as written words in certain cases (e.g., in comic books) (such as subtitles). These visual texts may survive on their own or can be used as part of a bigger textual composition. Readers have a certain amount of control over how they read dynamic text, which differs from the fixed text in a number of ways, including the absence of movement cues that allow readers to estimate the length and quantity of the text (such as the size of paper documents hidden in virtual space); different parts of the text and different text fragments are connected by hypertext links; and whether or not to display multiple summary texts in the search results. Readers will approach dynamic texts in a variety of ways as a result of these variances. Whenever readers engage in reading activities that include dynamic text, they must to a significant measure design their own reading paths. The term "text" was chosen over the term "information" because it is connected with written language and is more likely to convey reading of literature and information.

> ...It is our goal, to help people achieve their goals and develop their knowledge and potential while also participating in society, to capture all situations in which literacy plays a role, from the private to the public sphere, from school to the workplace, from formal education to lifelong learning and active citizenship.

"Achieving one's own goals" and "developing one's own knowledge and potential" demonstrate that long-term personal reading ability can help one achieve aspirations such as graduate school or job hunting, whereas those who are not very clear and directly enriched by reading do not demonstrate this ability (Gray & Rogers, 1956) PISA's definition of reading encompasses both traditional reading and innovative reading for the 21st century. It thinks that reading literacy is the foundation for full involvement in economic, political, public, and cultural life on a local, national, and international level. Society in the 21st century. The word "participation" is employed since it implies that the capacity to read is required for participation. People may make a positive contribution to society while still meeting their personal wants.

The PISA cognitive exam assesses reading ability via the use of processing activities and textual variables. The results of another questionnaire were used to determine aspects such as readers' motivation, personality, and previous experience The two most important considerations in the design of the PISA reading literacy assessment are, first, to ensure a broad coverage of what students read and what they read inside and outside of school, and second, to ensure that texts and tasks represent the natural difficulty range of texts and tasks for students worldwide. When it comes to reading ability, the PISA exam is based on three basic characteristics: Text refers to the variety of reading material available; process refers to the cognitive procedure used to determine how readers interpret the text; and context refers to the wide context or range of purposes in which reading takes place. In a scenario, the reader is given a task—a specified goal—that he or she must fulfill to be successful. All three will contribute to ensuring comprehensive coverage in this region. Text characteristics and task goals are both manipulable in the PISA test, which necessitates the use of many distinct cognitive processes to alter the complexity of the task. As a result, the goal of the PISA reading literacy exam is to determine whether or not students have mastered the process of reading (text). Readers may make use of the text (content, reading range) and the surrounding context (broad context or reading purpose related to a reading purpose). Although there may be individual variances in reader characteristics depending on the abilities and history of each reader, these differences are not altered using cognitive techniques but rather are discovered via questionnaire assessment. The implementation of these three qualities is required prior to the development of an evaluation that makes use of them. That is, you must provide a different acceptable value for each feature than the previous one. The materials and tasks that test developers create may be classified in this way, which can be used to arrange data reports and evaluate the findings.

### 1.2.2.2.1 Processes

It is necessary for people to be capable of performing a broad variety of procedures to obtain the reading skills outlined in this framework. Additionally, to effectively execute these processes, readers must possess the cognitive abilities, strategies, and motives that are necessary to support these processes. When it comes to reading literacy, the PISA 2018 Reading Framework highlights the goal-driven, critical, and intertextual aspects of this skill. The preceding component of reading has been updated and broadened to clearly reflect a more thorough process, and expert readers may draw upon it in a variety of ways depending on the precise work context and information environment in which they find themselves. Text processing and task management are two broad types of reading processes defined by the PISA 2018 study, which is more specific. The PISA 2018 cognitive exam is primarily concerned with textual processing. Text processing comprises a variety of tasks such as smooth reading, placing information, understanding, assessment, and reflection, among others. Reading fluency may be characterized as a person's capacity to correctly and automatically read words and texts, as well as the ability to phrase and process these words and texts to comprehend the overall meaning of the text (also known as text comprehension) (Kuhn & Stahl, 2003). In other words, fluency refers to how quickly and easily you can read a piece of material.

For the purpose of gaining positional knowledge, competent readers may read the whole text attentively, comprehend its essential concepts, and consider it in its entirety. In everyday life, readers, on the other hand, often employ text for the sole aim of obtaining precise location information, with little or no regard for the remainder of the text. Furthermore, when reading complicated digital material such as search engines and webpages, geographical information is a vital component of the reading process. For readers to discover information inside and between texts, Framework 2018 provides two processes: (1) searching within texts and (2) searching between texts. The ability to locate information in tables, sections of text, or whole volumes is a talent in and of itself. Readers' grasp of task requirements, their knowledge of text organizers (e.g., headers and paragraphs), and their ability to judge the relevance of the text all play a role in determining where information should be placed. Having a strategic understanding of their information demands and the capacity to swiftly disengage from irrelevant paragraphs are both required for readers to be able to access information effectively (McCrudden & Schraw, 2007). In addition, readers may be required to go through a sequence of paragraphs to find particular information in certain cases. This necessitates the capacity to modify reading speed and processing depth, as well as the ability to recognize when information in the text should be considered or ignored (Duggan & Payne, 2009). The access and retrieval problem on the PISA 2018 exam demands readers to scan text and recover target information that consists of many words, sentences, or values from a large amount of material. There is little or no need to comprehend text above the level of individual phrases. It is possible to recognize target information by matching queries and components in the text in a literal or near-literal manner; however, certain jobs may need reasoning at the word or phrase level. Reading skills are not limited to selecting information from a single paragraph; they also have the ability to pick information from numerous paragraphs. In the electronic world, the quantity of information accessible to the reader is often significantly more than the reader's real processing capability. With multi-text reading, the reader must pick which texts are the most significant, relevant, correct, or authentic. This is a difficult decision (Rouet & Britt, 2011). These determinations are based on readers' evaluations of the text's quality, which is based on incomplete and often opaque signs, such as the information included in web links, and are based on a variety of factors. As a result, the capacity of a person to search for and choose paragraphs from a collection of texts is an essential component of reading skill. Text search and selection tasks in PISA 2018 involve the use of text descriptors, such as the title, source information (such as the author, medium, and date), and embedded or explicit links, such as search engine results pages, to aid in the process.

For example, when it comes to comprehension, a big number of reading activities include the analysis and incorporation of long paragraphs of the text to develop a knowledge of the content provided by the paragraphs. Text comprehension (also known as comprehension) may be thought of as the process of constructing the reader's mental representation of the text's information. There are two fundamental processes that underpin the context model: the building of a literal memory representation and the integration of text content and previous knowledge via the process of mapping and reasoning. To comprehend the literal meaning of the text, the reader must first comprehend the phrase or paragraph in question. It is necessary to match the question directly or indirectly to the desired information in the text to successfully complete this job of text comprehension. Readers may find it necessary to sort or compress material on their own computers. It is necessary to go from a single phrase to an entire paragraph to create a comprehensive text representation. Readers will be required to develop a variety of sorts of reasoning, ranging from basic connection thinking (such as anaphora) to more complicated coherent linkages and ties between relationships (such as space, time, causality, or claim-argument links). Textual reasoning may be used to link distinct sections of a text together, as well as to relate the text to a question. Lastly, in the job where the reader must identify the underlying principal concept of a particular article, inference generation is necessary, for example, to develop an abstract or article title for the piece. It is possible that when readers are presented with several texts, they will be required to integrate and reason on the basis of information found in distinct texts. When integrating information across numerous text segments, it is possible that the information provided can be inconsistent or contradicting. This is a specific difficulty that might develop. As a result, readers must actively engage in the review process while also recognizing and managing conflicts (Braten et al., 2009; Stadtler & Bromme, 2014).

In terms of assessment and reflection, skilled readers may draw implications from a book that go beyond the literal or inferential meaning that the author intended. Their ability to critically analyze the quality and validity of the information included in the text is enhanced by their ability to reflect on the content and form of the text. Examine the product's quality and reputation. Competent readers may evaluate the validity, timeliness, accuracy, and/or fairness of the material included in the article, as well as its credibility and quality. The ability to analyze information needs readers to identify and evaluate the source of the information, including whether or not the author is competent, informed, and courteous. Take into consideration both the substance and the form. Competent readers must be able to evaluate the overall quality and style of the writing as well. To engage in this kind of reflection, you must be able to evaluate the writing's form and how the writing's content and form are connected to and conveyed by the author's purpose and ideas. Aspects of reflection that go beyond the text include the use of outside knowledge, ideas, or attitudes to connect the information presented in the book with one's own conceptual and experiential frame of reference. If you think about it, reflective projects are when you encourage your readers to compare and contrast, or speculate, various points of view based on their own experience or knowledge. Evaluation and reflection have always been an element of reading literacy, but with the rise in the quantity of information and heterogeneity that readers are confronted with today, their value has grown exponentially. Conflicts should be identified and dealt with. When confronted with contradictory texts, readers must be aware of the conflict and have a strategy for dealing with it (Britt & Rouet, 2012; Stadtler & Bromme, 2013, 2014).

In most cases, readers must assign contradicting assertions to their respective sources and evaluate the trustworthiness of the claims and/or the credibility of the sources to resolve disagreements. Because these abilities form the cornerstone of modern reading, determining the degree to which 15-year-old students are confronted with new problems in comprehending, comparing, and integrating numerous texts is an important question (e.g., Braten et al., 2011; Coiro et al., 2008; Goldman, 2004; Leu et al., 2015; Mason et al., 2010; Rouet & Britt, 2014).

Readers engage with the text in the context of any evaluation, as well as in many everyday reading contexts, since they are given a task or external signals to complete. Among the abilities required for reading literacy is the capability of an individual to accurately express reading needs in a specific situation, establish task-related reading goals, monitor progress toward achieving these goals, and discuss self-regulated reading abilities throughout the activity by self-regulating goals and strategies. Task-oriented objectives compel the reader to locate material and/or paragraphs that are relevant to the task. Finally, the process of monitoring (metacognition) allows the reader to dynamically adjust the target over the course of the reading session. Task management is based on text processing, and it stresses the fact that various degrees of metacognition may be achieved via text processing. Reading goals can be constructed in a variety of ways, including spontaneously generated goals based on personal interests and initiative. Although readers' understanding of task requirements is an important part of the task management process, the construction of reading goals goes beyond a clear task description. The PISA reading evaluation, on the other hand, only takes into account objectives that are generated when the reader is directed to accomplish a specific assignment. Aside from that, owing to implementation constraints, the task management process is represented in PISA 2018, but there is no direct and independent assessment of it. Some background surveys, on the other hand, will measure readers' understanding of reading methods. To evaluate task management abilities in future cycles, it may be necessary to employ computer-generated process metrics (e.g., how many times a student accesses a given text page or the number of times a student sees a question).

Briefly stated, the 2018 framework categorizes the cognitive processes involved in intentional reading activities in a complete and thorough way due to the fact that they unfold in a single or multiple textual contexts. Currently, it is not feasible to differentiate across processes within a single competency level due to design restrictions. Instead, the framework outlines a more condensed set of procedures that will serve as the foundation for future extension and report generation.

### 1.2.2.2.2 Texts

Read just the material that the reader needs. A paragraph or series of texts relevant to a certain task must have sufficient information in order for a trained reader to meaningfully grasp and solve the challenges posed by the task to pass the assessment. However, despite the fact that there are many distinct kinds of texts and that any evaluation should contain a diverse variety of texts, there has never been a widely accepted taxonomy for the many various types of texts that readers encounter. Due to the emergence of new text kinds and text-based communication services, some of which may not survive the next ten years and others of which may be whole new creations during that period, the issue has grown increasingly significant and difficult to resolve.

There are four primary dimensions to define the text in the prior frame of reference (2009), which are as follows: The following are the requirements: (1) media (print or electronic); (2) environment (creative or informational); (3) text format (continuous, discontinuous, mixed, or many); (4) text kind (description, story, explanation, argument, illustration, transaction). Digital reading assessment was given as an optional course in 2009 and 2012, respectively. Despite the fact that the exam was delivered on a computer, only the text from printed paper papers was utilized in the 2015 reading literacy assessment. For the sake of clarity, these texts are referred to as fixed and dynamic texts, rather than media, under the term "Text Display Space" (trying to clarify that although their origins are printed on paper, students actually read them on computer screens, therefore on electronic media). There were no new activities planned and implemented since reading was such a tiny area in 2015. As a result, dynamic texts, that is, texts such as websites with hyperlinks, menus, and other electronic media navigation elements, are excluded from the scope of the PISA 2015 assessment.

Reading was a significant area of focus in 2018, and the updated framework and expanded text may now be reflected in the assessment results. There are text categories that are typical of print media, and there are text categories that are characteristic of digital media that are ever-expanding. The same way that printed text is "static", certain digital text is "static" since it comes with a limited collection of interactive capabilities (scrolling, pagination, and search). A paper that is supposed to be printed but instead appears on a computer screen is an example of this (such as a word processing document or PDF file). Many digital texts, on the other hand, contain new functionalities that expand the potential of readers to engage with the content, which is why they are referred to as "dynamic texts". Embedded hyperlinks that direct readers to other parts, pages, or websites; sophisticated search facilities that temporarily scan search phrases and/or highlight these words in the text; and social activities, such as text-based exchanges e-mail, discussion forums, and instant messaging services are examples of communication medium.

This year's framework distinguishes between four types of text: single-source, multiple-source, organization and navigation structure (static and dynamic), format (continuous, discontinuous, mixed), and kind of text (textual) (description, narrative, elaboration, argument, guidance, interaction, and transaction). Making multiple test materials based on these four aspects will assure comprehensive coverage in this subject and will reflect both established and new reading habits and habits of mind.

The source in the PISA 2018 framework is represented by a text unit. When defining a single source text, the author (or group of authors), the date of authoring or publishing, and the reference title or number are all necessary. Depending on the medium (conventional printed books, for example), the concept of an author might be exact or more loosely defined (such as in a blog post or website sponsor). Although it is not explicitly stated, even a single source text may be understood in this manner since it is given to the reader in isolation from other texts. Multi-source texts are distinguished by the presence of many authors, the publication of multiple editions at various dates, the use of multiple titles, and the use of multiple reference numbers. Please keep in mind that the term "title" refers to the bibliographic catalog unit in the PISA framework. Long texts with titles and subtitles are nevertheless considered to be single texts since they were authored by a specific author (or group of writers) on a certain date in a specific location. An online publication with many pages is also considered a single source of text, provided there is no clear reference of various authors or dates on each page. On a single page, a variety of text sources may be shown. This is true for printed newspapers, numerous textbooks, discussion forums, consumer reviews, and Q&A websites, among other things. Finally, a single text may have embedded sources, which are references to other authors or texts that are included inside the text. As a result, the multi-text examined in the previous edition of the framework corresponds to the multi-source text considered in the 2018 PISA framework, so long as the text is derived from several sources. All other manuscripts are categorized as single-source texts, which are those that have just one source.

Screen sizes vary widely in the digital world, ranging from mobile phone displays that are smaller than conventional index cards to enormous multi-screen displays that show information from numerous Windows screens at the same time. This framework was created at a time when the display resolution of a common computer screen was 1024×768 pixels, which was lower than today's standard. In the case of standard font size, this is sufficient to show around half a page of A4 or American letters, which is a fairly small amount of text. A large number of tools are provided with digital text to enable users to access and display select paragraphs due to the fact that the "text landscape" presented on the screen is continually changing. Scroll bars and tabs (which are also found in many other software applications, such as spreadsheets and word processors) are examples of general-purpose tools. Other tools for adjusting the size or position of text on the screen include tools for navigating between embedded hyperlink text fragments and menus, which are examples of more specific tools such as moving between embedded hyperlink text fragments. There is increasing evidence that digital text navigation necessitates the development of specialized abilities (OECD, 2011; Rouet et al., 2012). The capacity to process text utilizing high-density navigation tools, as well as the ability to process text in general, must be evaluated. Simply put, the PISA 2018 framework differentiates between "static" and "dynamic" text for a variety of reasons. In contrast to "static", non-linear text that is difficult to organize and has a low density of navigation tools (typically one or more screen pages that are ordered in a linear way), "dynamic" text is more complicated, non-linear, and has a greater density of navigation devices. Keep in mind that the word "density" is preferable to "quantity" when describing the fact that dynamic text does not have to be any longer than static text. It is important to ensure broad coverage in this field while also maintaining consistency with the previous framework, so the 2018 framework retains the previously mentioned "format" and "type" of text classification dimensions, both of which are essentially the same as those in the previous framework.

In text categorization, differentiating between continuous and discontinuous text is a critical step. In addition, distinguishing between continuous and discontinuous text lies at the heart of the PISA 2000 framework and assessment structure. On the other hand, continuous writing is often made up of phrases that are grouped into paragraphs. These are appropriate for bigger structures such as chapters, chapters, and whole volumes, among others. Continuous and discontinuous text may be either fixed text or dynamic text. Discontinuous text is often represented as a matrix format based on a mix of lists. Mixed and rich text may be fixed text as well as dynamic text; however, it is more often than not dynamic text. In the following sections, we will go through each of the four forms in further depth. Other non-text format objects, particularly dynamic text, are often utilized for fixed text, as is the case with dynamic text. Pictograms and graphic pictures are often used to supplement fixed text and may be considered as part of the fixed text under certain circumstances. Still photos and video, as well as animation and audio files, are often accompanied by dynamic text and may be regarded to be a component of that text in certain cases. Although PISA does not include non-text items for the purpose of assessing reading ability, any such things may theoretically exist in PISA as part of the (spoken) text in the future. In practice, however, video and animation are only used in a relatively restricted number of the present exams. Audio is not utilized at all due to practical constraints, such as the need for headphones and audio translation, which prevent it from being used.

In terms of text format, differentiating between continuous text and discontinuous text is an essential way of text categorization, and it is also one of the tenets of the PISA 2000 framework and assessment organization, which are both based on the PISA 2000 framework and evaluation organization. On the other hand, continuous writing is often made up of phrases that are grouped into paragraphs. These are appropriate for bigger structures such as chapters, chapters, and whole volumes, among others. Discontinuous text is often presented in a matrix style that is comprised of a series of lists. Text that is continuous and discontinuous may be either fixed text or dynamic text. Mixed and rich text may be fixed text as well as dynamic text; however, it is more often than not dynamic text. In the following sections, we will go through each of the four forms in further depth. Other non-text format objects, particularly dynamic text, are often utilized for fixed text, as is the case with dynamic text. Illustrations and graphics Images are often shown in the form of fixed text, and they might be legally considered to be a part of that fixed text. Still photos and video, as well as animation and audio files, are often accompanied by dynamic text and may be regarded to be a component of that text in certain cases. Although PISA does not include non-text items for the purpose of assessing reading ability, any such things may theoretically exist in PISA as part of the (spoken) text in the future. In practice, however, video and animation are only used in a relatively restricted number of the present exams. Audio is not utilized at all due to practical constraints, such as the need for headphones and audio translation, which prevent it from being used. Continuous text is made up of paragraphs that are made up of sentences. The following are some examples of continuous text: newspaper reports and articles, novels and short tales, reviews, and correspondence. Text is arranged graphically or visually by using sentence and paragraph separation (such as indentation) and punctuation norms to create a logical flow. In addition, the text follows a hierarchical framework, including headers and material to assist readers in identifying the book's organizational structure. These tags also serve as cues as to where the text's limits are (e.g., to indicate the completion of a paragraph). It is generally simpler to discover information when multiple font sizes, font kinds (such as italics and bold), borders, and styles are used. The ability to read well while using typefaces and formatting suggestions is a vital skill. Discourse markers are also used to provide organizational information to the listener. Using sequence tags ("first", "second", "third", etc.), for example, might highlight the connection between each unit introduced into the next and the relationship between these units and the broader text around them. Causal connectives (e.g., "hence", "for this reason", "because", and so on) show the existence of a causal link between two or more components of a text. Because the structure of the discontinuous text and continuous text is different, various reading approaches must be used to read both. The majority of the disjointed text is composed of lists. Some are single, simple lists, but the majority are made of numerous simple lists that may or may not intersect with one another. The following are examples of discontinuous text objects: lists of words or numbers, tables of contents, charts and graphs, advertising, schedules, indexes, and tables. These text objects might be either static or dynamic in nature. Due to the way many fixed and dynamic texts are constructed as a single, cohesive product from several continuous and discontinuous format parts, they are referred to as mixed texts. For example, paragraphs containing illustrations or diagrams with legends are examples of mixed text. If a mixed text is properly constructed, the components (e.g., a chart or table with necessary prose explanations) will go through the levels of local (e.g., finding a city on a map) and global (e.g., discussing trends depicted in graphs) complexity. Printed periodicals, reference books, and reports often utilize a mixed text style in which writers use a variety of representations to convey information. If the author uses dynamic text, the author's web page will often have a mixture of text, including lists, prose paragraphs, and visuals. Continuous and discontinuous formatted text may also be seen in message-based text (e.g., online forms, emails, and discussion forums). According to the previous version of the framework, the "multi" format established in that version is now stated as a form of the new "source" dimension defined above.

### 1.2.2.3 Digital reading

In many diverse locations and for many different reasons, information and communication equipment based on digital technology is extensively utilized and readily available. In terms of similarities, the most significant thing to note is that they both allow for the display and reading of text. In reality, text messaging is used in almost all computer technology applications, including video games. Therefore, users of computers and network digital technologies are compelled to read digital language regardless of their purpose, mission, or objective.

In addition, digital technology has had a significant impact on the form, content, and life cycle of texts, which has in turn had an impact on the nature of reading itself. It is important for the government and society to be aware of these developments since they are beginning to have an impact on practically all elements of social life, including the government, education, employment, business, and civic life. Just a few examples: increasing numbers of taxpayers are completing forms online; students are searching for information on the Internet; job seekers are searching for job advertisements on recruitment websites; consumers are ordering goods from online retailers; and people are creating and maintaining online social communities. All of these actions, as well as many others, need the creation, diffusion, and reading of some kind of text.

#### 1.2.2.3.1 The addition of new capabilities to digital texts

The text shown on a computer screen may seem to be extremely similar to the text written on paper. They make use of the same fundamental symbology, the same grammar, and, to a certain degree, the same principles that are used to construct paragraphs and signal structures as well. A deeper inspection, on the other hand, will uncover significant discrepancies. One notable distinction is the physical size of the display area, sometimes known as the "page". A 15-inch computer screen is only the size of an A4 sheet of paper, making it far smaller than printed periodicals, catalogs, or supermarket flyers. Tablets and smartphones, which have significantly smaller displays than traditional electronic gadgets, have been more popular in recent years. Furthermore, because of the tiny size and poor quality of digital information, users of digital text are often confronted with issues such as diminished readability and fragmented information presentation. The excerpt from the printed page generally matches the display size of the page on the computer monitor or tablet. Digital text, on the other hand, should not be seen as a lesser quality replica of printed text. Digital technology is continuing to advance, and it may one day be able to compete with high-quality printing in terms of quality. Additional to this, the developers of digital documents have developed new publication standards to overcome the inherent shortcomings of digital media (e.g., consider increasingly popular web-based applications tailored for small screens). New techniques of conveying and arranging information have also been made possible by digital technology, some of which provide clear advantages to readers as compared with traditional printed text.

i. From static pages to dynamic Windows and frames

Readers may now travel between pages of text using digital text, which is a novel experience. Some of these issues are connected to the aforementioned constraints of digital displays, while others are the result of innovative innovations that give users novel methods to read and move through text content. When considering the influence of these new gadgets on digital reading abilities, it is important to note certain fundamental distinctions between printed text and digital text in terms of page layout and volume organization, which we will discuss later.

Physical objects are often mentioned in written text, which indicates that the content is linked to them. Text appears in two forms: as spoken knowledge and as tangible objects such as a page, a chapter, or a volume. Printed text may and should be saved and indexed in the same way that any other physical collection is. As a result, libraries have utilized a numbering system to arrange volumes and page numbers since at least the 16th century. In both circumstances, the number always refers to the item's position in the relevant collection's sequence, regardless of the case. As a result, catalogs and indexes have become widely used cataloging strategies for printed documents in recent years.

In digital text, on the other hand, the actual storage of information is structured independently of the reader's actions. Additionally, the page numbers of digital text are not reliant on the particular device on which they are presented. In the majority of circumstances, the page is bigger than the actual display screen or window on which it is shown. This is the primary distinction between printed text, which has a frame that is typically equivalent to a physical page and occasionally smaller, such as a newspaper page, and other types of text. The virtual nature of page content and format necessitates the use of indexing and retrieval methods other than page combination and numbering, which are not always feasible. Over the last 20 years, these technologies have progressed, and navigation devices have also changed their browser versions to keep up with the times. The electronic text is sent with a mechanism that enables readers to travel between and within the pages of the electronic text, if necessary. Vertical and horizontal scroll bars, index tabs, and expandable menu frames have all been popular navigational tools for digital sites during the last decade. None of these gadgets make any sense when it comes to the printed page.

ii. From linear arrangement to networking and hyperlinking

At the level of various text combinations, such as in e-books or websites, the most substantial disparities between printed and digital displays may be seen. The designers of digital documents have devised a variety of approaches to display the information of these compounds and to move the reader from one page to the next on the screen. The menu, which is a list of page titles from which readers may choose, is one of the early indexing strategies used in electronic publications and is still in use today. The digital menu is comparable to a table of contents, except that it does not always include page numbers as well. As an alternative, readers pick choices by directly clicking on the item or symbol that symbolizes the option, which enables the chosen page to be shown rather than the top of the menu page (that is, in a new window or TAB). However, since there is no page number, once a page is presented, the reader will not be able to determine where the page is in relation to the rest of the e-book. To give these hints, analogy symbols must be used in conjunction with other symbols. Menus may be layered, which implies that choosing a menu item will show another, more particular menu once it has been selected. A separate page or a section of a multi-text page may also be used to show the results. Menus are increasingly appearing in frames at the top or left of the display window when seen in the context of websites. This allows the reader to comprehend where he or she is in relation to the document collection by updating the remainder of the window while maintaining its menu structure.

Recently, with the introduction of mobile devices that can show vast quantities of multimedia information, the issue of building efficient menu systems for digital information systems has come back to the forefront of discussion. In addition, the construction of "hands-free" menu systems that are directed by eye motions or language is a current topic of active study and development. When it comes to digital text, one of the most noticeable characteristics is the hypertext link, which is a technique that was developed in the 1980s to connect information pages in huge electronic texts. It is a piece of information (typically a word or phrase) that logically connects to another piece of information, often known as a hypertext link, or hyperlink (usually a page). When you click on the hyperlink, you will be sent to a new page rather than the previous page or the top of the page that you were on. A list of hyperlinks (sometimes known as a menu) or an embedded content page may be used to show hyperlinks. When hyperlinks are embedded, they are often identified by a certain color or typeface. To generate multi-page documents with a network structure, hyperlinks should be employed. In contrast to lists or hierarchical structures, the placement of pages in a network structure is not a logical progression. Instead, it follows a semantic link that spans several pages. A hyperlink is a text link that allows the creator of a multi-page digital document to connect one page to another on the document. Hyperlinks encourage the growth of digital papers (hypertext), and the general organizational structure of digital documents differs from that of conventional documents. Initially, hypertext was hailed as a way of "liberating" readers from the stifling restrictions of so-called linear text, according to several early research. Scientific study on hypertext reading, on the other hand, has shown that network-like document arrangement often results in confusion and cognitive overload (Conklin, 1987). The capacity of the reader to mentally articulate the top-level structure of hypertext seems to be critical for navigation and direction in non-linear frameworks. Because global organizers commonly make use of well-known symbols and metaphors, it is often beneficial to appropriately depict the general structure of an information space built of hypertext pages (such as structured menus and content maps) to avoid confusion (Rouet & Potelle, 2005).

In brief, expertise with explicit and embedded hyperlinks, non-linear page structures, and global content display methods and tools is required for success in reading, navigating, and searching for information in digital text. According to the empirical findings thus far, viewing digital text is far from simple and may provide certain difficulties for some types of users in particular (such as the elderly).

iii. From illustrated text to multimedia and augmented reality

In addition, digital technology has provided new techniques for merging spoken text with other types of expressive expression. Instructions and comments may be shown by clicking on photographs and graphics on the internet. The use of text may be mixed with the use of animated images, graphics, and even video resources. When using augmented reality, users may blend their real-world surroundings with explanations and comments provided by digital gadgets. Individuals may now stroll the streets of cities, visit museums and exhibits, and study professional skills ranging from mechanics to surgeons thanks to the widespread usage of multimedia presentations on fixed and mobile digital devices, according to the latest statistics available. These enhancements are still considered too modest to be included in the 2009 edition of the PISA digital reading evaluation, but they will be progressively included in future PISA tests.

iv. From authored texts to online discussion and social networks

The transition from so-called certified text to message-based discussion forums, social networks, and Web 2.0 is another notable element of digital text. Internet use has grown in popularity, as has electronic display interactivity, which has enabled the development of new kinds of communication that bridge the gap between conventional written text and spoken discourse. It is becoming more usual to utilize the Internet to send and receive e-mail or text messages, engage in discussion groups, and maintain social contacts. It is necessary to master reading comprehension and writing abilities for these activities, even if the book in question is of a new genre and form to the participant. An investigation of the influence of these new kinds of discourse communication on the learning of skills is required.

### 1.2.2.3.2 New features of digital reading

As technology advances, people's reading and exchanging of information at home and in the office is changing at an alarming rate. From schooling to working in actual or virtual workplaces to dealing with personal affairs like as taxes, healthcare, and vacation arrangements, the Internet is becoming more pervasive in the lives of all residents. Persistent personal and professional growth is a lifetime activity, and future students will need to be comfortable with digital technologies to properly handle the growing amounts and complexity of information.

In parallel with the movement from printed materials to computer displays to smartphones as the medium through which we acquire information, the structure and format of text have also evolved. This, in turn, necessitates the development of new cognitive methods and the clarification of objectives in the context of intentional reading. As a result, excellent reading ability no longer consists just in the capacity to read and comprehend written language. However, while the extended ability to understand and interpret continuous texts (including literary texts) is still valuable, success also requires the deployment of complex information processing strategies, such as the analysis of relevant information from multiple texts (or information) and the integration of relevant information from multiple texts (or information). And explain where the information came from. Furthermore, to be successful and productive citizens, they will need to employ knowledge from a variety of subjects (such as physics and mathematics) as well as technology to efficiently search, organize, and filter vast volumes of information. Developing these abilities will be essential for full involvement in the 21st century job market, continued education, and participation in social and civic activities (OECD, 2013b).

As a result of the widespread use of ICT by the general population, there has been a considerable change in reading habits from print to digital formats. This transition has had a significant influence on the way reading is defined as a talent in today's society. For starters, the material that individuals read on the Internet differs from the content that they read in conventional printed form. Digital gadgets need online readers to work beyond limitations such as smaller displays, cluttered screens, and difficult websites to make use of rich information, communication, and other services. Aside from that, other forms of digital communication have evolved, including e-mail, text messaging, discussion forums, and social networking programs. However, it must be stressed that, with the advancement of digital technology, individuals must read more selectively but also more often and for a broader variety of reading reasons than they have in the past. As a result, readers must be familiar with these new text-based genres as well as social and cultural behaviors.

In addition, readers in the digital age must learn a number of new abilities. They must have a basic understanding of information and ICT to comprehend and operate equipment and applications. Additionally, they must use search engines, menus, links, tags, and other paging and scrolling capabilities to locate and obtain the information they need. Because of the abundance of information available on the Internet, readers must exercise caution when selecting information sources and must evaluate the quality and authenticity of the information they are receiving before using it. Finally, the reader must go through the document to verify the facts, discover any discrepancies and conflicts, and work to resolve such conflicts and differences. The following are some examples of the significance of these new abilities:

v.  Accessing texts of interest

For the printed text to be effective, the reader must first locate a significant artifact, then utilize the categories and organizers to locate material relevant to the item. Readers must search for terms in digital text, scan for unexpected links, and utilize navigation gadgets to navigate through it. The latter must be able to produce vocabulary, evaluate the importance of language expression (while ignoring interference), and comprehend the information layer in the menu tree. To be a skilled digital text reader, one must be acquainted with the operation of navigational equipment and instruments, among other things. In addition, he or she must be able to mentally visualize the movement of the window on the text page in order for it to move in the right direction. This includes the ability to work around apparent discrepancies, such as the fact that the down arrow on the scroll bar actually pushes the text up rather than down. As early as 1989, Foss observed that certain users had a tendency to get disoriented in the Windows labyrinth on the computer screen; early human factor research generally determined that for the majority of readers, just two side-by-side windows seem to be a reasonable compromise (Wiley, 2001; Wright, 1993). The ability to open, arrange, and close several windows is a talent in and of itself. There is evidence to suggest that reading sophisticated digital text requires not just language processing skills, but also visual and spatial ability (Pazzaglia et al., 2008; Naumann et al., 2008).

vi.  Integrate information across texts

Regardless of the medium employed, integration is defined as the comparison and connection of multiple text fragments that need comparable processing. Reading multiple texts in one sitting is more likely to happen when digital material does not follow a stable categorization system, and when digital media makes it so simple to cross-reference text, readers are more likely to find themselves skipping different readings in one sitting. In addition, the Internet provides readers with the ability to gather a huge number of various sources for any given issue at their leisure. Because of this, the accumulation of information from several pieces has become a characteristic of digital writing that is read in a continuous fashion. For young readers, cross-text integration necessitates the development of complicated reading abilities and techniques that are not readily accessible to them (Britt & Rouet, 2012). Even though these abilities are not specific to digital reading, they may account for a significant portion of a reader's digital reading aptitude in general.

vii. Evaluating texts for quality and credibility

A vast variety of content is available to users of web-based papers because of the open and uncontrolled nature of internet publishing. The majority of retrieval systems today are based on semantic matching between queries and material, regardless of whether the query is of a certain kind, whether it is accurate, if it is authoritative, or whether it is credible. Readers need to be aware of not just the substance of the piece, but also its author, publisher, publishing date, intent, and any possible biases included within it. These attributions are often supported in the print world by a number of perceptual and contextual clues (such as the appearance and position of the text) as well as the presence of human media (such as librarians, booksellers, and reviewers). On the Internet, however, these cues and mediators are mostly absent, and readers must rely on their own inferences to determine the quality of the material (Britt & Gabrys, 2000). It is becoming increasingly clear that evaluating online information is a difficult aspect of digital reading for most teenagers, despite the fact that they increasingly rely on the Internet to obtain new information on topics of interest (Dinet et al., 2003; Kuiper et al., 2005).

### *1.2.2.4 Assessing reading literacy*

In this part, we will discuss the usage of scenarios, the elements that influence the complexity of the project, the dimensions that should be used to guarantee that all domains are covered, and other significant topics that should be considered while designing and executing the evaluation.

#### 1.2.2.4.1 Scenarios

Reading is an intentional action that takes place in a certain target setting, such as a classroom. When taking a standard reading assessment, applicants will be given a series of unconnected essays on a variety of broad themes to complete. In each article, students are required to respond to a series of irrelevant questions before moving on to the next irrelevant article. Students are really intended to "forget" what they have read before while answering the questions in the next paragraphs, according to the typical design of the course. As a result, reading has no other primary function except to provide answers to distinct inquiries. Student engagement in assignments may be increased using scenario-based assessment approaches, which allows for more accurate evaluation of students' skills. Unlike the traditional independent PISA reading unit, the 2018 PISA assessment will include scenarios in which students will be required to read a series of topics-related articles to complete more advanced tasks (such as answering some larger comprehensive questions or writing recommendation letters based on a set of articles), such as the traditional PISA reading unit. Reading objectives provide a set of goals or criteria that students may use to search for information, evaluate sources, read comprehension, and/or integrate literature into their learning. This may encompass everything from chosen literary masterpieces to textbooks to e-mails to blogs to websites to policy papers to historical materials and anything in between. Candidates may not be able to choose related texts for their own reading and personal purposes from the prompts and tasks derived from this framework; however, the purpose of this assessment is to allow candidates to have a certain degree of freedom in choosing the source and path of the text used in response original hint. The effectiveness of goal-driven reading may be assessed within the limits of large-scale assessment in this manner.

### 1.2.2.4.2 Responsibilities

Each scenario has one or more activities that must be completed. Text-related questions may be asked in each task, ranging from traditional comprehension items (locating information and formulating arguments) to more complex tasks such as synthesizing and integrating multiple texts, evaluating web search results, and confirming the information in multiple texts, among others. To complete each job, one or more processes defined in the framework must be evaluated. Students' talents may be measured by assigning them activities in the scenario that is progressively more demanding from low to high in difficulty. Consider the following scenario: a student is presented with an initial assignment in which he or she must locate a certain document from a list of search results. Students may be required to respond to questions pertaining to the material included in the article for the second assignment. In the final activity, students may be required to decide if the author's points of view in the first article are consistent with those expressed by the author in the second piece. It is possible to construct the tasks in each instance such that, if the student does not locate the proper document in the first assignment, he or she will be provided with the correct document for completion of the second work in each circumstance. It will not be possible to "totally or entirely deactivate" the complicated multi-part scenario in this manner, but it will be possible to triangulate various student ability levels via a series of realistic activities. The scenarios and problems used in the 2018 PISA reading exam, as well as the units and projects used in the prior assessment, are a direct reflection of this. It is more realistic than conventional context-based evaluation since it models the way people interact with and utilize sources of information, as well as reading and writing. This course exposes students to real-world issues as well as problems that need to be addressed. It requires the use of both fundamental and advanced reading and thinking abilities. A logical extension of the standard cell-based PISA approach, this scenario provides a step forward. The PISA 2012 problem-solving assessment and the PISA 2015 collaborative problem-solving exam both employed a scenario-based method to test problem-solving skills.

Introduction 35

It is anticipated that each task will test one of the three basic cognitive processes described above. In this case, they might be considered to be different types of assessment items. Items from past PISA reading ability examinations will be utilized to track trends in reading ability. As a result, to achieve the required proportion of tasks containing multiple texts, and because previous PISA assessments concentrated on tasks containing only one text, the development of new projects will primarily require the creation of tasks containing multiple texts (e.g., searching and selecting related texts, understanding the reasoning of multiple texts, and confirming/handling conflicts), among other things. However, you must give a sufficient number of individual text items to guarantee that subsequent trend items fill the full frame at the same time.

### 1.2.2.4.3 Factors affecting item difficulty

The PISA Reading Assessment is designed to track and report on students' reading abilities at the completion of their compulsory schooling, which is 15 years old. Each activity in the assessment is designed to obtain real evidence of this capacity by imitating reading experiences in which readers may choose to engage or withdraw from the school environment (as a teenager or adult). Tasks in PISA reading literacy vary from simple placement and comprehension exercises to more difficult activities that include the integration of information from many texts. It is possible to alter the complexity of the work by modifying the program and text format settings.

### 1.2.2.4.4 Factors improving the coverage of the domain

Different reading scenarios may be created to emulate different possible reading situations. Context is a word that is most often used to describe the context and use of a text in which the reader is involved. In most cases, context is employed to match a certain text type and author with a specific text type and author. In the case of textbooks, they are often created for students who will utilize them in a formal educational setting. As a result, context is often used to refer to the context in which the text is being read, as well as the intended audience and purpose of the writing. However, in some cases, different types of texts are involved, such as when history students record first-hand events (such as personal diaries or court testimony) and academic papers written long after the event, such as when history students record first-hand events (such as personal diaries or court testimony) and academic papers written long after the event. These circumstances might be either private or public, professional or educational in nature. It should be underlined again that many writings may be classified in more than one way depending on the circumstance they are written for. In practice, an article may be written for amusement and guidance (both personal and educational), to offer professional advice, which is also general information, or to provide professional advice, which is also general information (professional and public). It is the goal of extracting texts from various settings to increase the amount of material available for the PISA reading literacy exam.

The goal and internal arrangement of the text are referred to as the text's construction in the text type. Among the most common sorts of text are description, narrative, elaboration, argumentation, direction, and transactional information. Real-world texts have a tendency to breach the boundaries of text genres and are thus difficult to categorize. It is, nonetheless, beneficial to categorize text by text type (based on the primary features of the text) in tests such as PISA to guarantee that a diverse variety of reading kinds is represented in the data set. Werlich's (1976) work was utilized to develop the text type categorization system that was used in PISA 2018. In a similar vein, many texts may be classified as belonging to many text kinds at the same time.

### 1.2.2.4.5 Response formats

Student talents are shown in a variety of ways, and how they are demonstrated is determined by the sort of data gathered as well as any inherent constraints of large-scale evaluations. Like any large-scale assessment, there is a limit to the number of project forms that may be used. However, computer-based assessment makes it possible to use answer forms that include textual activities, such as highlighting and drag-and-dropping, in addition to traditional response formats. Computer-based examinations, like paper-based tests, may incorporate multiple-choice questions as well as brief responses (students write their own answers). Students with different personalities exhibit varying levels of performance as a result of the various response formats. PISA data have been used in a variety of studies, all of which have shown that the manner of the answer has a major influence on the performance of various groups. In light of this discrepancy, it is critical to keep a comparable percentage of the answer formats of the items used in each PISA cycle to track changes over the course of the study.

The fact that open structured response questions are especially significant in the evaluation, reflection, and evaluation process is yet another aspect in the context of reading literacy assessment. The assessment method is often geared to evaluate the quality of students' thinking rather than the final solution itself, as opposed to the final answer itself. However, since the assessment is primarily focused on reading rather than writing, structured answer questions should not place an undue emphasis on the evaluation of writing abilities such as spelling and grammar, for example. Finally, pupils from different nations are not aware of the many types of replies that are available. As a result, including a variety of course formats in the curriculum is likely to give opportunity for all students, regardless of country, to encounter both familiar and unexpected forms. For the most part, regardless of whether or not the teaching model changes, the PISA reading literacy assessment will continue to use multiple-choice questions and open-ended structured answer questions to ensure adequate coverage of abilities, fair treatment of observed differences between countries and genders, and effective assessment of reflection and evaluation processes. Any large changes in the distribution of item types will have a negative impact on the measurement of trends in electronic reading exams as compared with paper-based assessments.

### 1.2.2.4.6 Assessing ease and efficiency

The PISA 2018 reading literacy assessment will include an assessment of reading fluency, which is defined as the ease and efficiency with which students can read simple texts for comprehension (OECD, 2019). This will provide a valuable indicator for describing and understanding the differences between students, especially those with lower reading levels (OECD, 2019). Students with low basic reading skills may spend too much attention and cognitive effort on lower-level skills such as decoding, word recognition, and sentence parsing, resulting in insufficient resources to complete single or multiple texts. This finding applies to young people and young readers.

The PISA 2018 computer management and scoring program measures the difficulty and efficiency of reading text accurately for 15-year-old children. Although as mentioned above, not all slow reading is bad reading, there is a lot of evidence showing how and why a person's lack of automaticity in basic reading becomes a bottleneck to higher levels of reading ability and is related to comprehension. Poor ability is related (Rayner et al., 2001). Therefore, it is very valuable to have a simple and effective indicator to better describe and explain the low-level performance of the PISA reading comprehension task. The basic indicators of reading speed under low-demand conditions can also be used for other purposes, such as investigating the degree to which students adjust reading speed or strategic processes when faced with more complex tasks or larger amounts of text. More importantly, with the exponential growth of text content on the Internet, students in the 21st century need not only skilled readers but also effective readers. Although there are many ways to define, manipulate, and measure the ease of use, efficiency, or fluency of reading, the most common way for readers to not read aloud when using silent reading tasks is as an indicator of accuracy and speed. The measurement of oral reading fluency, that is, readers reading aloud, can also be used to assess the reader's rhyme and expressive ability, but unfortunately, oral reading fluency cannot be implemented and scored in all PISA languages. In addition, it is uncertain whether the measurement of oral reading fluency will increase the value of silent reading accuracy and reading rate indicators (Eason et al., 2013; Kuhn et al., 2010). Therefore, silent reading task design is the most feasible in PISA management.

To better understand the challenges faced by 15-year-olds who score low in the PISA reading ability assessment, a specific task can be performed at the beginning of the assessment to measure the ease of use and efficiency of reading. The performance of this task can be measured and reported independently of the primary proficiency scale. As mentioned above, poor reading efficiency may be a symptom of poor basic skills. However, some people, such as non-native English speakers, may have a relatively slow reading speed, but through compensation or strategic processes, when they have enough time to complete complex tasks, they can become higher-level readers. Therefore, the most prudent approach seems to be to use readability indicators as descriptive variables to help distinguish students who may lack basic skills from students who are slow but proficient in reading. In addition, ease of use and reading efficiency can be used as one of several indicators to determine the level of student health testing (see "Precautions for Health Testing" below). However, due to the reasons mentioned in the previous paragraph, this method is not suitable as the only indicator of reading level. In other surveys, a task that has been effectively used as an indicator of reading difficulty and efficiency requires students to read sentences and judge their credibility based on the general knowledge of the sentence or the logical consistency within the sentence. The test not only considers the accuracy of students' understanding of the article but also considers the time it takes to read and answer.

Data from complex reading literacy tasks will not be used to measure reading fluency in the 2018 PISA test. The task of reading fluency should be specific to the structural design and guidance of reading fluency. Therefore, the text needs to be simple and short so that students will not use strategies or compensation processes when answering questions. In addition, the task requires minimal reasoning to avoid confusion between decision time and reading time. The more complex the task, the less likely it is to assess reading fluency alone. However, it is recommended to analyze the log files of this cycle to evaluate whether the new PISA reading literacy task set has indicators that are closely related to sentence-level efficiency tasks.

#### 1.2.2.4.7 Assessing students' reading motivation, reading practices and awareness of reading strategies

Since PISA 2000, the Reading Literacy Framework has emphasized the importance of reader motivational attributes (such as their attitudes towards reading) and the importance of reading practice; therefore, items and scales to measure these structures have been developed in the student questionnaire. It should be noted that reading motivation and reading strategies vary depending on the context and text type. Therefore, the questionnaire items that assess motivation and reading strategies should involve a series of situations that students may discover. In addition to being more relevant, being more specific can also reduce the risk of bias in scoring and self-reported responses.

Motivation and participation are powerful variables and levers that we can use to improve reading and narrow the gap between student groups. In the previous PISA cycle, reading literacy was the main area (PISA 2000 and PISA 2009), and the main motivation structure of the survey was reading interest and intrinsic motivation. The scale that measures interest and intrinsic motivation also includes reading avoidance, which is a lack of interest or motivation and has a strong negative correlation with achievement, especially among readers with dyslexia. According to the 2018 PISA research, the PISA questionnaire will investigate two other factors: self-efficacy (a person's perceptual ability to perform a specific task) and self-concept (a person's perceptual ability to perform a specific field). Reading exercises were previously measured by self-reported frequency of reading different types of text in various media (including online reading). For PISA 2018, the list of online reading exercises will be updated and expanded to take account of combined exercises (such as e-books, online searches, text messages, and social networks).

Metacognition is a person's ability to think and control reading comprehension strategies. By using these strategies, readers can effectively interact with the text and regard reading as a problem-solving task, requiring strategic thinking to complete reading comprehension. In previous PISA cycles, participation and metacognition have proven to be reliable predictors of reading performance, mediators of gender or socioeconomic status, and potential levers for closing performance gaps. The questionnaire has updated and expanded the measurement standards of motivation, metacognition, and reader practice to take into account recent and emerging reading practices, as well as better measurement standards for teaching practices and classroom support that support reading growth. Proficiency in reading requires students to understand and apply strategies to optimize the knowledge they gain from the text, while taking into account their goals and objectives. For example, students must know when it is appropriate to read an article, or when the task requires continuous and complete reading of the article. PISA 2009 collected information about reading strategies through two reading scenarios. In the first scenario, students are required to evaluate the effectiveness of different reading and text comprehension strategies in achieving information summarization goals; in the second group, students must evaluate the effectiveness of other strategies for comprehension and memorization of the text. According to the new characteristics of the reading process, Pisa 2018 will also collect reading strategy knowledge related to the evaluation of the material quality and credibility goals, especially digital reading and reading multiple articles.

There is strong research evidence that classroom practice, such as direct teaching of reading strategies, can help improve reading skills. In addition, teachers' support and support for autonomy, ability, and task ownership have improved students' reading skills, strategic awareness, and reading participation. In most education systems, reading is no longer a math and science subject for 15-year-old children, and some reading instruction may be explicit or incidental to language courses and other subjects (such as social sciences, science, foreign languages, civics, or ICT). The scattered challenge in reading teaching is to determine the questionnaire items that measure classroom practice and opportunities to learn reading strategies that can best support the development of students' reading skills, practice, and motivation.

The deployment of computer assessments in PISA creates opportunities for adaptation testing. Adaptability testing allows each student to use fewer items to achieve a higher level of measurement accuracy. This is done by showing students items that match their ability level. Adaptability testing has the potential to improve the resolution and sensitivity of evaluation, especially at the low end of the distribution of student performance. For example, students who perform poorly on reading fluency assessment projects may have difficulty with highly complex multi-text projects. Future PISA cycles can provide these students with additional low-level texts to better assess specific aspects of their understanding.

### *1.2.2.5 Reporting proficiency in reading*

In terms of proficiency, PISA measures student accomplishment in a way that may be interpreted in terms of educational policy considerations. Reading literacy assessment results are summed in a single comprehensive reading literacy scale with an average of 500 and a standard deviation of 100 in PISA 2000, which is a reading literacy exam that focuses on reading proficiency. In addition to the comprehensive scale, students completed five subscales: three process (aspect) subscales (information retrieval, text interpretation, reflection, and assessment), two text format subscales, and one text format subscale (information retrieval and text interpretation) (continuous and discontinuous). Using the average score and distribution of each component of reading literacy construction, these five subscales may be used to compare results across various subgroups and nations. Despite the fact that these subscales are closely connected, there are some notable variances between the subscales themselves. There are many ways to look for and relate these disparities to the curriculum and teaching techniques used in the respective nation. Reading has once again emerged as a prominent focus of PISA 2009, which this year includes complete scales and subscales as well as individual measures.

When the reading was a secondary subject in the PISA exams in 2003, 2006, 2012, and 2015, and the students taking the test had fewer reading questions, the single reading literacy scale was reported on the comprehensive scale, rather than the comprehensive scale. In 2018, reading re-established itself as the main area, and reports based on sub-scales were once again made available to students. The following subscales will be included in the PISA 2018 report: (1) location information, which includes activities requiring students to search for and pick relevant texts, as well as challenges requiring students to find relevant information within the text. (2) Comprehensiveness, which necessitates that students articulate the meaning of the text effectively and integrate knowledge, as well as complete the reasoning job. (3) Evaluation and reflection: Students are expected to evaluate the quality and trustworthiness of the information they have received, reflect on the content and form of the text they have read, identify, and resolve conflicts that exist within or between texts.

Literacy activities are evaluated according to the difficulty and abilities required to complete the work successfully in the same way as students may be ranked from lowest to maximum competence on a single scale. The context, text style, task requirements, and difficulty of the reading ability tests utilized in the PISA study all differ significantly. The scope of a project is determined via a process known as project mapping. The task map serves as a visual depiction of the reading literacy abilities shown by students at various levels of proficiency in reading. The length, structure, and intricacy of the text all contribute to the difficulty of the task. While the total difficulty will vary based on how the question or description is defined, the connection between the reader and the text will also influence the overall difficulty. It has been determined that a number of variables may contribute to the difficulty of any literacy task. These variables include the complexity of mental processes (such as retrieval and interpretation) that are critical to the task, the amount of information that readers must absorb, and the level of familiarity or new information readers must learn from within the text, among other things.

It is represented in PISA 2000, which demonstrates the intricacy and difficulty of this procedure. A total of six levels are defined by the comprehensive reading literacy scale and each subscale of the scale (below levels 1, 1, 2, 3, 4, and 5). In 2009 and 2015, PISA trends were measured using the International Student Assessment 2000 Comprehensive Scale Program, which is described as the International Student Assessment 2000 Comprehensive Scale Program. As a result of the newly established project, a more accurate description of the present performance level is provided, as is a description of a performance level that is greater or lower than that indicated by PISA. The scale was enlarged to six levels in 2000, with the first level being separated into two classes, Class 1A and Class 1B. This level offers an effective way for examining the development of reading literacy demands on comprehensive scales and subscales at the elementary and middle school levels. The scale represents a person's abilities as well as the difficulty of completing a task. Students who draw on a single scale and those who reflect the project are more likely to finish activities drawn on the same scale (or lower), but they are less likely to complete tasks drawn on a higher scale, according to the findings.

With no present upper limit on the greatest degree of reading literacy, it is possible to say that the upper limit on the reading ability of top pupils is indeterminate at this time. These kids, on the other hand, may nevertheless be classified as completing things at the maximum possible degree of competency. Students who are at the bottom of the reading literacy rankings are more likely to have significant difficulties. Despite the fact that their reading skill might be lower than 1b at this point, their reading ability—that is, what they can accomplish with their reading—is ineffable. Prior to designing new materials for the Pisa 2018 event, researchers want to gauge participants' present reading ability and comprehension at or below the 1B level.

In comparison to standard Item Response Theory (IRT) estimates like Maximum Likelihood Estimates or Weighted Maximum Likelihood Estimates, plausible values have significant methodological advantages. Indeed, plausible values provide unbiased estimates of (1) population performance parameters such as mean, standard deviation, or decomposition of variance; (2) percentages of students per proficiency level because they are on a continuous scale, as opposed to non-continuous estimates; and (3) bivariate or multivariate indices of relations between performance and background variables because this information is included in the psychometric model (OECD, 2013a).

On each performance scale, each student is usually assigned five realistic values. Statistical analyses should be run independently on each of these five possible values, and the results should be combined to get the final statistics estimates and standard errors. It is important to note that these standard errors will include sampling uncertainty as well as test unreliability. To obtain the final estimate of the parameter and its standard error, the plausible value methodology, combined with the replicates, requires that the parameter, such as a mean, a standard deviation, a percentage, or a correlation, be computed 405 times (i.e., five plausible values by one student final weights and 80 replicates). Working with one plausible value instead of five will give you an unbiased estimate of population parameters, but it won't tell you about the imputation error, which indicates the influence of test unreliability on parameter estimation. This imputation error is minor when dealing with a large dataset. The imputation error, on the other hand, increases as the sample size decreases.

As a summary, this section provides a high-level review of PISA's fundamental material, including its definition, what it assesses, how it is tested, and its influence as a large-scale assessment across nations, among other things. Because this book is primarily concerned with PISA reading, it goes into great depth on the evolution of the idea of PISA reading as well as the changes that have occurred in the PISA reading framework. In particular, since the fourth round of the PISA study in 2009, new aspects of digital text and digital reading have been deliberately developed to encourage the integration of digital reading into everyday life. When it comes to studying PISA reading, the field is wide open, and researchers can use a variety of variables to examine the relationship between students' paper reading and computer reading (Hahnel et al., 2018). For example, gender of students (e.g., Zhang et al., 2013), immigrant background (e.g., Marks, 2005), and socioeconomic status (e.g., Jahangir et al., 2015) at the individual level, school mean SES (e.g., Tang & Zhang, 2020) and school average achievement (e.g., Nagengast & Marsh, 2012). According to expectations, more and more research will be conducted in the near future, which will provide new problems to students' reading as well as raise more concerns concerning students' reading characteristics and reading habits. PISA will continue to offer a valuable contribution to researchers in the area of reading by serving as a dependable source of research questions pertaining to student reading achievement.

## 1.3 Research scopes

The quick spreading and incremental development of machine learning techniques have provided a new perspective for the examination of students' reading performances based on large-scale assessment. Therefore, this study aimed to analyze the synergistic impact of the factors/variables on high- and low-performing digital readers based on the latest-released PISA 2018 dataset. A powerful classification machine learning approach, namely, the support vector machine (SVM), as well as the SVM–recursive feature elimination (SVM–RFE) techniques were used to differentiate these two cohorts of students from a total of 146 contextual variables/factors.

In Chapter 2, the basic ideas of EDM is presented, followed by an introduction to the dynamic model of educational effectiveness. Accordingly, the student-level factors, classroom-level factors, school-level factors, and country-level factors of digital reading performance are carefully reviewed. Previous studies about the application of EDM approaches to analyze large-scale educational data are also presented. Chapter 3 basically addresses the three commonly-used methods in the exploration of educational data, namely, machine learning, hierarchical linear modeling, and structural equation models, and delineates the detailed process of data analytical process in this research. Chapter 4 presents the results obtained from the machine learning methods, where the performance of the SVM model, the optimal feature set, and the detailed descriptions of the key features are included. Chapter 5 discusses the results of the experiment following the classification of the factors of learning effectiveness (i.e., student-level factors, classroom-level factors, and school-level factors). In Chapter 6, the conclusions and research limitations are provided. With studies on PISA based on big data analysis forming the overarching theme, the book could be regarded as a guidance for utilizing machine learning algorithm in examining the mass global database. In an attempt to provide direct insights into the organization and development of PISA, the author writes this book for the purpose of identifying the origins and formations of every domain assessed, explaining tools employed to analyze data, giving further interpretations of PISA results and changes in results throughout the rounds, as well as allowing for growing attention to education amelioration and an appeal to more discussions on education.

## References

Abu, A. (2016). Educational data mining & students' performance prediction. *International Journal of Advanced Computer Science and Applications*, 7(5), 212–220. https://doi.org/10.14569/ijacsa.2016.070531

Alejandro, P. A. (2014). Educational data mining: A survey and a data mining-based analysis of recent works. *Expert Systems with Applications*, 41(4), 1432–1462. https://doi.org/10.1016/j.eswa.2013.08.042.

Alonso-Fernández, C., Calvo-Morata, A., Freire, M., Martínez-Ortiz, I., & Fernández-Manjón, B. (2019). Applications of data science to game learning analytics data: A systematic literature review. *Computers & Education*, 141, 1–14. https://doi.org/10.1016/j.compedu.2019.103612

Baker, R. S. (2015). *Big data and education* (2nd ed.). New York: Teachers College, Columbia University.

Binkley, M., Erstad, O., Herman, J., Raizen, S., Ripley, M., Miller-Ricci, M., & Rumble, M. (2011). Defining twenty-first century skills. In P. Griffin, B. McGaw, &

E. Care (Eds.), *Assessment and Teaching of 21st century skills* (pp. 17–66). Dordrecht: Springer Netherlands. http://doi.org/10.1007/978-94-007-2324-5_2

Braten, I., Britt, M., Stromso, H., & Rouet, J. (2011). The role of epistemic beliefs in the comprehension of multiple expository texts: Toward an integrated model. *Educational Psychologist, 46*(1), 48–70. http://doi.org/10.1080/00461520.2011.538647

Braten, I., Stromso, H., & Britt, M. (2009). Trust matters: Examining the role of source evaluation in students' construction of meaning within and across multiple texts. *Reading Research Quarterly, 44*(1), 6–28. https://doi.org/10.1598/rrq.44.1.1

Britt, M., & Rouet, J. (2012). Learning with multiple documents: Component skills and their acquisition. In J. Kirby, & M. Lawson (Eds.), *Enhancing the quality of learning: Dispositions, instruction, and learning processes* (pp. 276–314). New York: Cambridge University Press. http://doi.org/10.1017/CBO9781139048224.017

Britt, M. A., & Gabrys, G. (2000). `Teaching advanced literacy kills for the world wide web. In C. Wolfe (Ed.), *Webs we weave: Learning and teaching on the world wide web* (pp. 73–90). New York: Academic Press.

Coiro, J., Knobel, M., Lankshear, C., & Leu, D. J. (2008). Central issues in new literacies and new literacies research. In J. Coiro, M. Knobel, C. Lankshear, & D. J. Leu (Eds.), *Handbook of research on new literacies* (pp. 1–21). New York: Lawrence Erlbaum Associates, Taylor & Francis Group.

Conklin, J. (1987). Hypertext: An introduction and survey. *Computer, 20*(9), 17–41. https://doi.org/10.1109/MC.1987.1663693

Cunningham, A. E., & Stanovich, K. E. (1997). Early reading acquisition and its relation to reading experience and ability 10 years later. *Developmental Psychology, 33*(6), 934–945. https://doi.org/10.1037/0012-1649.33.6.934

Dinet, J., Marquet, P., & Nissen, E. (2003). An exploratory study of adolescent's perceptions of the web. *Journal of Computer Assisted Learning, 19*(4), 538–545. http://doi.org/10.1046/j.0266-4909.2003.00056.x

Duggan, G. B., & Payne, S. J. (2009). Text skimming: The process and effectiveness of foraging through text under time pressure. *Journal of Experimental Psychology: Applied, 15*(3), 228–242. http://doi.org/10.1037/a0016995

Eason, S. H., Sabatini, J., Goldberg, L., Bruce K., & Cutting, L. E. (2013). Examining the relationship between word reading efficiency and oral reading rate in predicting comprehension among different types of readers. *Scientific Studies of Reading, 17*(3), 199–223. http://doi.org/10.1080/10888438.2011.652722

Gantasala, P. V., Gantasala, S. B., & Naikgari, K. N. C. (2009). Knowledge management: An integrated approach. *International Journal of Knowledge. Culture and Change Management, 9*(1), 11–23. https://doi.org/10.18848/1447-9524/cgp/v09i01/50725

Goldman, S. (2004). Cognitive aspects of constructing meaning through and across multiple texts. In N. Shuart-Faris & D. Bloome (Eds.), *Uses of intertextuality in classroom and educational research* (pp. 313–347). Charlotte, NC: Information Age Publishing. Retrieved from: https://www.researchgate.net/publication/236116001_Cognitive_aspects_of_constructing_meaning_through_and_across_multiple_texts

Gray, W. S., & Rogers, B. (1956). *Maturity in reading: Its nature and appraisal.* Chicago: University of Chicago Press.

Guleria, P., Arora, M., & Sood, M. (2013). Increasing quality of education using educational data mining. In *Proceedings of the 2013 2nd International Conference on Information Management in the Knowledge Economy, IMKE 2013* (pp. 118–122). New York: Institute of Electrical and Electronics Engineers Inc.

Hahnel, C., Goldhammer, F., Kroehne, U., & Naumann, J. (2018). The role of reading skills in the evaluation of online information gathered from search engine environments. *Computers in Human Behavior, 78,* 223–234. https://doi.org/10.1016/j.chb.2017.10.004

Hu, J., Dong, X. & Peng, Y (2021). Discovery of the key contextual factors relevant to the reading performance of elementary school students from 61 countries/regions: Insight from a machine learning-based approach. *Reading and Writing, 35*(1), 93–127. https://doi.org/10.1007/s11145-021-10176-z

Jahangir, E., Lipworth, L., Edwards, T. L., Kabagambe, E. K., Mumma, M. T., Mensah, G. A., . . . Sampson, U. K. A. (2015). Smoking, sex, risk factors and abdominal aortic aneurysms: A prospective study of 18782 persons aged above 65 years in the southern community cohort study. *Journal of Epidemiology and Community Health, 69*(5), 481–488. https://doi.org/10.1136/jech-2014-204920

Križanić, S. (2020). Educational data mining using cluster analysis and decision tree technique: A case study. *International Journal of Engineering Business Management, 12,* Article 1847979020908675. https://doi.org/10.1177/1847979020908675

Kuhn, M., & Stahl, S. A. (2003). Fluency: A review of developmental and remedial practices. *Journal of Educational Psychology, 95*(1), 3–21. http://doi.org/10.1037/0022-0663.95.1.3

Kuhn, M. R., Schwanenflugel, P. J., & Meisinger, E. B. (2010). Aligning theory and assessment of reading fluency: Automaticity, prosody, and definitions of fluency. *Reading Research Quarterly, 45*(2), 230–251. http://doi.org/10.1598/RRQ.45.2.4

Kuiper, E., Volman, M., & Terwel, J. (2005). The web as an information resource in K-12 education: Strategies for supporting students in searching and processing information. *Review of Educational Research, 75*(3), 285–328. http://doi.org/10.3102/00346543075003285

Leu, D. J., Forzani, E., Rhoads, C., Maykel, C., Kennedy, C., & Timbrell, N. (2015). The new literacies of online research and comprehension: Rethinking the reading achievement Gap. *Reading Research Quarterly, 50*(1), 37–59. https://doi.org/10.1002/rrq.85

Marks, G. N. (2005). Accounting for immigrant non-immigrant differences in reading and mathematics in twenty countries. *Ethnic and Racial Studies, 28*(5), 925–946. http://doi.org/10.1080/01419870500158943

Mason, L., Boldrin, A., & Ariasi, N. (2010). Searching the web to learn about a controversial topic: Are students epistemically active? *Instructional Science, 38,* 607–633. https://doi.org/10.1007/s11251-008-9089-y

McCrudden, M. T., & Schraw, G. (2007). Relevance and goal-focusing in text processing. *Educational Psychology Review, 19*(2), 113–139. http://doi.org/10.1007/s10648-006-9010-7

Nagengast, B., & Marsh, H. W. (2012). Big fish in little ponds aspire more: Mediation and cross-cultural generalizability of school-average ability effects on self-concept and career aspirations in science. *Journal of Educational Psychology, 104*(4), 1033–1053. https://doi.org/10.1037/a0027697

Naumann, J. (2008). Log File Analysis in hypertext research: An overview, a meta-Analysis, and some suggestions for future research. In J. J. Cañas (Ed.), *Workshop on cognition and the web: Information processing, comprehension and learning* (pp. 53–57). Granada: University of Granada.

OECD. (2000). *Measuring student knowledge and skills.* Paris: OECD Publishing. https://doi.org/10.1787/9789264173125-en

OECD. (2009). *PISA data analysis manual: SAS, second edition*. Paris: OECD Publishing. https://www.oecd.org/pisa/pisaproducts/pisadataanalysismanualspssandsassecondedition.htm

OECD. (2011). *PISA 2009 results: Students on line. Digital technologies and performance (Volume VI)*. Paris: OECD Publishing. http://doi.org/10.1787/9789264112995-en

OECD. (2013a). *OECD skills outlook 2013: First results from the survey of adult skills*. Paris: OECD Publishing. http://doi.org/10.1787/9789264204256-en

OECD. (2013b). *PISA 2015 draft frameworks*. Paris: OECD Publishing. http://www.oecd.org/pisa/pisaproducts/pisa2015draftframeworks.htm

OECD. (2019). *PISA 2018 results (Volume I): What students know and can do*. Paris: OECD Publishing. https://doi.org/10.1787/5f07c754-en

Pazzaglia, F., Toso, C., & Cacciamani, S. (2008). The specific involvement of verbal and visuospatial working memory in hypermedia learning. *British Journal of Educational Technology*, *39*(1), 110–124. https://doi.org/10.1111/j.1467-8535.2007.00741.x

Rayner, K., Foorman, B. R., Perfetti, C. A., Pesetsky, D., & Seidenberg, M. S. (2001). How psychological science informs the teaching of reading. *Psychological Science in the Public Interest*, *2*(2), 31–74. http://doi.org/10.1111/1529-1006.00004

Romero, C., & Ventura. S. (2010). Educational data mining: A review of the state of the art. *IEEE Transactions on Systems, Man, and Cybernetics, Part C (Applications and Reviews)*, *40*(6), 601–618. https://doi.org/10.1109/TSMCC.2010.2053532

Romero, C., & Ventura, S. (2017). Educational data science in massive open online courses. *Wiley Interdisciplinary Reviews: Data Mining and Knowledge Discovery*, *7*(1), Article e1187. https://doi.org/10.1002/widm.1187

Romero, C., & Ventura, S. (2020). Educational data mining and learning analytics: An updated survey. *Wiley Interdisciplinary Reviews: Data Mining and Knowledge Discovery*, *10*(3), Article e1355. https://doi.org/10.1002/widm.1355

Rouet, J. F., & Britt, M. (2011). Relevance processes in multiple document comprehension. In M. McCrudden, J. Magliano, & G. Schraw (Eds.), *Text relevance and learning from text*. Charlotte, NC: Information Age Publishing.

Rouet, J. F., & Britt, A. (2014). Multimedia learning from multiple documents. In R. Mayer (Ed.), *Cambridge handbook of multimedia learning* (pp. 813–841). Cambridge: Cambridge University Press.

Rouet, J. F., & Potelle, H. (2005). Navigational principles in multimedia learning. In R. E. Mayer (Ed.), *The Cambridge handbook of multimedia learning* (pp. 297–312). Cambridge: Cambridge University Press.

Rouet, J. F., Vörös, Z., & Pléh, C. (2012). Incidental learning of links during navigation: The role of visuo-spatial capacity. *Behaviour & Information Technology*, *31*(1), 71–81. https://doi.org/10.1080/0144929x.2011.604103

Stadtler, M. & Bromme, R. (2013). Multiple document comprehension: An approach to public understanding of science. *Cognition and Instruction*, *31*(2), 122–129. https://doi.org/10.1080/07370008.2013.771106

Stadtler, M. & Bromme, R. (2014). The content–source integration model: A taxonomic description of how readers comprehend conflicting scientific information. In D. Rapp, & J. Braasch (Eds.), *Processing inaccurate information: Theoretical and applied perspectives from cognitive science and the educational sciences* (pp. 379–402). Cambridge: The MIT Press.

Tang, X., & Zhang, D. (2020). How informal science learning experience influences students' science performance: A cross-cultural study based on PISA 2015. *International*

*Journal of Science Education*, 42(4), 598–616. https://doi.org/10.1080/09500693.2020.1719290

Vlahos, G. E., Ferratt, T. W., & Knoepfle, G. (2004). The use of computer-based information systems by German managers to support decision making. *Journal of Information & Management*, 41(6), 763–779. https://doi.org/10.1016/j.im.2003.06.003

Werlich, E. (1976). *A text grammar of English*. Heidelberg: Quelle and Meyer.

Wiley, J. (2001). Supporting understanding through task and browser design. In *Proceedings of the Twenty-third Annual Conference of the Cognitive Science Society*, New Jersey, 1136–1143.

Wright, P. (1993). To jump or not to jump: Strategy selection while reading electronic texts. In C. McKnight, A. Dillon, & J. Richardson (Eds.), *Hypertext: A psychological perspective* (pp. 137–152). New York: Ellis Horwood.

Zhang, N., Baker, H. W., Tufts, M., Raymond, R. E., Salihu, H., & Elliott, M. R. (2013). Early childhood lead exposure and academic achievement: Evidence from detroit public schools, 2008–2010. *American Journal of Public Health*, 103(3), e72–e77. https://doi.org/10.2105/AJPH.2012.301164

# 2
# LITERATURE REVIEW

## 2.1 The definition and overview of educational effectiveness

Educational effectiveness research (EER) indicates the indispensable role of schools and education in cultivating students' academic performance and well-being (Creemers & Kyriakides, 2008). The basic question of EER could be briefly summarized as what factors are associated with a "good" school and through which way we could produce more "good" schools (Reynolds et al., 2014). The development of the research models in this field went through three different phases and was documented in previous literature. Chronologically speaking, they are the economic approach, the approach that examines variables at the student level, and the approach with a multilevel structure (Creemers & Kyriakides, 2006).

The first approach explores the association between the supply of certain schooling inputs and students' academic outcomes regardless of the influence of background variables. One typical model that can be categorized into this approach is the "education production" models (e.g., Elberts & Stone, 1988). From an input-output economic point of view, the model was based on assumption that if the inputs in education increase, the educational outcomes will improve. However, a large number of studies questioned this argument by providing a series of different findings. For instance, increasing the amount of funding for education per student does not contribute to higher student outcomes (Hedges et al., 1994). In research on digital reading education, researchers have found that factors including digital resources at school and teachers' instructional behaviors were not significant predictors of students' reading capability (Cho et al., 2021).

Different from the first approach, the second approach further considers some antecedent conditions (i.e., a number of student-level and socioeconomic factors) that may exert influences on students' academic performance. The former centers on students' attitudinal and personal factors, including but not limited to learning aptitudes, personality, and motivation. The latter not only investigates the effects of students' SES, social capital, and peer group on their learning outcomes but also school's capability to narrow the gap between student outcomes. The two dimensions of educational effectiveness, namely, quality and equity, were thus derived from this perspective. However, the second approach has not yet introduced the idea of the interactions and dynamics of multilevel factors. Partly due to technological restrictions, the complex relationships among factors of different levels remain unanswered.

The third method, however, is mainly about a more complicated perspective of the multilevel effectiveness factors, which intricately integrate the essence of School Effectiveness Research (SER), Teacher Effectiveness Research (TER), and the early input-output studies. With the advancement of methodology, particularly the emergence and availability of program and software for the analysis of multilevel and multimodal data, the estimation and examination of school effectiveness with higher efficiency can be achieved (Goldstein, 2003). Models of this approach (e.g., the dynamic model of educational effectiveness) thus focused factors of different levels. EDM's main goal is to deliver high-quality education to students to improve their academic performance, which is influenced by a variety of elements and variables, including personal, academic, behavioral, and environmental characteristics. To this regard, the dynamic model could clearly reflect the interaction between students and the environment, which is a comprehensive and well-established model for SER (Muijs, 2008).

## 2.2 The dynamic model of educational effectiveness

The dynamic model of educational effectiveness is a multilevel model that delineates factors at four seemingly separate but inherently associated levels (see Figure 2.1): student, classroom/teacher, school, and country (Creemers & Kyriakides, 2008), where each factor was measured on five dimensions, that is, frequency, focus, stage, quality, and differentiation. The other four dimensions qualitatively analyze features of each factor's functioning, aside from frequency, which is a quantitative approach to gauging efficacy. A mixture of different measuring dimensions, as opposed to a single dimension, could provide a more comprehensive review (Kyriakides, 2008).

## 2.3 Student-level factors and digital reading performance

Student-level factors of digital reading performance are well-documented in the previous literature. Students' socioeconomic status (SES) (Vazquez-Lopez & Huerta-Manzanilla, 2021) and home resources (Cho et al., 2021), especially cultural capital (Rasmusson, 2016), were found to have a significant relationship with their digital reading performances. In terms of student gender, some researchers found that female students outperform their male counterparts in

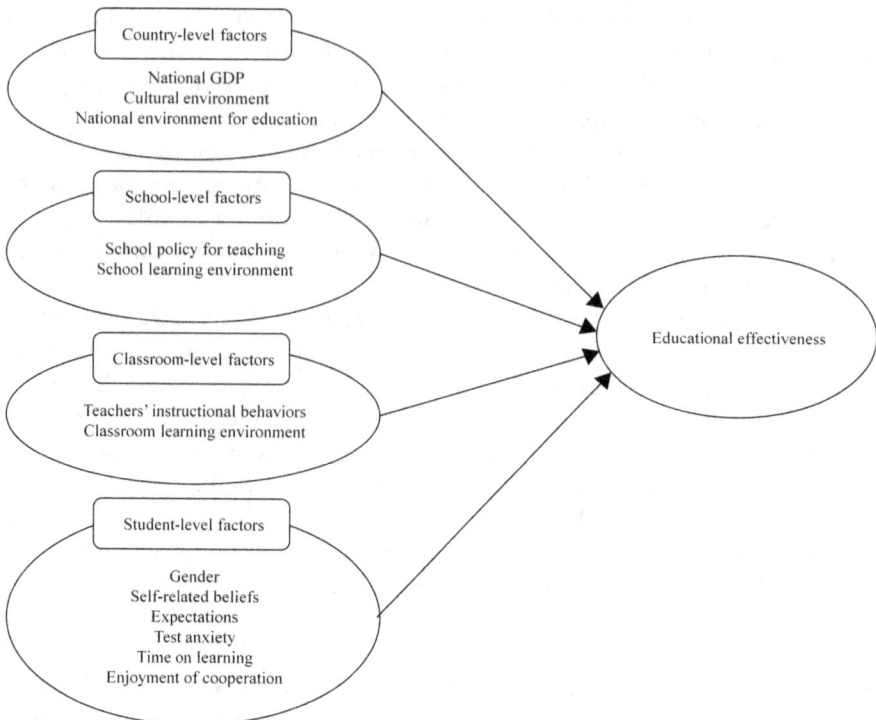

**FIGURE 2.1** The dynamic model of educational effectiveness.

computer-based reading assessments, but this environment seemed to narrow the gender gap (Lim & Jung, 2014). Yet the impacts of gender could not be simply explained because studies have mentioned that gender could react with various factors (Lim & Jung, 2019).

Furthermore, students' reading skills were also examined, showing significant influences. It is identified that previous learning experience, inferential reasoning strategies, and self-regulated reading habits could contribute to successful online reading (Coiro & Dobler, 2007). Affective factors also play an indispensable role. For one thing, reading self-concept and reading self-efficacy could be conducive to both print and digital reading literacy (Chapman & Tunmer, 2003; Cho et al., 2021). For another thing, reading attitudes are generally regarded as a significant predictor of students' digital reading literacy. The impacts of reading attitudes are diverse when it comes to different forms of reading materials. Results showed that attitudes toward academic digital reading are positively associated with, while attitudes toward recreational digital reading are negatively associated with students' performance (Jang & Ryoo, 2019; Keskin et al., 2016).

Affective factors and personal skills and knowledge related to ICT are of paramount importance. Students' affective factors exert mixed effects on their reading performances. Researchers have identified the positive effects of self-confidence, interest, and autonomy in ICT tasks on students' traditional reading performances (HU et al., 2018; Petko et al., 2016; Salmerón et al., 2018) and digital reading performances (Lim & Jung, 2019); yet, students' enjoyment of social interaction around ICT negatively correlates with their reading performances (HU et al., 2018). A new finding suggests a slightly different pattern: although students who hold positive views towards ICT perform better in digital reading assessments, their performances are likely to be influenced by opinions on ICT of peers at the same school (HU & Yu, 2021). Additionally, necessary skills for surfing (e.g., control/metacognitive strategies, navigation skills, and self-regulated learning) are proven to positively contribute to digital reading literacy (Salmerón et al., 2018; Vazquez-Lopez & Huerta-Manzanilla, 2021). It is worth noticing that knowledge of metacognitive strategies could positively mediate the relationship between ICT use and digital reading literacy (Chen et al., 2021).

Additionally, a great number of studies have proposed that different purposes of using ICT resources could lead to diverse effects on students' academic outcomes. A small number of them explored the effects of the aim of using ICT on students' digital reading performances. Most researchers found that academic use of ICT resources, especially reading frequency of the Internet for informational purposes could to a large extent explain digital reading performance (Gil-Flores et al., 2012; Salmerón et al., 2018). Online social recreational activities, however, are found to have either positive (Gil-Flores et al., 2012) or negative influences (Naumann, 2015) on digital reading. This might be due to the different frequencies of use; that is, social reading activities could help build familiarity with digital devices, but once the students transcend the "optimum threshold", their competence will be damaged (OECD, 2011). Interestingly, researchers found that computer games play a contributive role in students' digital performances, benefiting boys more compared with girls. This might be partly because engaging in computer games could improve students' visual–spatial skills, which is highlighted in digital reading rather than in print reading (Rasmusson & Åberg-Bengtsson, 2015).

## 2.4 Classroom-level factors and digital reading performance

The role of teachers came to the forefront of shaping the complex literacy worlds inhabited and co-constructed by the young (Kucirkova, 2020). The importance of teachers' capability of coordinating the use of digital and print reading during class was highlighted (Kucirkova, 2020). For instance, objective-focused fast extensive reading can be utilized by teachers to cultivate students' online reading interest, showing remarkable results (Sun et al., 2016). General instructional support is found not significant in predicting digital reading performances (Cho et al., 2021), while some specific teaching strategies (e.g., digital storytelling) could help develop components of students' digital reading capability such as fluency and vocabulary (Morgan, 2012).

The influences of ICT-infused instruction on digital reading are widely reported in previous studies, showing mixed results. Scholars not only perceived teachers' professional development of ICT use as a significant predictor of students' digital reading skills (Hatlevik et al., 2015), but also highlighted the necessity and quality of incorporating digital texts in instruction in teaching (Kesson, 2020). Overall, studies suggest that the teachers should properly utilize the ICT resources and adequately assign digital reading tasks during class to improve students' digital reading literacy. For instance, Nielen et al. (2018) found that guidance from a digital Pedagogical Agent (PA) during class could improve students' reading motivation and incidental vocabulary learning. This result has further proven the importance of the introduction, coordination, and innovation of digital resources in reading; teachers are considered the key facilitators in the process.

## 2.5 School-level factors and digital reading performance

School type and the equity dimension should be regarded as important predictors of students' digital reading performances (Amiama-Espaillat & Mayor-Ruiz, 2017; Rasmusson, 2016). Other factors mainly include school disciplinary climate (Lim & Jung, 2014), provision of reading-related activities (Lim & Jung, 2019), the rapport of student-teacher relationships (Vazquez-Lopez & Huerta-Manzanilla, 2021) and schools' partnership with parents (Kucirkova, 2020). Recent research found that school SES also plays an indispensable role. While performance in high-SES schools is largely influenced by educational factors (e.g., metacognitive strategies and achievement motivation), performance in low-SES schools is more susceptible to some country-level socioeconomic indicators (e.g., GDP), and individual educational indicators are relegated to a secondary level (Gamazo & Martínez-Abad, 2020).

It is interesting that there are mixed findings about the association between school resources and students' digital reading literacies. Some studies argued that the abundance of e-resources (e.g., the availability of laptop, mobile phone, and the Internet) at school could promote their digital reading performances, with male students more susceptible to the accessibility of ICT resources than female students (Divya & Mohamed, 2020). Others, however, argue that neither possession of online mobile devices nor digital resources at the school level is a significant predictor of students' performances in digital reading (Cho et al., 2021), which might be explained by inappropriate use of these equipment.

## 2.6 Country-level factors and digital reading performance

Most of the studies that examine students' digital reading performance either focus on a particular country or utilize cross-national data. According to previous literature, we could safely conclude that a number of country-level indicators (e.g., GDP per capita, the Information Development Index, or IDI expenditure on education, characteristics of education system, and national policies and curriculum) have effects on students' reading performances. Most of the studies have established three-level models using data from the large-scale assessment, and the GDP per capita is usually set as the controlled variable (e.g., HU et al., 2021; HU & Yu, 2021) Some studies indeed evaluated students' digital reading and made comparisons between performances. For instance, researchers have found that for Norway, parental pressure has a substantial effect on the overall reading factor on the school level; while for Sweden, the effects of school type are more prominent (Rasmusson, 2016). However, due to the complexity of the constructs and measurements of other indicators, few studies have taken them into consideration, and these country-level data in large-scale assessment are often missing. Future research should try to include a more comprehensive evaluation of the country-level factors that may influence students' digital reading and other academic performance.

## 2.7 The application of EDM approaches to analyze large-scale educational data

An emerging body of research applied methods of EDM to the analysis of PISA data, providing new perspectives to help improve the productivity of educational research derived from PISA. The tree algorithm is one of the most commonly used methods in the exploitation of large-scale educational dataset. Asensio et al. (2018) analyzed the six context questionnaires from a metric perspective using regression trees to identify the predictors of the performance of Spanish students. Gamazo and Martínez-Abad (2020) used the C4.5 algorithm to obtain a predictive model of school performance in reading, math, and science. They found that performance of high-SES schools is largely influenced by educational factors, performance in low-SES schools is more susceptible to some country-level socioeconomic indicators (e.g., GDP). Other scholars also used C4.5 to construct decision trees to identify students' science learning patterns and effectiveness based on the PISA dataset (e.g., Liu & Whitford, 2011; Martínez-Abad, 2019). It is noteworthy that Martínez-Abad et al. (2020) present an innovative methodological proposal by combining the HLM and decision trees to examine the factors associated with school effectiveness.

Other studies take some large international educational database into consideration, such as Trends in International Mathematics and Science Study (TIMSS) and Progress in International Reading Literacy Study (PIRLS) conducted by the International Association for the Evaluation of Educational Achievement (IEA), and National Assessment of Educational Progress (NAEP). Depren et al. (2017) explored the TIMSS 2011 data using the EDM methods and found that logistic regression outperforms other algorithms. The factor of student confidence has also been identified as the most effective factor in mathematics performance. Liu and Ruiz (2008) reported a study on using two data mining approaches, namely, C4.5 and M5 to predict K-12 students' competence levels on test items related to energy using data from TIMSS and NAEP. Results have shown that the decision tree and linear function agree with each other on predictions, and cognitive demands have been identified as the most significant predictors. Some studies used a combination of both unsupervised and supervised learning algorithms to predict student performance on math scores.

## 2.8 Research gaps and research questions

Scholars conducted research on new forms of digital learning to determine precisely how elements of different levels are associated with students' digital reading performance (Coiro et al., 2011; Naumann, 2015; Salmerón et al., 2018). However, many issues about the effects of individual, societal, and environmental factors that may work together to exacerbate the performance gap in student competency in digital reading remain unsolved (Forzani, 2018). There is a definite need to continue accumulating information from large-scale data analyses to supplement previous research on how such factors influence digital reading ability (Naumann, 2015).

This study aims to identify the key factors that collectively contribute to students' digital reading performances. First, it is based on a large-scale analysis grounded in multiple countries with large sample size, namely, 81,904 students from 38 OECD countries, which ensures the generalizability of the findings. Second, our study covers a large range of contextual factors at different levels, which contributes to the high efficiency of the classification results. Third, considering the large sample size and high-dimensional data, we use the novel machine learning approach, namely support vector machine (SVM) to provide a new perspective for the EER and reading research. Fourth, thanks to the superiority of SVM in identifying the synergistic effects of an optimal feature set, the delicate interaction between factors of different levels could be identified. Specifically, we address the following three research questions in our study:

1. What are the most influential factors for predicting students' digital reading performances?
2. How accurately could the proposed model composed of key factors collaboratively predict students' as top- or non-top-performing digital readers?
3. What are the detailed influences of these most influential factors on students' digital reading performances?

## References

Amiama-Espaillat, C., & Mayor-Ruiz, C. (2017). Digital reading and reading competence: The influence in the Z generation from the Dominican Republic. *Comunicar*, 25(52), 105–114. https://doi.org/10.3916/c52-2017-10

Asensio, M. I., Carpintero, M., E., Exposito, C. E., & Lopez, M. E. (2018). How much gold is in the sand? Data mining with Spain's PISA 2015 results. *Revista Española de Pedagogía*, 76 (270), 225–245. https://doi.org/10.22550/REP76-2-2018-10

Chapman, J. W., & Tunmer, W. E. (2003). Reading difficulties, reading-related self-perceptions, and strategies for overcoming negative self-beliefs. *Reading & Writing Quarterly, 19*(1), 5–24. https://doi.org/10.1080/10573560308205

Chen, J., Zhang, Y., & HU, J. (2021). Synergistic effects of instruction and affect factors on high- and low-ability disparities in elementary students' reading literacy. *Reading and Writing: An Interdisciplinary Journal, 34*(1), 199–230. https://doi.org/10.1007/s11145-020-10070-0

Cho, B. Y., Hwang, H. J., & Jang, B. G. (2021). Predicting fourth grade digital reading comprehension: A secondary data analysis of (e)PIRLS 2016. *International Journal of Educational Research, 105*, 101696. https://doi.org/10.1016/j.ijer.2020.101696

Coiro, J., & Dobler, E. (2007). Exploring the online reading comprehension strategies used by sixth-grade skilled readers to search for and locate information on the internet. *Reading Research Quarterly, 42*(2), 214–257. https://doi.org/10.1598/rrq.42.2.2

Coiro, J., Castek, J., & Guzniczak, L. (2011). Uncovering online reading comprehension processes: Two adolescents reading independently and collaboratively on the Internet. In P. L. Dunston, L. B. Gambrell, K. Headley, S. K. Fullerton, P. M. Stecker, V. R. Gilles & C. C. Bates (Eds.), *60th Yearbook of the Literacy Research Association* (pp. 354–369). Oak Creek, WI: Literacy Research Association.

Creemers, B. P. M., & Kyriakides, L. (2006). Critical analysis of the current approaches to modelling educational effectiveness: The importance of establishing a dynamic model. *School Effectiveness and School Improvement, 17*(3), 347–366. https://doi.org/10.1080/09243450600697242

Creemers, B. P. M., & Kyriakides, L. (2008). *The dynamics of educational effectiveness: A contribution to policy, practice and theory in contemporary schools*. London: Routledge.

Depren, S. K., Aşkın, Ö. E., & Öz, E. (2017). Identifying the classification performances of educational data mining methods: A case study for TIMSS. *Educational Sciences-Theory & Practice, 17*(5), 1605–1623. https://doi.org/10.12738/estp.2017.5.0634

Divya, P., & Mohamed Haneefa, K. (2020). Factors influencing digital reading behavior of students: A study in universities in Kerala. *DESIDOC Journal of Library and Information Technology, 40*, 313–320. https://doi.org/10.14429/djlit.40.5.15672

Elberts, R. W., & Stone, J. A. (1988). Student achievement in public schools: Do principles make a difference. *Economics Education Review, 7*(3), 291–299. https://doi.org/10.1016/0272-7757(88)90002-7

Forzani, E. (2018). How well can students evaluate online science information? Contributions of prior knowledge, gender, socioeconomic status, and offline reading ability. *Reading Research Quarterly, 53*(4), 385–390. https://doi.org/10.1002/rrq.218

Gamazo, A., & Martínez-Abad, F. (2020). An exploration of factors linked to academic performance in PISA 2018 through data mining techniques. *Frontiers in Psychology, 11*, Article 575167. https://doi.org/10.3389/fpsyg.2020.575167

Gil-Flores, J., Torres-Gordillo, J. J., & Perera-Rodríguez, V. H. (2012). The role of online reader experience in explaining students' performance in digital reading. *Computers and Education, 59*, 653–660. https://doi.org/10.1016/j.compedu.2012.03.014

Goldstein, H. (2003). *Multilevel models in educational and social research* (3rd ed.). London: Edward Arnold.

Hatlevik, O. E., Ottestad, G., & Throndsen, I. (2015). Predictors of digital competence in 7th grade: A multilevel analysis. *Journal of Computer Assisted Learning, 31*(3), 220–231. https://doi.org/10.1111/jcal.12065

Hedges, L. V., Laine, R., & Greenwald, R. (1994). Does money matter? A meta-analysis of studies of the effects of differential school inputs on student outcomes. *Educational Researcher, 23*(3), 5–14. https://doi.org/10.3102/0013189x023003005

HU, J., Dong, X., & Peng, Y (2021). Discovery of the key contextual factors relevant to the reading performance of elementary school students from 61 countries/regions: Insight from a machine learning-based approach. *Reading and Writing, 35*(1), 93–127. https://doi.org/10.1007/s11145-021-10176-z

HU, J., & Yu, R. (2021). The effects of ICT-based social media on adolescents' digital reading performance: A longitudinal study of PISA 2009, PISA 2012, PISA 2015 and PISA 2018. *Computers & Education, 175*, 1–20. https://doi.org/10.1016/j.compedu.2021.104342

HU, X., Leung, F., & Yuan, T. (2018). The influence of culture on students' mathematics achievement across 51 countries. *International Journal of Science and Mathematics Education, 16*(1), S7–S24. https://doi.org/10.1007/s10763-018-9899-6

Jang, B., & Ryoo, J. (2018). Multiple dimensions of adolescents' reading attitudes and their relationship with reading comprehension. *Reading and Writing, 32*(7), 1769–1793. https://doi.org/10.1007/s11145-018-9926-6

Keskin, H. K., Baştuğ, M., & Atmaca, T. (2016). Factors directing students to academic digital reading. *Egitim Ve Bilim-Education and Science, 41*, 177–129. http://doi.org/10.15390/EB.2016.6655

Kesson, H. (2020). Reading digital texts: Obstacles to using digital resources. *English Teaching, 19*, 155–168. http://doi.org/10.1108/ETPC-02-2019-0019

Kucirkova, N. (2020). Toward reciprocity and agency in students' digital reading. *Reading Teacher, 73*, 825–831. https://doi.org/10.1002/trtr.1893

Kyriakides, L. (2008). Testing the validity of the comprehensive model of educational effectiveness: A step towards the development of a dynamic model of effectiveness. *School Effectiveness and School Improvement, 19*(4), 429–446. https://doi.org/10.1080/09243450802535208

Lim, H. J., & Jung, H. K. (2014). Students' reading engagement in print and digital reading achievement: Using a multilevel structural equation modeling. *Journal of Curriculum and Evaluation, 17*, 123–151. Retrieved from https://www.kci.go.kr/kciportal/ci/sereArticleSearch/ciSereArtiView.kci?sereArticleSearchBean.artiId=ART001895920

Lim, H. J., & Jung, H. (2019) Factors related to digital reading achievement: A multi-level analysis using international large-scale data. *Computers & Education, 133*, 82–93. https://doi.org/10.1016/j.compedu.2019.01.007

Liu, X., & Ruiz, M. E. (2008). Using data mining to predict K-12 students' performance on large-scale assessment items related to energy. *Journal of Research in Science Teaching, 45*(5), 554–573. Scopus. https://doi.org/10.1002/tea.20232

Liu, X., & Whitford, M. (2011). Opportunities-to-learn at home: Profiles of students with and without reaching science proficiency. *Journal of Science Education and Technology, 20*, 375–387. https://doi.org/10.1007/s10956-010-9259-y

Martínez-Abad, F. (2019). Identification of factors associated with school effectiveness with data mining techniques: Testing a new approach. *Frontiers in Psychology, 10*, Article 2583. https://doi.org/10.3389/fpsyg.2019.02583

Martínez-Abad, F., Gamazo, A., & Rodríguez-Conde, M. J. (2020). Educational data mining: Identification of factors associated with school effectiveness in PISA assessment. *Studies in Educational Evaluation, 66*, Article 100875. https://doi.org/10.1016/j.stueduc.2020.100875

Morgan, H. (2012). Using digital story projects to help students improve in reading and writing. *Reading Improvement, 51*, 20–26. Retrieved from https://chinesesites.library.ingentaconnect.com/content/prin/rimp/2014/00000051/00000001/art00004

Muijs, D. (2008). Educational effectiveness and the legacy of Bert P. M. Creemers. *School Effectiveness and School Improvement, 19*(4), 463–472. https://doi.org/10.1080/09243450802535224

Naumann, J. (2015). A model of online reading engagement: Linking engagement, navigation, and performance in digital reading. *Computers in Human Behavior, 53*, 263–277. https://doi.org/10.1016/j.chb.2015.06.051

Nielen, T. M., Smith, G. G., Sikkema-de Jong, M. T., Drobisz, J., van Horne, B., & Bus, A. G. (2018). Digital guidance for susceptible readers: Effects on fifth graders' reading motivation and incidental vocabulary learning. *Journal of Educational Computing Research, 56*(1), 48–73. https://doi.org/10.1177/0735633117708283

OECD. (2011). *PISA 2009 results: Students on line. Digital technologies and performance (Volume VI)*. Paris: OECD Publishing. http://doi.org/10.1787/9789264112995-en

Petko, D., Cantieni, A., & Prasse, D. (2016). Perceived quality of educational technology matters: A secondary analysis of students' ICT use, ICT-related attitudes, and PISA 2012 test scores. *Journal of Educational Computing Research, 54*(8), 1070–1091. http://doi.org/10.1177/0735633116649373

Rasmusson, M., & Aberg-Bengtsson, L. (2015). Does performance in digital reading relate to computer game playing? A study of factor structure and gender patterns in 15-year-olds' reading literacy performance. *Scandinavian Journal of Educational Research, 59*(6), 691–709. https://doi.org/10.1080/00313831.2014.965795

Rasmusson, M. A. (2016). A multilevel analysis of Swedish and Norwegian students' overall and digital reading performance with a focus on equity aspects of education. *Large-Scale Assessments in Education, 4*(1), 1–25. https://doi.org/10.1186/s40536-016-0021-7

Reynolds, D., Sammons, P., de Fraine, B., van Damme, J., Townsend, T., Teddlie, C., & Stringfield, S. (2014). Educational effectiveness research (EER): A state-of-the-art review. *School Effectiveness and School Improvement, 25*(2). https://doi.org/10.1080/09243453.2014.885450

Salmerón, L., García, A., & Vidal-Abarca, E. (2018). The development of adolescents' comprehension-based Internet reading activities. *Learning and Individual Differences, 61*, 31–39. https://doi.org/10.1016/j.lindif.2017.11.006

Sun, Z., Yang, X. M., & He, K. K. (2016). An extensive reading strategy to promote online writing for elementary students in the 1:1 digital classroom. *Computer Assisted Language Learning, 29*(2), 398–412, https://doi.org/10.1080/09588221.2014.974860

Vazquez-Lopez, V., & Huerta-Manzanilla, E. (2021). Factors related with underperformance in reading proficiency, the case of the programme for international student assessment 2018. *European Journal of Investigation in Health, Psychology and Education, 11*(3), 813–828. https://doi.org/10.3390/ejihpe11030059

# 3
# METHODOLOGY

## 3.1 Methods review: Machine learning, HLM, and mediation analysis

### 3.1.1 Machine learning algorithms

#### 3.1.1.1 The definition and classification of machine learning algorithms

1. The classification of machine learning algorithms
    Generally, the data mining methods could be classified into two major types, namely, supervised and unsupervised methods (Cios et al., 2007). Supervised methods are suited for the situation when the subjects are evident and aim to train a classifier to classify the subjects accurately so that it could be generalized to other data sets; while the unsupervised methods are suited for the situation when the subjects are obscure, and aims to clearly separate groups based on their distinguished features (Qiao & Jiao, 2018) (Figure 3.1).
2. The development of machine learning
    Considering that machine learning could be regarded as a subset of Artificial Intelligence (AI), we should first understand how it falls within the broad set of AI.
    The AI process loop is provided as follows in Figure 3.2:

#### 3.1.1.2 An introduction to several frequently-used algorithms

Machine learning methods such as naive Bayes (NB), decision tree (DT), neural network (NN), support vector classification (SVC), logistic regression (LR), and random forest (RF) were used to predict students' learning performance in previous studies (e.g., Lu et al., 2018; Oladokun et al., 2008; Romero et al., 2013; Yoo & Kim, 2014).

DOI: 10.4324/9781003351108-3

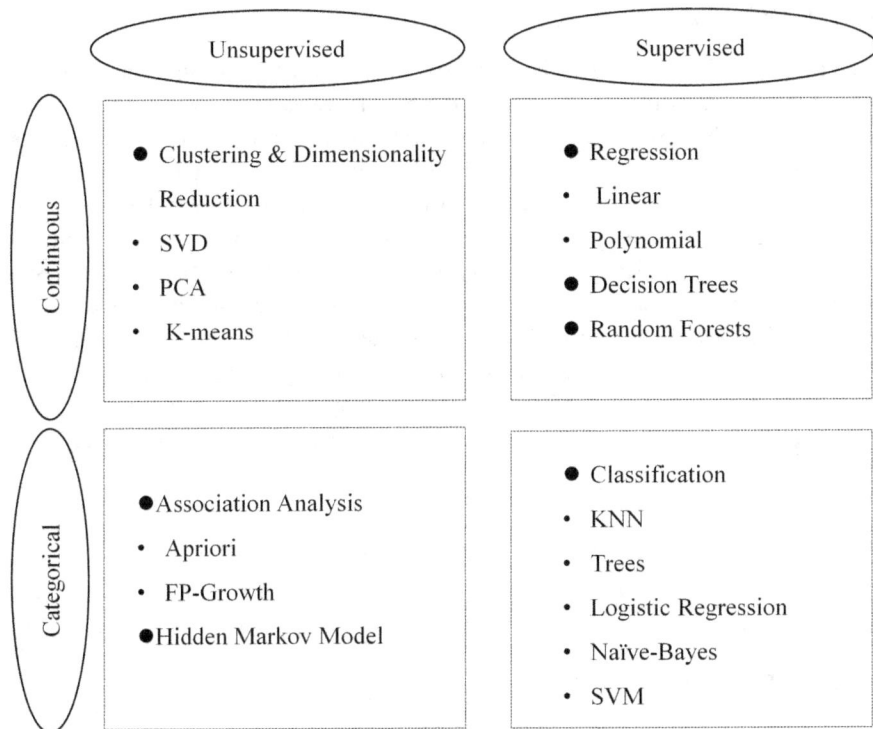

**FIGURE 3.1** The classification of machine learning algorithms.

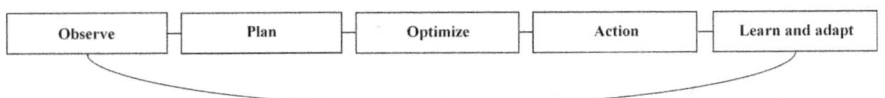

**FIGURE 3.2** The AI process loop.

### 3.1.1.2.1 Decision tree (DT)

A DT is a predictive model in machine learning that depicts a mapping relationship between object properties and object values. Müller and Guido (2016) found that DT learns a hierarchy of yes/no questions, resulting in a DT. It is made up of the three sections, namely, the decision node, the state node, and the result node.

Take the binary classification of high performers and low performers by DT for an example (Figure 3.3). First, students are classified according to their scores. If their scores are high, they go to the left node, otherwise the right. The left students continue to be classified according to their attendance rate. If it is high, they go to the left node, otherwise the right. The left students continue to be classified according to their number of questions answered during class and the number of assignments submitted. At last, the high performers and low performers are identified.

## 3.1.1.2.2 Random forest (RF)

DT can be used not only for classification but also for the calculation of probability for dichotomous and categorical dependent variables. It has the advantage of being straightforward to understand, implement, and use. However, it has a number of drawbacks, the most significant of which is that DT is unstable, meaning that slight changes in the data might result in significant changes in the resulting tree. Breiman and colleagues (1984) proposed the RF model, which is an extension of classification and regression trees (CART). In a similar fashion to CART, RF has been extended in numerous ways so that, in addition to survival times, dichotomous, unordered categorical, and ordered categorical dependent variables, as well as continuous dependent variables, can now be handled (Gordon & Olshen, 1985). It is a robust way to replace existing machine learning methods such as NNs by enhancing the model's prediction accuracy

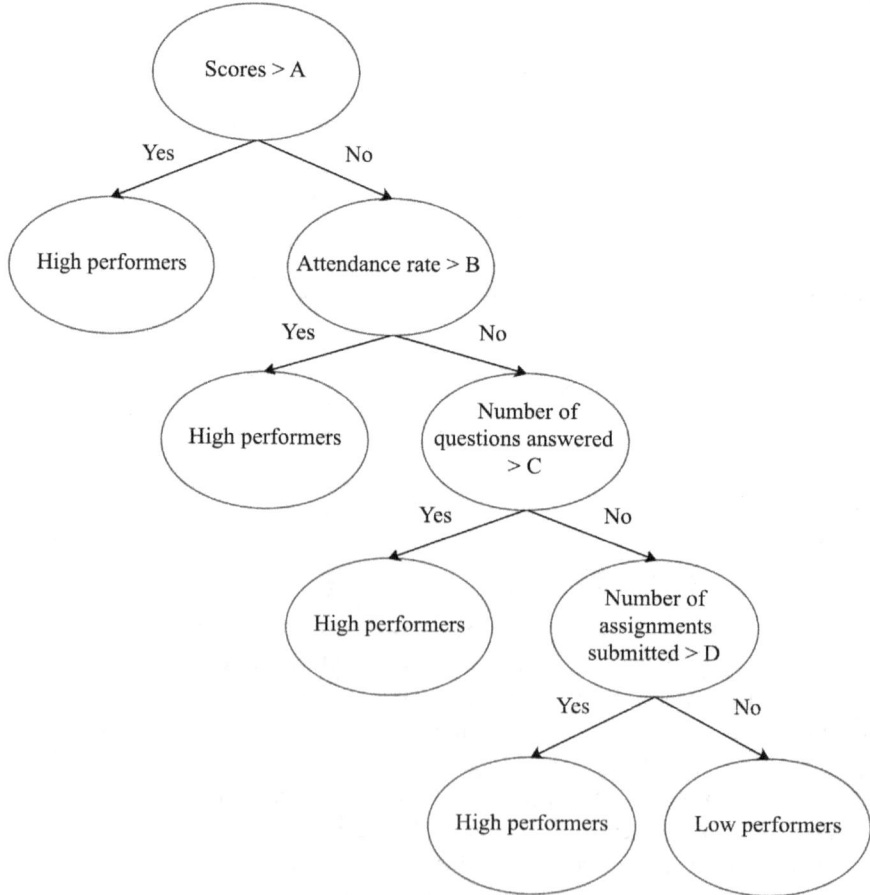

**FIGURE 3.3** An illustrative example of DT binary classification about high performers and low performers in the study.

by summarizing a large number of classification trees (Loh, 2011). Furthermore, the RF tree-building method inherently allows for feature interaction and high correlation between features (Ziegler & Konig, 2014).

The combination of machines may provide advantages in three areas. First, due to the vast hypothesis space of learning tasks, there may be several hypotheses obtaining the same performance in the training set from a statistical standpoint. When a single machine is employed in this situation, the generalization performance may be harmed owing to incorrect selection, but integrating many learners reduces the danger. Second, learning algorithms have a chance to shrink into local minima, some of which have poor generalization performance, but the danger of going into bad local minima can be minimized by integrating them after repeated runs. Third, the genuine hypothesis of some learning tasks may not be in the hypothesis space evaluated by the current learning algorithm from the standpoint of representation. If a single learner is used at this time, it will almost probably be invalid. It is feasible to acquire a better approximation by merging many learners due to the extension of the relevant hypothesis space.

RF has advanced significantly in recent years and is now widely regarded as one machine learning method among several for a wide range of problems. It has been used in a broad range of applications, including genome-wide association studies (Kruppa et al., 2012) and protein–protein interaction prediction (Lin et al., 2005). The remarkable flexibility of RFs explains this wide range of application possibilities (Ziegler & Konig, 2014). It should be mentioned, however, that the use of RF is still limited by natural science. Future EDM research should fully utilize the RF's capabilities so that the model's performance may be significantly enhanced (Figure 3.4).

### 3.1.1.2.3 Extreme gradient boosting (XGBoost)

The XGBoost classifier (XGBoost for short) is an ensemble model consisting of a number of decision classification trees proposed by Chen and Guestrin (2016). When learning irregular patterns, a single DT must divide to attain a homogenous class, resulting in overfitting and erroneous results. XGBoost is an enhancement on the gradient boosting technique that solves the extreme value of the loss function using Newton's approach, expands the loss function Taylor to the second order, and adds a regularization term to the loss function. The gradient boosting algorithm loss is the first portion of the objective function during training time, while the regularization term is the second part. As a result, XGBoost uses the gradient boosting ensemble technique to repeatedly combine weak base learners into a strong model. Each successive tree is built in a sequential manner, learning from its predecessor to decrease residual error and enhance the model's overall performance. The relative significance of an input variable may also be accessed as DT. The algorithm has been used in a variety of disciplines, and its superior performance has been repeatedly demonstrated (Xiao et al., 2017;

**62** Methodology

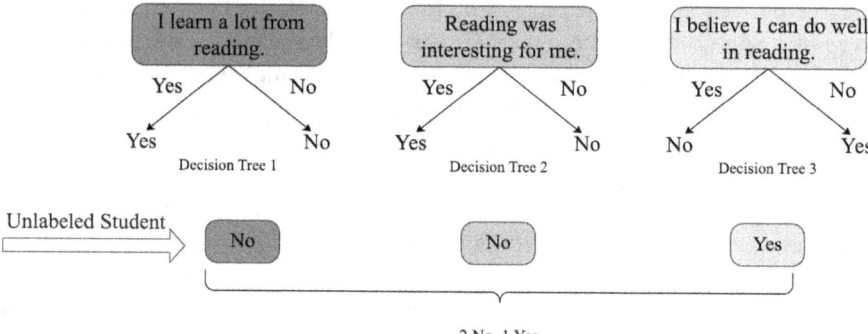

**FIGURE 3.4** An illustrative example of RF binary classification of high performers and low performers in reading.

Zhang et al., 2018). An illustrative example of XGBoost classification of good readers and poor readers is provided below in Figure 3.5 for ease of reference.

### 3.1.1.2.4 Bayesian network

In Figure 3.6, the basic mechanism of a Bayesian network is depicted. Grades, course difficulty, IQ, SAT scores, letters of reference, and other factors all affect a student's performance. The link between these variables may be described using a directed acyclic graph. Students' grades are decided by the course's difficulty and intellect, SAT scores by intelligence, and recommendation letter quality by scores. Each variable in the model has a conditional probability distribution associated with it, which is used to determine a distribution of the value of the variable when each potential joint assignment of its parent node is known. The conditional probability distribution for nodes without parent nodes is based on a collection of empty variables. A Bayesian network is made up of this network topology and a conditional probability distribution.

The advantage of the naive Bayesian model is based on classical mathematical theory and has a solid mathematical foundation as well as a consistent

Methodology  63

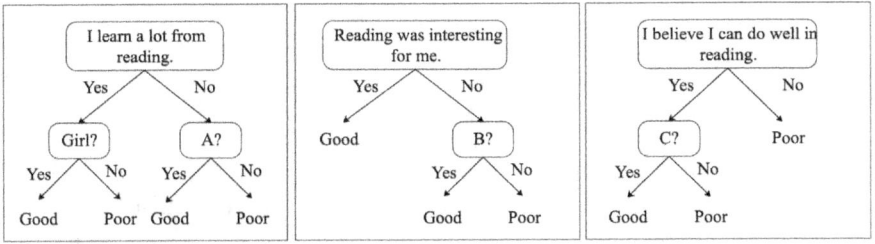

**FIGURE 3.5**  An illustrative example of XGBoost classification of good readers and poor readers.

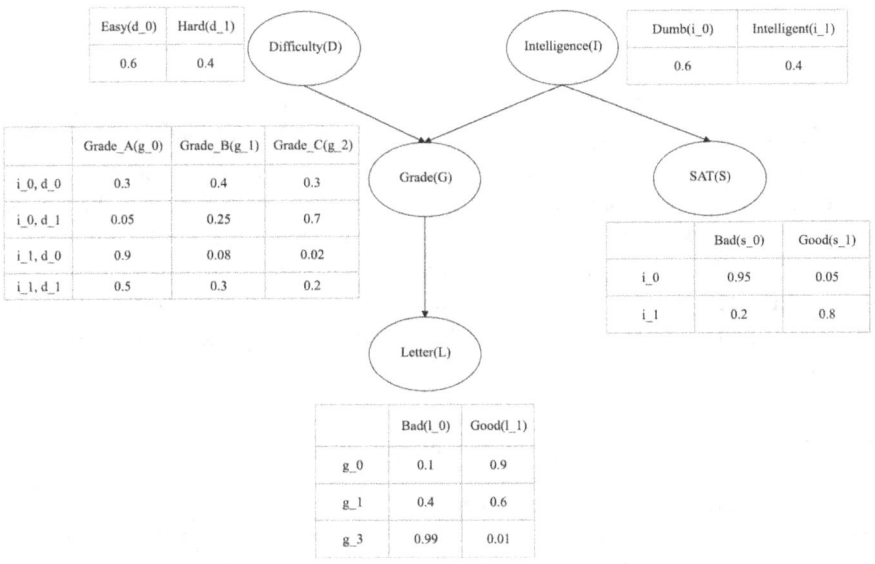

**FIGURE 3.6**  An illustrative example of Bayesian network about the determinants of the quality of recommendation letter.

classification efficiency. It works well with tiny amounts of data, can handle numerous categorization jobs, and can be trained incrementally. It is unaffected by missing data, and the procedure is straightforward. It is frequently employed in the categorization of text. Disadvantages include the requirement to determine a prior probability; the categorization decision's error rate; its sensitiveness to the phrasing of the input data.

### 3.1.1.2.5 Artificial neural networks (ANNs)

ANN is a network structure formed by various interconnected processing units (neurons), which is an abstraction, simplification, and simulation of the human brain mechanism. The structure of ANNs is provided in Figure 3.7.

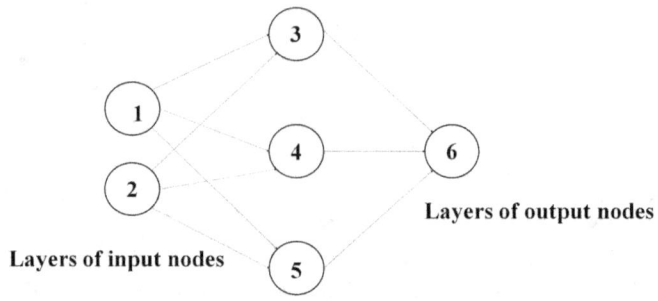

**FIGURE 3.7** The structure of ANNs.

The ANNs are suitable for the analysis of Programme for International Student Assessment (PISA) data set. This is because the student data were embedded in the school in PISA, which could be regarded as a "nested" structure. While students from a certain school were taking the student questionnaires, the school questionnaire was delivered to the principal of this school. It means that we could acquire information about students' schools according to the school questionnaire fulfilled by the principal. As a result, in data processing, we could assign the school-level information to each sample student based on their school ID. The structure of PISA data is depicted in Figure 3.8.

### 3.1.1.3 SVM: A novel and powerful ML algorithm

Support vector machine (SVM) is a pattern recognition classifier created from the extended portrait method, which was first proposed by Vapnik and coworkers in 1963 (Cortes & Vapnik, 1995). The gradual progress of SVM theories in the 1970s, with Cover's (1965) theoretical study of the maximum margin decision boundary in pattern recognition.

Bernhard, Guyon, and Vapnik introduced nonlinear SVM using the kernel approach in 1992. Following that, in 1995, Cortes and Vapnik created a soft margin nonlinear SVM and used it to recognize handwritten characters. Since its publication, this study has received a lot of attention, and it serves as a reference for the usage of SVM in a variety of domains. After its initial appearance, SVM has already outperformed competing techniques in several sectors as a principled and strong machine learning algorithm. Because of its superior performance in text categorization (Joachims, 1998), it swiftly became a key machine learning tool and the embodiment of the statistical learning craze of the time. SVM has been extensively researched since then, and it is currently being investigated in both methodological and pragmatic applications. It has become a commonly utilized technique in research of numerous subjects after weathering all of the

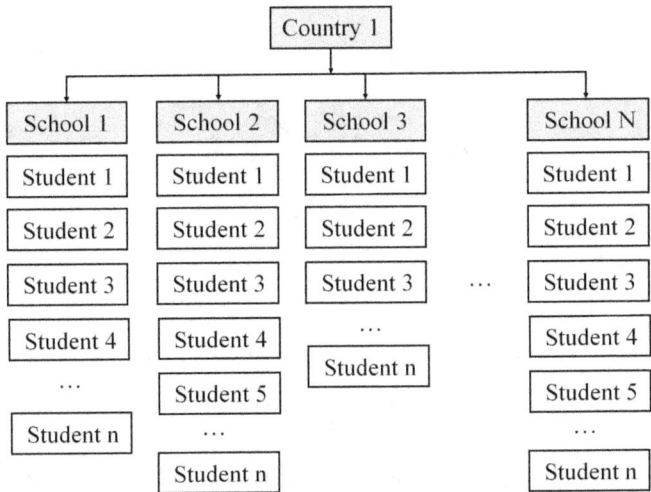

**FIGURE 3.8** The structure of PISA data.

obstacles throughout the years without a scratch (Cristianini & Shawe-Taylor, 2000).

SVM is a powerful and versatile machine learning model that can perform pattern recognition, regression analysis, and, most importantly, binary classification. This is accomplished by creating a multidimensional hyperplane and mapping input data to a feature space with kernel functions, effectively dividing the data into two categories of descriptors (Cortes & Vapnik, 1995). Essentially, the goal of the SVM classifier is to create the hyperplane with the greatest margin (maximum distances between the two nearest data points, namely, support vectors, and the hyperplane). The algorithm of it is elaborated below.

Given a training data set $D = \{(x\_1, y\_1), (x\_2, y\_2), ..., (x\_n, y\_n)\}$, $y\_i \in \{+1, -1\}$. To distinguish distinct types of samples, the basic principle of classification is to locate one hyperplane in the sample space based on training set $D$. Obviously, there are a variety of hyperplanes that may be used to split the training samples. A fitted hyperplane, on the other hand, is projected to be the most "tolerant" of local training sample disruption. The best such function is obtained by maximizing the margin between the two classes, which is what SVM guarantees. The margin, on the surface, corresponds to the shortest distance between the data points nearest to the hyperplane. In this case, the hyperplane in the "center" of the two types of training samples, which is the bold line in Figure 3.9, should be determined. This hyperplane has the best classification performance as well as the most generalization capability.

The basic model of SVM is provided in Figure 3.10. Generally, the hyperplane in the sample space can be described as $wx + b = 0$. Here $w$ represents the weight vector, which decides the direction of the hyperplane; $b$ represents the

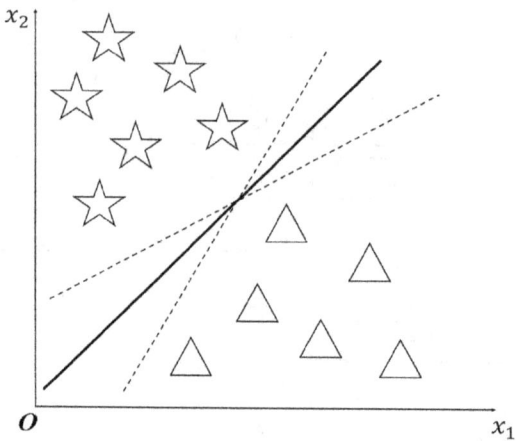

**FIGURE 3.9** Various hyperplanes that could divide the training data into two groups.

bias, which decides the distance between the hyperplane and the origin. Since $w$ and $b$ collectively set the location of the hyperplane, the hyperplane could be marked down as $(w, b)$. The distance between a random dot $x$ in the sample space and $(w, b)$ is

$$r = \frac{|wx + b|}{\|w\|} \qquad (3.1)$$

Supposing the hyperplane $(w, b)$ could classify the samples correctly. Given $(x_i, y\_i) \in D$, if $y_i = +1$, then we have $wx_i + b > 0$; if $y_i = -1$, then we have $wx_i + b < 0$. Let

$$\begin{cases} wx_i + b \geq +1, y_i = +1 \\ wx_i + b \geq -1, y_i = -1 \end{cases} \qquad (3.2)$$

Accordingly, training sample dots closest to the hyperplane $(w, b)$, which are called "support vectors", meet (2).

The distance formula of a point to a line is two-dimensional space is

$$d = \frac{|Ax + By + C|}{\sqrt{A^2 + B^2}} \qquad (3.3)$$

So that the distance between the two heterogeneous support vectors and $(w, b)$ is called "margin", which is given as

$$\gamma = \frac{2}{\|w\|} \qquad (3.4)$$

where

$$\|w\| = \sqrt{w_1^2 + \cdots + w_n^2} \qquad (3.5)$$

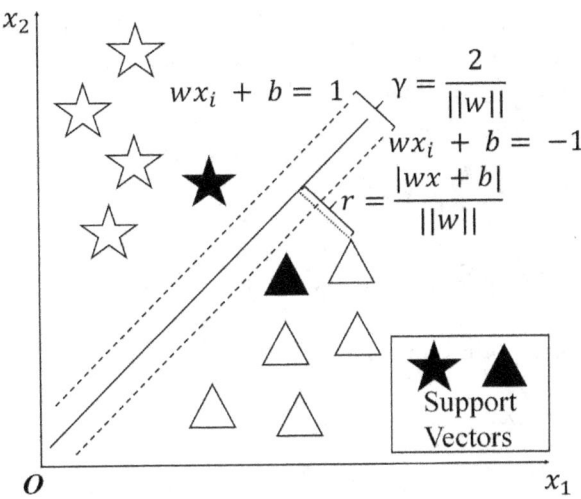

**FIGURE 3.10** The basic model of SVM.

To find the partition hyperplane with maximum margin means to find the parameters $w$ and $b$ that can satisfy the constraints in (2) which produce the largest $\gamma$, namely

$$\max_{w,b} \frac{2}{\|w\|} \tag{3.6}$$

s.t. $y_i(wx_i + b) \geq 1, \quad i = 1, 2, \ldots, m$

Evidently, to maximize the margin, we need to maximize $\|w\|^{-1}$, which equals to minimize $\|w\|^2$, so (4) could be rewritten as

$$\min_{w,b} \frac{\|w\|^2}{2} \tag{3.7}$$

s.t. $y_i(wx_i + b) \geq 1, \quad i = 1, 2, \ldots, m$

Given that it is difficult to solve the original optimization problem, we can turn the original problem into a dual problem that is easy to calculate.

Since the objective function

$$f(x) = \frac{\|w\|^2}{2} \tag{3.8}$$

and the constraint function

$$g_i(x) = 1 - y_i(wx_i + b) \tag{3.9}$$

**68** Methodology

are both continuous differentiable convex functions on $\mathbf{R}^n$, the original optimization problem can be transformed into a dual problem for solution. We can use the Lagrange multiplier method to establish a dual problem.

The Lagrange function for the original problem is

$$L(w,b,\lambda) = f(x) + \sum_i \lambda_i g_i(x) \tag{3.10}$$

$$L(w,b,\lambda) = \frac{\|w\|^2}{2} + \sum_i \lambda_i \left(1 - y_i(wx_i + b)\right) \tag{3.11}$$

The original problem thus turns into

$$\min_{w,b} \max_{\lambda} L(w,b,\lambda) \tag{3.12}$$

s.t. $\lambda \geq 0$

The dual problem of the original problem is defined as

$$\max_{\lambda} \min_{w,b} L(w,b,\lambda) \tag{3.13}$$

s.t. $\lambda \geq 0$

If the original problem and the dual problem have optimal values $d$ and $p$ respectively, then there should be

$$d = \max_{\lambda} \min_{w,b} L(w,b,\lambda) \leq \min_{w,b} \max_{\lambda} L(w,b,\lambda) = p \tag{3.14}$$

By transforming the original problem into a dual problem, we can easily calculate $\min_{w,b} L(w,b,\lambda)$. In this way, the calculation difficulty could be greatly reduced.

There are many software packages for SVM, among which LIBSVM (Chang & Lin, 2011) and LIBLINEAR (Fan et al., 2008) are well-known. According to the number of references, LIBSVM developed by the Institute of information engineering of Taiwan University is now the most widely used SVM tool. As an SVM library, it provides the users with easy access, winning itself a pleasurable reputation in the machine learning area (Chang & Lin, 2011). The basic idea of LIBSVM is to train a data set to find out the optimal model and then utilize it to process a testing set. Here is an example of the classification of apples using three descriptive features.

### 3.1.1.3.1 SVM-recursive feature elimination (SVM-RFE)

The SVM-RFE approach was originally used in medical areas to determine the genetic differences between sick and healthy persons as an embedded feature selection tool (Guyon et al., 2002). The SVM-principal RFE's job is to rank all components according to their effect on classification outcomes (Guyon et al., 2002). Essentially, the SVM-RFE operates by deleting the feature with the least weight at each iteration, and this process continues until all factors have been eliminated. Following this feature removal approach, a few SVM models based on these selected features are constructed again. Last but not least, the new models' performance is compared to the previous models' performance with all features included.

The SVM-RFE has been shown to be more resistant to data overfitting than other feature selection algorithms, and it has excelled in a variety of applications. Gorostiaga and Rojo-Alvarez (2016) used SVM-RFE to fully exploit the virtues of SVM-RFE in a study of Spanish students' PISA results, owing to its superiority in concurrently recognizing the numerous variables that separate the cohorts.

### 3.1.1.3.2 SVM-RFE-cross-validation (SVM-RFE-CV)

Cross-validation (CV) is a commonly-used procedure to find the best hyperparameters of SVM to reach the highest accuracy. It could assess the generalization ability of a model to an independent data set. The basic idea of CV is to use a "testing set" to test the discrimination ability of the machine to the new samples, and then take the "testing error" on the testing set as the approximation of the generalization error of the machine. It is noted that the samples selected for "testing set" should not be overlapped with the "training set", which thus refers to the remaining samples.

Given a data set $D = \{(x_1, y_1), (x_2, y_2), \ldots, (x_n, y_n)\}$. In CV, data set $D$ is usually divided into $k$ mutually exclusive subsets, according to the consistency of data distribution through stratified sampling. Then, each time the union of $k - 1$ subset is used as the training set, and the remaining subset is used as the test sets, so that the k-group training/test set can be obtained, which means that $k$-times training and testing could be carried out. Finally, the mean value of the $k$-time results is obtained. Five-fold, ten-fold, and leave-one-out CV being the three most typical types (James et al., 2013; Meijer & Goeman, 2013), CV is in this regard also called $k$-folds CV. Figure 3.11 provides the detailed process of tenfold CV as an example for further understanding.

### *3.1.1.4 Model evaluation and selection*

### 3.1.1.4.1 Empirical error and over-fitting

For example, a set of data 1, 2, 4, 5. Use threshold 3 to divide it into two categories. Suppose the classification results of the learner are 1 and 2, 4, and 5. But the actual results are 1, 2, and 4, 5. The wrong 2 is the error. What is an empirical error? In fact, it is the error in the training set, which is also called training error. Compared with the empirical error, there is also the generalization error that we often encounter. The generalization error is the error in the new sample (test set).

**FIGURE 3.11** The graphic illustration of ten-fold cross-validation.

Obviously, we all want to generalize the learner with small errors. However, we don't know what the new sample is like in advance. In fact, what we can do is minimize the empirical error of the learner. In most cases, we can learn a learner with little empirical error and good performance on the training set. If all training sets are classified correctly, that is, the classification error rate is 0, but is such a learner good?

However, when the model learns the training samples "too well", it is likely that some characteristics of the training samples themselves have been regarded as the general properties of all potential samples. This phenomenon is called "over-fitting" in machine learning, and "under-fitting" is opposite to over fitting, which means that the general properties of training samples have not been learned well.

### 3.1.1.4.2 Three ways to evaluate the model

i. Hold-out

The data set $D$ is directly divided into two mutually exclusive sets, one as the training set s and the other as the test set t, that is, $d = s \cup T, s \cap t = \emptyset$. After training the model on $S$, $t$ is used to evaluate its test error as the estimation of generalization error. Taking the second classification task as an example, assuming that $D$ contains 1,000 samples, s contains 700 samples and $t$ contains 300 samples, after training with s, if the model has 9 sample classification errors on $T$, the error rate is $(90/300) \times 100\% = 30\%$, and the corresponding accuracy is $1-30\% = 70\%$. When using the hold-out method, we need to pay attention to the following points:

First, the division of training/test set shall maintain the consistency of data distribution as much as possible to avoid the impact on the final results due to additional errors introduced in the data division process. For example, in the classification task, at least keep the category proportion of samples similar. If the data set division process is viewed from the perspective of sampling, the sampling method that retains the category proportion is usually called "stratified sampling". If the proportion of sample categories in S and t is very different, the error estimation will deviate due to the proportion of training/test data distribution.

Second, even after the sample proportion of the training/test set is given, there are still many ways to segment the initial data set $D$. Different partitions will lead to different training/test sets, and the results of model evaluation will be different accordingly. Therefore, the estimation results obtained by the single use of the set-aside method are often not stable and reliable. When using the set-aside method, it is generally necessary to take the average value after several random divisions and repeated experimental evaluations as the evaluation results of the set-aside method.

Third, we hope to evaluate the performance of the model trained with $D$, but the set-aside method needs to divide the training/test set, which will lead to a dilemma: if the training set s contains most samples, the trained model may be closer to the model trained with $D$, but the evaluation result may not be stable and accurate because $t$ is relatively small; If the test set $t$ contains more samples, the difference between the training sets $s$ and $D$ is greater, and the evaluated model may be significantly different from the model trained with $D$, thus reducing the fidelity of the evaluation results.

ii. Cross-validation

CV is a machine learning technique that is commonly used to develop models and test model parameters, as well as to assess the performance of a machine learning model. CV is frequently used to accomplish model selection.

CV entails repeatedly utilizing the data, slicing and dicing the resulting sample data into separate training and testing sets, training the model with the training set, and evaluating the model's prediction with the testing set. On this foundation, we may create a variety of training and test sets, and a sample from one training set may become a sample from the next test set, a process known as "Crossover".

When there isn't enough data, CV is utilized. We employ CV to train the best selection model if the data sample size is less than 10,000. If the sample size is greater than 10,000, the data is normally divided into three groups at random: one for the training set, one for the validation set, and one for the test set. The validation set is used to verify the model's prediction and pick the model and its relevant parameters, while the training set is used to train the model. The final model is then utilized to pick which model and associated parameters to employ in the test set.

### 3.1.1.4.3 Indicators to measure the performance of the model

A general-purpose machine learning algorithm and a domain-specific kernel function are included in the SVM (HU et al., 2021). The SVM training technique is used to create a training model that can then predict which category a new sample instance belongs to (Dong & HU, 2019). When given a set of training samples, each sample is labeled with one of two categories. A confusion matrix is used to evaluate the performance of SVM models (Figure 3.12) (see Table 3.1).

Generally, based on the confusion matrix, an array of indicators that ranges from 0 to 1 is used to evaluate the classification ability of a machine learning algorithm (Baldi et al., 2000); these include an accuracy score (ACC), a sensitivity score (SEN, also called the recall score), a specificity score (SPE), a precision score, an F1-score, the Matthews correlation coefficient (MCC) and the area under the receiver operating characteristic (ROC) curve (AUC). Technically, the mathematical formulae used to produce these values are provided as follows:

$$ACC = (TN + TP) / (TP + TN + FP + FN) \tag{3.15}$$

$$SPE = TN / (TN + FP) \tag{3.16}$$

$$Precision = TP / (TP + FP) \tag{3.17}$$

$$SEN = TP / (TP + FN) \tag{3.18}$$

$$F1\text{-score} = 2T\big((TP / (TP + FP)) \times SEN\big) / (TP / (TP + FP) + SEN) \tag{3.19}$$

$$MCC = (TP \times TN - FP \times FN) / \sqrt{((TP + FP)(TP + FN))(TN + FP)(TN + FN)} \tag{3.20}$$

$$AUC = \int_0^1 ROC(t)\,dt \tag{3.21}$$

The proportion of real findings in the selected population, encompassing both positive and negative results, is represented by ACC. This is one of the most often

**TABLE 3.1** The confusion matrix

|  | Positive (Predicted) | Negative (Predicted) |
|---|---|---|
| Positive (Actual) | True Positive (TP) | False Negative (FN) |
| Negative (Actual) | False Positive (FP) | True Negative (TN) |

Note: Positive: Observation is positive; Negative: Observation is negative.

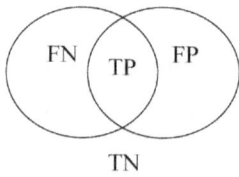

**FIGURE 3.12** The different types of classification results.

used metrics for evaluating classifier performance. When our classes are almost balanced and precise forecasts of those classes are equally significant, we employ the accuracy measure.

Precision reflects the proportion of projected positive instances among the actual number of positive cases, whereas SPE refers to the percentage of real negative findings that are accurately diagnosed. When compared to a model with lesser accuracy, a model with high precision will identify a larger percentage of positive classes. When we're more interested in discovering the most number of affirmative classes possible, even if total accuracy suffers, precision becomes more crucial.

The proportion of genuine positives that are accurately identified as such is represented by SEN/Recall. In circumstances when we want to catch the most number of instances of a certain class, even if it raises our false positives, it becomes an essential indicator of classifier performance. Consider bank fraud: a model with a high recall will provide us with a greater number of prospective fraud scenarios. However, it will assist us in raising the alert in the majority of questionable instances. The code below calculates recall for our model predictions.

AUC is a ranking-based classification performance metric that can identify a randomly selected positive example from a randomly selected negative example.

Even though the size of two classes differs, MCC is employed to measure model quality.

The harmonic mean of accuracy (another performance metric) and recall is the F1-score.

Although each indicator is powerful and valuable for measuring classification ability, recent research usually utilizes a combination of the SPE, SEN, Precision, AUC, F1-score, MCC, and ACC (e.g., Chen et al., 2021a, 2021b; HU et al., 2021). This is because employing diverse indicators might result in a wide range of evaluation outcomes, yet using different performance measures can improve the quality of performance evaluation. It should be highlighted, however, that these performance indicators should be used as a guide rather than a final judgment, because the efficiency of a model is determined by the inextricable mix of the algorithm, data, and job requirements.

### 3.1.1.4.4 Hyperparameter tuning strategies

Most learning algorithms have some parameters that need to be set. Different parameter configurations often lead to significant differences in the performance of the learned model. Therefore, when evaluating and selecting the model, in addition to selecting the applicable learning algorithm, it is also necessary to set the algorithm parameters, which is commonly referred to as parameter tuning. There is no essential difference between parameter adjustment and algorithm selection: train the model for each parameter configuration, and then take the value of the corresponding counties within the name in the real number range.

Therefore, for each parameter, there is one thing to note: many parameters of the learning algorithm take value in the real number range. Therefore, it is not feasible to train the model for each parameter configuration. In reality, it is common to select a range and change step for each parameter. For example, if the step is 0.05 within the range of [0,0.2], there are actually five candidate parameter values to be evaluated, and the selected value is finally generated from these five candidate values. Obviously, the selected parameter value is often not the "best" value, but it is the result of a compromise between calculation overhead and performance estimation. Through this compromise, the learning process becomes feasible. In fact, even after such a compromise, it is still very difficult to adjust parameters. It can be easily estimated that the algorithm has three parameters, and each parameter takes only five candidate values, so there are 125 models for each training/test set. Many powerful learning algorithms have a large number of parameters to be set, which will lead to a great amount of parameter adjustment work, so that in many application tasks, whether the parameters are adjusted well often has a key impact on the final model performance.

Given the data set $D$ containing m samples. We only use part of the data to train the model in the process of model evaluation and selection. Therefore, after the model selection is completed, the learning algorithm and parameter configuration have been selected. At this time, the model should be retrained with data set D. This model uses all m samples in the training process, which is the model we finally submit to users.

### 3.1.1.5 The advantages and disadvantages of machine learning approaches in EDM

As we have mentioned in Chapter 1, EBD is featured by a series of unique properties, including large sample size and hierarchy, which synergistically spawn the high-dimensional features. Machine learning algorithms, however, enjoy the hard-wired virtue in EDM. When it comes to large educational data sets decorated with a large amount of data with complex variables, traditional methods are often dwarfed by SVM (Chen et al., 2021a). In general, multiple linear regression and hierarchical linear modeling, are of great use for interpreting and estimating low variable dimensions and small sample sizes. However, to decode the complexity of data sets involves clarifying the complex interactions between predictor variables and problems undefined with no clear algorithmic solutions which is often beyond the reach of conventional methods (Kasgari et al., 2013). Machine learning method, however, is suitable for the statistical analysis of problems with a considerable number of samples with high dimensionality, and it is effective to discover the collective effects triggered by a feature set with great influences (Shoaib et al., 2022). Compared with other conventional methods, machine learning outperforms in extracting information from complex relationships between numerous variables, and detecting the underlying patterns in a large database without strong preconceptions (Livieris et al., 2017). SVM is regarded as the most commonly used and effective classifier due to its excellent generalization ability. Compared with other machine learning methods, it excels in avoiding overfitting and providing classifications with high accuracy and robustness (Mitchell, 1997).

Objectively speaking, there are also some drawbacks found when utilizing the machine learning and deep learning approach. Regarding SVM, it is not the optimal method when dealing with small-sized sample with low variable dimensions; it is time-consuming when dealing with the data and producing the final results; the noise of the data could also exert negative effects on its efficiency and performance (Kotsiantis, 2012). Worse still, considering the transparency of methods, the computational process for machine learning is not visualizable. Nevertheless, this view fails to foresee the development of interpretable AI, in the wake of which the "black box" once received widely will become a "glass box" in the near future. (Witten et al., 2016). Thus, we can safely conclude that utilizing machine learning in educational research could be a favorable choice, echoing throughout the literature relevant to big data analysis.

### *3.1.2 Hierarchical linear models (HLM)*

Hierarchical linear modeling (HLM) is a sophisticated and versatile regression model for evaluating complicated nested data structure, in which lower-level analysis units are stacked within higher-level analysis units. It is extremely adaptable, allowing researchers to specify relationships across many educational levels. Hierarchical linear modeling is discussed in this chapter. To begin with, this chapter analyzes the application of HLM to PISA reading and related research, describes its development, mechanism, use, and explains why it is effective in PISA reading-based investigations. The HLM idea is introduced, as well as the issues that will be discussed in this section. This chapter also includes a general introduction to cross-sectional HLM models, as well as an illustrated example contrasting the outcomes of two different models, introducing readers to the core concepts of HLM as applied to cross-sectional and longitudinal data. HLM is a complicated subject, and no assumptions are made about the reader's knowledge with it beyond a fundamental comprehension of regression. As a result, this chapter is devoted to understanding HLM analyses and key judgments made by HLM when creating complicated models. It begins with a quick overview of clustered data structures and some of the issues that arise. The major components of a two-level model using a cross-sectional data structure are then introduced, and key considerations are highlighted.

### *3.1.2.1 An introduction to HLM*

Hierarchical linear model, also known as a linear mixed-effects model, multilevel modeling, or covariance components model (Leyland & Goldstein, 2001), is eminently suitable for analyzing complex multilevel nested relationships as well as nested structure of the data, that is, lower-level units of analysis are clustered within higher-level units of analysis. It's particularly well suited to assessing changes in student achievement using growth models and longitudinal data. These varied models can be used to examine how people change over time and how specific variables at each level might predict where people start and/or how quickly they evolve. For example, we may look at data from a group of children in urban and rural schools as they progressed from kindergarten through fifth grade. We could then see if students in urban schools performed better in kindergarten than students in rural schools, and if these same pupils advanced at different rates over the course of the study's five years. We could also look into the kids' other traits. For example, we may look at the pace at which kids with one impairment, such as autism spectrum disorder advanced compared to students with a different condition (such as learning disabilities), and see if the observed association held true for students in both urban and rural schools.

When data is clustered, for example, students are clustered within schools and the influence of predictor variables on some result is contingent on that nesting, it's vital to account for it in the model to prevent misrepresenting the effects. Individuals nested within a higher-level unit are often more similar than they are different, and their membership in that higher-level unit may influence the observed outcome of a therapy (e.g., students attending School A instead of School B). Individual residuals inside the unit will be correlated if the data are reliant on the higher-level unit, which violates the normal single-level regression assumption of observation independence (Raudenbush & Bryk, 2002).

In most cases, failing to account for nested data structures leads to aggregate bias, misestimated standard errors, and regression heterogeneity. When a variable is aggregated, it has a different meaning than when it is disaggregated. This is known as aggregation bias. When you use the aggregated variable as a predictor variable in a model, the results may be skewed toward the aggregated meaning of the variable. For example, as Raudenbush and Bryk (2002) point out, the overall composition of the student population in specific schools may have an impact on individual kids in addition to the effect of individual FRL eligibility. HLM can easily handle these complex interactions, as will be discussed later in the study.

We get misestimated standard errors when we don't account for the dependence on higher-level units or when the independence of observations assumption is broken. By integrating higher-level units in the model, HLM corrects the estimates, resulting in independent observations within a unit. Heterogeneity of regressions occurs when the connection between a predictor variable and a certain result varies by a higher-level unit. For instance, the relationship between student achievement and FRL may be fairly robust in some institutions but significantly weaker in others. This heterogeneity would be ignored by standard single-level regression, which implies a consistent link across schools, while HLM may test and adjust for heterogeneous associations directly.

### 3.1.2.2 HLM: A powerful model in detecting nested data sets
#### 3.1.2.2.1 The universality of hierarchical data

A wide variety of statistical applications involve hierarchical data structures or multilevel structures. In transnational studies, researchers explore how disparities in national economic growth mixed with the educational outcomes of adults affect fertility rates. A combination of economic indicators retrieved at the national level and household data for analysis. Specifically, the data structure is with households clustered within countries, and the underlying data structure is hierarchical or multilevel. Organizational studies, in which researchers look at how firm-internal variables like organizational culture, knowledge integration, and core competency affect individual workers' performance by using a similar nested data structure. Both the firm and the workers can be considered units in this study, with workers nested within firms.

Moreover, in developmental studies, several observations in statistics are collected over time on a set of candidates, involving repeated measurement design for their change trajectory. Among this kind of research, psychologists are more concerned with how internal factors of individuals, as well as variation in their contextual exposure, produce effects on their change trajectories. Traditionally, it is common to view a design as people crossing occasions at the same number of points in time, but this is not always the case. A study conducted by Huttenlocher et al. (1991) examined how language exposure in the home predicts how a child's vocabulary develops over time. In spite of this, we may consider occasions to be nested within people because the number of time points and the spacing between them vary from person to person.

Hierarchical linear models also give a general statistical framework for varieties of studies, along with for quantitative synthesis of findings. For example, researchers tend to explore how different the display among research of treatment implementations, research methods, research subjects or research contextual background with regard to the treatment effect estimates. In this case, research subjects are clustered within these studies.

Another prime example can be seen in the educational or linguistic studies, Broadly, researchers might investigate factors related to the school, such as school location, school size, school SES, teachers (e.g., teaching method, teacher–student relationship), and students themselves (e.g., students' self-efficacy, and motivation). Each of these elements that influence student academic achievement can be thought of as several degrees of clustering; for example, children in Level 1 are grouped together in classrooms (at Level 2), which are also clustered within schools (at Level 3), and to investigate how contextual factors affects students' academic achievements by considering school and country background information. Cases in this area are quite challenging as it often includes double nested structure of repeated measurement for individuals. Specifically, students represent the first level, schools represent the second level and the country represents the third level. Such data have a three-level hierarchical structure with students clustered within the school; schools clustered within the country. The entire data set is interdependent and always be interlaced or corresponded to each other simultaneously.

For hundreds of years, researchers are often lukewarm about the top-down or cross-level interactions of how many distributions can the higher-level factors (e.g., school-level or country-level information) have on the lower-level factors (e.g., individual performance). For example, the individual difference within different schools or countries could be the same or not, the relationship between different variables is based on the variation of schools or countries. Individual behaviors are always affected by their own characteristics and their surrounding environment. Specifically, in the education area, students' academic achievements are likely to be influenced by their own internal motivation or self-expectation, as well as their contextual factors (e.g., school background or family background) at the same time. The former effects are individual effects, while the later effects are "big-fish-small-pond" effects, called background effects or group effects.

For half a century, although researchers are more concerned with differentiating effects across levels of analysis, for example, individual effects and group effects (e.g., Dansereau et al., 1984), the analytical challenges for empirically and simultaneously testing these multilevel effects and detailed recommendations for addressing them have not yet been offered. Researchers have made substantial efforts on exploring to distinguish group effects and background effects, where they first proposed the "aggregation" and "disaggregation". Essentially, that is the choice between individual effects and group effects. Researchers like psychologists are more concerned with individual effects and ignore their group effects at the same time, causing the affection for the accuracy of correlation parameters. Since it seems that there is a greater similarity index among the individual outside the group than the similar background individuals within the group. On the other hand, a mistake could be amplified because the observed effects not only involve the group effects but also the individual effects. For example, when the individual variables are extracted from the groups that exist naturally, their relationship reflects two kinds of things: the individual effects and the covariation between the groups, that is, how much contribution that the covariation coefficient of $X$ can make to the covariation coefficient of $Y$. In this circumstance, the variables $X$ and $Y$ are likely to be closely linked with each other, while this correlation coefficient can be reduced if we add another relevant variable with variable $X$ and variable $Y$.

Another sign of the evolution of statistical analysis is Within Analysis Between Analysis (WABA). The algorithm of WABA is based on the following calculations of the same data set. First, the calculation is conducted in the individual level within the group, considering their within-group effect; Second, to calculate the average of second-level statistics, considering their between-group effect; finally, to conclude all the statistics, considering their total effect. To some extent, it is capable of reflecting the within-group and between-group variance proportion, whereas it fails to analyze what factors contribute to these results and why there is a difference in within-group effects between different groups.

Even with the prevalence of hierarchical data structures in social or scientific research, past studies have not explored the data analysis method in-depth and have not been concerned with the limitation of traditional regression methods adequately, since hierarchical data poses several problems when analyzing it. On the whole, traditional regression models [(e.g., analysis of variance (ANOVA)] are languished because it is incapable of addressing the dependency problem across levels and analyzing the entire data set with two or more layers simultaneously. It is unable to test with all the student-level, school-level, and country-level data simultaneously, whereas it can only conflate the single-level data effects. If one continues to use traditional regression models that assume data are organized at a single level, the violation of the assumption of independence will lead to aggregation bias and inaccurate estimation (Hofmann, 1997; Raudenbush & Bryk, 2002). For example, it is thought that individuals within hierarchies are more similar to each other than if they were randomly selected from the population as a whole. Due to the assignment of students to classrooms based on geography factors, students in one class are more likely to be similar to each other than those drawn from the entire school district or the national cohort. As a result, students in a given class tend to come from a community group that is more homogeneous than the population as a whole in terms of morals and values, socioeconomic status (SES), family background, and so on. In addition, the characteristics of individuals within the same class or school tend to be similar, for example, they may be influenced by their social environment, family background, demographic factors, or others, therefore, observations based on these individuals are not entirely independent.

### 3.1.2.2.2 The development of HLMs statistical theories

Hierarchical linear models were first proposed by Lindley and Smith (1972) as part of their seminal contribution to Bayesian estimation of linear models. In this context, Lindley and Smith (1972) constructed a general framework for analyzing multiple levels of this nesting of data structures. However, it fails to proceed since the problem of covariance components estimation of unbalanced data is unable to be solved. Therefore, in the early 1970s, there is no general estimation method was feasible. Then, Dempster et al. (1977) proposed an EM algorithm and provided a possible way to bridge the problem of covariance components estimation. Dempster et al. (1981) elaborate on the practicability of this algorithm to hierarchical data structures. Laird and Ware (1982) put it into the study of growth, along with Mason et al. (1983), put this approach into practice to cross-sectional data with a nature of clustered data structure.

In the following years, other substantial number of researches related to covariance components estimation was provided by giving the advantages of the application of iteratively reweighted generalized least squares (GLS) as well as a Fisher scoring algorithm (Goldstein, 1986; Longford, 1987). Moreover, an increasing number of statistical computing programs or software packages are fitting these hierarchical linear models, for example, HLM (Raudenbush et al., 2000), MLWIN (Rasbash et al., 2000), SAS Proc Mixed (Littel et al., 1996) and so on.

i. Early applications of HLM

As described above, Hierarchical or multilevel data is universal in social and behavioral studies. That is, individuals might be clustered within organizational units, and the organizational units data might be clustered within communities, and even within countries or states. For example, people exist in structures such as homes, companies, schools, or countries. In an educational area, students exist in a hierarchical social structure that may involve their family (e.g., parents), classroom, peers, grade, school location, and state. Each level of this hierarchical structure has its own sub-model, and the sub-models' data contribute to expressing relationships among these predictors or variables within the given level. It could be expressed in terms of how a certain variable at one level influences variables at another level, as well as its relationship with other variables. Although any number of levels can be depicted, the fundamental two-level structure has all of the important statistical properties.

The early applications instructed in the following will emphasize three general research goals. First, to improve the accurate estimation of individual effects within organizational units such as developing a regression model for an individual school by taking the advantage of the fact that similar estimates are presented in other schools. Second, to test or formulate the hypothesis about the cross-level effects such as how various school types or school locations influence the relationship between social status and academic outcomes within school levels. Third is to partition the variance and covariance components across different levels such as decomposing the covariation among different predictors or variables within the individual level into within- and between-school components.

Researchers may now apply the hierarchical models to a broader range of data types due to these advances in statistics and computation. For instance, Rumberger (1995) investigated the predictors of pupils dropping out of school using a two-level model. He found a number of risk factors for early dropout at the student and school levels. The level-1 model was an LR model in which student background attributes influenced the log-odds of early dropout. As a function of school variables, level-1 coefficients differed between schools. In the setting of repeated measures, Homey et al. (1995) present an application, which was to see if high-rate offenders' tendency to commit crimes varies depending on their living circumstances, such as job and marital status. The result was binary, with each participant either committing or not committing a crime in the previous month. Some explanatory variables changed over time (e.g., employed versus jobless), while others changed among individuals but were time-invariant. Using an LR model, the level-1 model examined how individual odds of committing a crime changed over time. Individual log-odds of committing crime changed in the level-1 model, which was an LR model. At level 2, the parameters of individual alterations were different. Sampson et al. (1997) use count data as the result (the number of homicides per community), to study the youngsters nested within communities.

ii. Improved estimation of individual effects

The use of standardized test scores to select minority applicants to graduate business schools was a source of concern for Braun et al. (1983). Many schools utilize test scores to predict future academic success in part to make admissions choices. However, because white people make up the majority of MBA applicants, their data dominates the calculated prediction equations. As a result, these calculated prediction equations may not give a sufficient ordering for minority student selection. In theory, a separate equation for minority candidates in each school would be more equitable; however, predicting such equations is challenging due to the fact that most schools have few minority students and hence insufficient data on which to base credible predictions. In a study of 59 graduate business schools by Braun et al. (1983), in 14 schools, there were no minorities, whereas in 20 schools, there were one or three minorities. However, it would have been impossible to create prediction equations for minorities in these institutions using normal regression methodologies. Furthermore, even in the 25 schools where there was enough data to allow a separate calculation, the minority samples were still small, resulting in inaccurate minority coefficient estimates.

Alternatively, the data might be aggregated across all schools, ignoring student nesting inside schools, although this presents its own set of challenges. A failure to account for these selection artifacts could result in skewed prediction coefficients because minorities are significantly more likely to attend some schools than others. To overcome this problem, Braun et al. (1983) employed a hierarchical linear model. They were able to efficiently employ all of the available information by borrowing strength from the complete ensemble of data to offer each school different prediction equations for whites and minorities. The estimator for each school was a weighted combination of the information from that school and the relationships that exist across the entire sample (Morris, 1983; Rubin, 1987). As one might assume, the relative weights assigned to each component are determined by its precision.

iii. Modeling cross-level effects

The second common application of a multilevel model is to develop and evaluate hypotheses about how variables measured at one level influence relationships at a higher level. As cross-level effects are prevalent in behavioral and social research, this modeling framework represents a significant improvement over previous approaches. Mason et al. (1983), for example, looked at the impact of mother education and urban versus rural domicile on fertility in 15 nations. It is commonly established that high levels of education and urban living predict reduced fertility in many nations. However, the researchers reasoned that such impacts could be influenced by country characteristics such as the level of national economic growth and the intensity of family planning activities. A study conducted by Mason et al. discovered that higher maternal education was linked to reduced fertility rates in all states studied. On the other hand, the disparities between urban and rural fertility rates vary by country, with the largest disparities occurring in countries with high GDPs and few family planning programs. Another example comes from developmental psychology. Word acquisition is thought to be based on two factors: exposure to acceptable speech and fundamental differences in the ability to learn from such exposure, according to language development researchers. It is usually accepted that observed disparities in children's vocabulary development are mostly due to fundamental variances in ability. However, there is little actual evidence to support this notion. According to heritability studies, parental scores on standardized vocabulary tests could account for 10%–20% of the variance in their children's performance on identical exams. Experiments on humans haven't fared any better. The majority of individual diversity in vocabulary acquisition is yet unknown.

Researchers have traditionally studied exposure effects using two-time-point designs. At 14 months of age, a child's vocabulary could be examined for the first time, as well as information on the mother's verbal skills or language use. The size of the children's vocabulary would then be reviewed at a later date, say 26 months. After controlling for children's "starting ability", the data would be evaluated using a traditional linear model with the goal of assessing the maternal speech effect on 26-month vocabulary size. Huttenlocher et al. (1991) gathered longitudinal data on certain children who were monitored seven times between the ages of 14 and 26 months. This allowed for the creation of a customized vocabulary growth trajectory for each child based on repeated observations. A set of parameters defined each child's development. To forecast these growth factors, a second model incorporated information about the children, such as the child's sex and the amount of mother speech in the home setting. Based on a hierarchical linear model, the researchers discovered that exposure to language throughout infancy played a far larger influence on vocabulary growth than previously thought. In fact, the impacts were much larger than would have been observed if the first and last time points had been used in traditional analysis. This application highlights the difficulties of using traditional methods to make reliable judgments regarding growth correlates.

iv. Partitioning variance–covariance components

The estimate of variance and covariance components using imbalanced, nested data is the third use of hierarchical linear models. Educational scholars, for example, frequently aim to investigate the development of individual students within the context of classrooms and schools. A three-level model is required for the formal modeling of such phenomena. An analysis of only a small subset of Sustaining Effects Study longitudinal data is presented by Bryk and Raudenbush (1988). They analyzed arithmetic achievement data from 618 kids in 86 schools who were tested five times between Grades 1 and 3. They started with a model of academic accomplishment for each child within each school based on individual growth (or repeated measures). The three-level methodology allowed the heterogeneity in these individual growth trajectories to be broken down into within-school and between-school components. The findings were startling: between-school growth rates accounted for 83% of the variation in growth rates. In contrast, schools accounted for just around 14% of the variance in beginning status, which is consistent with the findings of cross-sectional studies of school impacts. Because conventional models do not account for the p, this research discovered significant disparities between schools that would have gone undetected by traditional approaches.

### 3.1.2.2.3 The algorithm of HLM

In general, HLM allows for explicitly analyzing the nested nature of data by simultaneously estimating the influence of predictors of different levels on the outcome variable at the individual level and meanwhile keeping these predictors at the appropriate analysis level, which will contribute to the development of multilevel theories since researchers must keep in mind which level the particular variable belongs to as well as its relationships with other variables in carrying out the analysis (Kozlowski & Klein, 2000; Raudenbush & Bryk, 2002). In addition, HLM enables analysts to take advantage of the overall data to improve the coefficient estimates of lower-level variables by generating Empirical Bayesian estimates, which are of substantial significance to the estimation of the fixed effects of higher-level variables (Raudenbush et al., 2004). In estimating the fixed effects of higher-level variables using HLM, GLS, instead of ordinary least squares (OLS), is employed to give greater weight to the more reliable and accurate lower-level estimates. HLM also utilizes the interactive computing of unbalanced data to give valid estimates of variance–covariance components, which cannot be achieved by traditional regression methods such as Analysis of Covariance (ANCOVA). Moreover, HLM provides robust estimates of standard error, which can be a very useful way to circumvent the pesky heteroscedasticity problem. As for the assumption of homogeneity of regression slopes, HLM explicitly models the variability of the relationship between covariates and the outcome variable, thus overcoming possible problems relevant to this assumption. Again, as mentioned above, the assumption of independence can be cast aside since HLM is especially designed to take into consideration the variation between groups (Raudenbush & Bryk, 2002).

i. Aggregation and disaggregation

Variables can be defined at any level of hierarchy in hierarchical linear modeling research. Analyses can be conducted directly in terms of some variables at their "natural" level. It might, for example, assess school size and style at the school level, as well as intellect and school success at the individual level. Additionally, researchers can use aggregation or disaggregation to move variables from one level to another. Aggregation, in this context, refers to the process of shifting variables from a lower to a higher level, such as moving to the school level and calculating the school average of students' intelligence scores. The term "disaggregation" refers to the process of aligning variables.

The lowest level (level 1) is usually expressed by the individuals. However, there are still other cases existing. For example, Galtung (1967) defines roles within an individual as the lowest level, and repeated measurements within an individual are the lowest level in a longitudinal design.

At each level of the hierarchy, there are varieties of types of variables. The following categories is based on the typology provided by Lazarsfeld and Menzel (1961). In addition, some distinctions between global variables, structure variables, and context variables are offered in the following paragraph. A global variable is a variable that refers only to the level at which it is defined and does not refer to other units or levels. At the student level, a global variable such as student intellect or gender will be a variable. At the school level, the number of students will be a global variable. Global variables are measured at their true level of existence.

Structure variables operate by referring to lower-level subunits. They consist of lower-level variables.

The school variable "average intelligence" is the average of the intelligence scores of students at that school. In multilevel analysis, it is a common process to use the mean of a lower-level variable as the higher-level explanatory variable. Lower-level variables can be used in other functions, though they are less common. For example, using the standard deviation of the lower-level variable as the higher-level explanatory variable can be used to test assumptions about the effect of population heterogeneity on the output variable. These variables are referred to as configurational variables by Klein and Kozlowski (2000), who emphasize the necessity of capturing patterns of individual variables in a population. Their studies also show how to portray group characteristics using functions other than the average of individual scores. Aggregation is required to create structural variables from lesser levels of data. Furthermore, because context variables are linked to super units, all variables at the lower level receive the value of a variable for the higher-level super-unit to which they belong.

It is not necessary to assign each variable to its proper category to analyze hierarchical linear models. The scheme's conceptual advantage is that it makes it clear to which level a measurement belongs. Prior to LR, hierarchical linear models were used to assign all variables to a single level of interest by aggregation or disaggregation and then analyze them using regression or analysis of variance. Analyzing variables from several levels at a single common level, on the other hand, is insufficient and leads to two unique types of issues.

The statistical issue is the first. When data is aggregated, it combines several data values from many sub-units into a smaller number of values for a smaller number of higher-level units. As a result, a significant amount of data is lost, and the statistical analysis loses its power. Data disaggregation, however, leads to the 'inflating' of a large number of values for a very small number of sub-units from a few values from a small number of super-units. Ordinary statistical tests consider all of these disaggregated data values to be independent data from a much larger sample of sub-units. Of course, the number of higher-level units is the appropriate sample size for these variables. Increasing the sample size to include a greater number of disaggregated cases increases the likelihood of rejection of the null hypothesis significantly more than the nominal alpha level predicts. To put it another way, investigators come up with a lot of significant outcomes that are completely false.

The second issue is about conceptual. If the researcher does not exercise caution when interpreting the results, he or she may fall victim to the fallacy of the wrong level, which involves studying data at one level and drawing conclusions at a different level. Ecological fallacy, also known as the 'Robinson effect', refers to the interpretation of data aggregated at the individual level (Robinson, 1950). Robinson elucidates aggregated data from nine geographic regions in 1930, indicating the relationship between the percentage of blacks and the level of illiteracy. The ecological correlation, or the relationship between aggregated variables at the regional level, is 0.95. On the contrary, there is a 0.20 individual-level connection between these global variables. In practice, an ecological correlation is very definitely not equivalent to its corresponding individual-level correlation. Making higher-level inferences based on lower-level analysis can be equally deceptive. The atomistic fallacy is a type of cognitive bias. The 'Simpson's paradox' is a related but separate fallacy (Lindley & Novick, 1981). If aggregated data taken from various populations is compacted and evaluated as if it originated from a single homogeneous population, Simpson's dilemma describes the problem of utterly erroneous conclusions being reached. Alker (1969) provides a comprehensive categorization of such fallacies.

A better method to approach multilevel data is to recognize that there is no single 'correct' level at which to interpret the data. Rather, each level of the data is significant in its own right. When we look into cross-level hypotheses or multilevel problems, this becomes evident. A multilevel problem is one in which the relationships between variables assessed at multiple hierarchical levels are investigated. One recurrent question is how a variety of individual and group variables interact to influence a single individual outcome variable. Some of the higher-level explanatory factors are often the averaged group means of lower-level individual variables. The purpose of the study is to see if the individual- and group-level explanatory variables have a direct effect on individual-level relationships, and if group-level explanatory variables serve as moderators of individual-level associations. If lower-level associations are moderated by group-level variables, this is manifested as a statistical interaction between explanatory variables at different levels. Previously, similar data were typically evaluated by adopting traditional multiple regression (MR) analysis, with one dependent variable at the individual level (first level) and other explanatory variables retrieved from all levels (Boyd & Iversen, 1979).

ii. Cross-classified hierarchical linear models

Multilevel data isn't always strictly hierarchical. Children, for example, can be nested both within the schools they attend and within the communities in which they live. When it comes to schools and communities, though, the nested structure may not be as obvious. Although most students choose to attend school in their local neighborhood, there are exceptions. Some pupils will attend school in places other than their home areas. Schools near the border between the two communities, in particular, may attract kids from both areas. As a result, unambiguous student hierarchies in schools and communities are impossible to develop. Of course, we can create such a model structure at any time, but we'll need to include certain schools multiple times because they're found in multiple communities. We're most certainly dealing with a cross-classified data structure whenever we run across such issues. Students are nested in schools and communities, for example, but schools and communities cross paths. When we look at the educational accomplishment, we may believe that both schools and communities can impact it.

Therefore, the model must take school and community as the source of achievement change, but in this way, students are nested in the cross-classification of school and community. Cross-classified data structures can appear at any level of a hierarchical data set. If we nest Students in the cross-classification of school and community, school and community are the second level, and students are the lowest level. However, there can also be cross-classification at the lowest level. Taking students as an example, they must perform a set of complex analysis tasks in computer class. There are several parallel classes, taught by different teachers. To maintain the same scoring policy for all students, all computer homework is graded by all teachers. Therefore, at the student level, we will give scores for several different exercises by several different teachers. One way to approach this issue is to divide the class's level into the highest level. The teacher is at the next lower level below this, and the practice is at the lowest level, which is below the teacher. This is a decent four-level hierarchical data structure. On the other hand, the class level can be divided into the highest level. Students are at a lower level than this, activities are at a higher level, and teachers are at a lower level than this. This is also a four-layer, four-layer hierarchical data structure. We appear to be able to model these facts using two contradictory data structures. Every time we run into this issue, it's a sign that we're dealing with a cross-classified data structure. We nested the students in the class in the scoring example, and the cross categorization and exercises of the teachers (raters) were nested in the students. Because variances between classes and pupils are possible, this cross-classification of exercises and teachers would be described at the most basic level, with pupils within classes nested within pupils. In such cases, generalizability theory can be used to model the dependability of the student's combined grade (Cronbach et al., 1972). We must partition the entire variation of the awarded grades as the sum of contributions from classes, students, exercises, and instructors to analyze the generalizability of the students' cumulative grades across exercises and teachers using generalizability theory. Cross-classified multilevel analysis is a smart technique to get the estimations you need for your project (Hox & Maas, 2006).

Multilevel models with cross-classification are useful in a wide range of circumstances. So far, the examples presented have all been from the realm of education. In longitudinal research, the non-response model is used, in which respondents are interviewed multiple times, sometimes by the same interviewer, and sometimes by different interviewers. The interviewer's personality traits may influence the interviewees' willingness to cooperate. The interviewees are nested within the interviewer, and the multilayer model analysis is used (Hox et al., 1991).

In longitudinal investigations, the prior interviewer may be significant, therefore we have a cross-classified structure with respondents nested within the present and previous interviewer's cross-classification. Pickery and Loosveldt (1998), O'Muircheartaigh and Campanelli (1999), and Pickery et al. (2001) are examples of multilevel cross-classified analyses in panel interview studies. Members of groups both provide and receive popularity ratings from other group members, hence cross-classified multilevel models have been used for sociometric choice data (van Duijn et al., 1999). See Rasbash and Goldstein (1994) for further instances.

iii. Longitudinal data in HLM

Longitudinal data, or repeated measurement data, can be regarded as multilayer data and repeated measurements clustered in individuals. In the simplest form, this leads to a two-layer model with a series of repeated measurements at the lowest level and individual subjects at the highest level. Longitudinal measures can be fixed or on different occasions. Multilevel analysis of longitudinal data can deal with both cases. Since multilevel modeling does not require balanced data, it is not a problem if the number of available measures is different for all individuals. This is an important benefit if there are missing panels or other forms of missing measurement individuals.

If data is collected to examine individual changes over time, the study's structure must be quantified on a scale that is comparable in each case.

This will not generate complex complications if the time duration is short. For instance, Tate and Hokanson (1993) reported on a longitudinal study in which students' baker depression scale scores were gathered three times during the academic year. We can presume that the research equipment remains identical throughout the investigation in this application, especially when well-validated measuring devices are used. On the other hand, a study investigated the improvement of reading ability of school-age children aged 5–12. It is obvious that we can't use the same tool to measure reading ability at different ages. Here, we must ensure that different measurement tools are calibrated, which means that a specific score has the same psychometric significance at all ages, independent of the actually used reading test. These problems are the same as those in cross-cultural comparison.

Another requirement is that there is a sufficient time interval between the two measurements so that the memory effect will not be a problem. In some applications, this may not be the case. For example, if the data collected are closely spaced in time, we may expect a considerable correlation between the data collected at close intervals, partly due to the memory effect. These effects should be included in the model, resulting in relevant errors in the model. Developing a multilevel model for this situation is quite complex. Some multilevel software has a built-in function of modeling related errors. The models discussed in this section are all data models for repeatedly measuring individuals over a period of time. Within the framework of multilevel model, we can also analyze the data of repeated measurement at a higher level. For example, we track the data of the same group of schools for several years. Of course, there are different students every year. The model of such data is similar to that discussed in this chapter. This repeated cross-sectional data is discussed by DiPrete and Grusky (1990), as well as Raudenbush and Chan (1993). The latent curve modeled by the structural equation by Kline (2011) was discussed.

Multilevel analysis of repeated measurements is usually applied to the data of large-scale group surveys. In addition, it can also be a valuable analytical tool in various experimental designs. If we have a pre-posttest design, the usual analysis is the ANCOVA, with the experimental group and the control group as factors and the pre-test as covariates. In the multilevel framework, we analyze the change of slope with time and use the virtual variables of the experimental group or control group to predict the difference in slope. If we only have a pre-posttest design, this will not provide more than the usual covariance analysis. However, in multilayer framework, it is meaningful to add more measurement occasions between pre-test and post-test. Maxwell (1998) shows that the ability to test the difference between the experimental group and the control group can be significantly improved by adding a few waves of additional data collection. If there is a midway exit, especially if it is not completely random, ANCOVA also has an advantage. Multilevel analysis of repeated measures can include incomplete cases, which is a major advantage when incomplete data do occur.

It's important to distinguish between repeated measurements taken at the same time or at various times. If the measurement is done on a set date, everyone does it on the same set of dates, usually at regular intervals, such as once a year. We take different measures against different people at different times depending on the circumstances. For example, this information can be found, for example, in growth research, which examines the physiological and psychological aspects of a group of people at various stages of development. Data can be collected at a set period of year, although everyone's age is different at that time. Alternatively, the original design is a fixed occasion design; however, data gathering is not completed on time due to scheduling issues. The distinction between fixed and changeable occasions is not significant for multilevel analysis of outcome data.

### 3.1.2.2.4 Most commonly used models of HLM

The purpose of this part is to clarify a series of the commonly used hierarchical linear model and to present the use of the techniques of estimation and hypothesis testing in the above part. For each model, we elaborate on the estimation of the fixed effects, random effects as well as variance–covariance components. In addition, we demonstrate the use of appropriate hypothesis testing procedures for these various parameters.

In general, there are five hierarchical linear models that are commonly used, namely, one-way ANOVA with random effects, means-as-outcomes regression, one-way ANCOVA with random effects, random-coefficients regression model, as well as a model with nonrandomly varying slopes.

i. One-way ANOVA with random effects

A one-way ANOVA with random effects model is one of the simplest conceivable hierarchical linear models. In this case, $\beta_{1j}$ in the level 1 model is set to zero for all j, yielding

$$y_{ij} = \beta_{0j} + r_{ij} \qquad (3.22)$$

We assume that each level-1 error, $r_{ij}$ is normally distributed with a mean of zero and a constant level-1 variance. It should be noticed that this equation predicts the outcome within each level-1 unit with just one level-2 parameter, the intercept, $\beta_{0j}$. In this case, $\beta_{0j}$ is just the mean outcome for the jth unit.

The level-2 model for the one-way ANOVA with random effects is as follows:

$$\beta_{0j} = \gamma_{00} + u_{0j} \qquad (3.23)$$

where

$\gamma_{00}$ represents the grand-mean outcome in the population, and $u_{0j}$ is the random effect associated with unit $j$, and is assumed to have a mean of zero and variance $\gamma_{00}$.

Combining the above Equations may arise the following equation, yielding

$$Y_{ij} = \gamma_{00} + u_{0j} + r_{ij} \qquad (3.24)$$

which is, indeed, the one-way ANOVA model with grand mean $\gamma_{00}$; with a group (level-2) effect, $u0j$; and with a person (level-I) effect, $r_{ij}$. It is a random-effects model because the group effects are construed as random. Notice that the variance of the outcome is

$$Var\left(y_{ij}\right) = Var\left(u_{0j} + r_{ij}\right) = \gamma_{00} + o^{-2} \qquad (3.25)$$

In a hierarchical data analysis, estimating the one-way ANOVA model is typically beneficial as a preliminary step. The grand mean $\gamma_{00}$ is given a point estimate and a confidence interval. More importantly, it offers data on the outcome variability at both levels. The $o^{-2}$ parameter represents the within-group variability and $\gamma_{00}$ captures the between-group variability. We refer to the hierarchical model of the above equations as fully unconditional in that no predictors are specified at either level 1 or 2. A useful parameter associated with the one-way random-effects ANOVA is the intraclass correlation coefficient. This coefficient is given by the following formula,

$$\rho = \gamma_{00} / (\gamma_{00} + o^{-2}) \qquad (3.26)$$

and measures the proportion of the variance in the outcome that is between the level-2 units.

ii. Means-as-outcomes regression

Another common statistical problem involves the means from each of many groups as an outcome to be predicted by group characteristics. This submodel consists of the above model as the level-1 model and, for the level-2 model,

$$\beta_{0j} = \gamma_{00} + \gamma_{01}W_j + u_{0j} \qquad (3.27)$$

where in this simple case we have one level-2 predictor $W_j$, combining the above model can achieve a model as follows:

$$Y_{ij} = \gamma_{00} + \gamma_{01}W_j + u_{0j} + r_{ij} \qquad (3.28)$$

It is worth noting that $u_{0j}$ now has a different meaning. Whereas the random variable $u_{0j}$ had been the deviation of unit $j$'s mean from the grand mean, it now represents the residual

$$u_{0j} = \beta_{0j} - \gamma_{00} - \gamma_{01}W_j \qquad (3.29)$$

Similarly, the variance in $u_{0j}$, $\gamma_{00}$ is now the residual or conditional variance in $\beta_{0j}$ after controlling for $W_j$.

iii. One-way ANOVA with random effects

Based on the full model, let us constrain the level-2 coefficients $\gamma_{00}$ and $\gamma_{01}$ and the random effect, $u_{0j}$ (for all $j$) equal to 0. The resulting model would be a one-factor ANCOVA with random effects and a single level-1 predictor as a covariate. That is,

$$Y_{ij} = \beta_{0j} + \beta_{1j}\left(X_{ij} - \bar{X}..\right) + r_{ij} \qquad (3.30)$$

The Level-2 model refers to

$$\beta_{0j} = \gamma_{00} + u_{0j} \qquad (3.31)$$
$$\beta_{1j} = \gamma_{10} \qquad (3.32)$$

The combined model is

$$Y_{ij} = \gamma_{00} + \gamma_{10}\left(X_{ij} - \bar{X}..\right) + r_{ij} + u_{0j} \qquad (3.33)$$

The only difference between this Means-as-Outcomes Regression and the standard ANCOVA model is that the group effect here $u_{0j}$ is conceived as random rather than fixed. As in ANCOVA, $\gamma_{10}$ is the pooled within-group regression coefficient of $Y_{ij}$ on $X_{ij}$. Each $\beta_{0j}$ is now the mean outcome for each level-2 unit adjusted for differences among these units in $X_{ij}$.

An extension of the random effects of ANCOVA allows for the introduction of level-2 covariates. For example, if the coefficient is nonfull, the combined model becomes

$$Y_{ij} = \gamma_{00} + \gamma_{01}W_j + \gamma_{10}\left(X_{ij} - \bar{X}..\right) + r_{ij} + u_{0j} \qquad (3.34)$$

This model provides for a level-2 covariate, $W_j$, while also controlling for the effect of a level-1 covariate, $X_{ij}$, and the random effects of the level-2 units, $u_{0j}$.

iv. Random-coefficients regression model

All of the sub-models discussed above are examples of *random-intercept models*. Only the level-1 intercept coefficient, $\beta_{0j}$, was regarded as random. The level-1 slope did not exist in the one-way ANOVA or the means-asoutcomes cases. In the random-effects ANCOVA model, $\beta_{1j}$ was included but constrained to have a common effect for all groups.

Studies in which level-1 slopes are considered as varying randomly over the population of level-2 units are a key class of hierarchical linear model applications. The random-coefficients regression model is the most basic example of this class. Both the level-1 intercept and one or more level-1 slopes fluctuate randomly in these models, but there is no attempt to forecast this variation.

The level-2 model becomes,

$$\beta_{0j} = \gamma_{00} + +u_{0j} \qquad (3.35)$$
$$\beta_{1j} = \gamma_{10} + +u_{1j} \qquad (3.36)$$

where

$\gamma_{00}$ is the average intercept across the level-2 units;
$\gamma_{10}$ is the average regression slope across the level-2 units;
$u_{0j}$ is the unique increment to the intercept associated with level-2 unit $j$;
and $u_{1j}$ is the unique increment to the slope associated with level-2 unit $j$.

The dispersion of the level-2 random effects as a variance–covariance matrix:
Var
where

Var($u_{0j}$)= $\gamma_{00}$ represents unconditional variance in the level-1 intercepts;
Var($u_{0j}$)= $\gamma_{11}$ represents unconditional variance in the level-1 slopes; and
Cov($u_{0j},u_{1j}$)= $\gamma_{01}$, represents unconditional covariance between the level-1 intercepts and slopes

Note that we refer to these as unconditional variance–covariance components because no level-2 predictors are included in either equation.

Substitution of the expressions for $\beta_{0j}$ and $\beta_{1j}$ in equations can be a mixed model as

$$Y_{ij} = \gamma_{00} + \gamma_{10}\left(X_{ij} - \overline{X_{.j}}\right) + r_{ij} + u_{0j} + u_{1j}\left(X_{ij} - \overline{X_{.j}}\right) \qquad (3.37)$$

This model implies that the outcome $Y_i$ is a function of the average regression equation, $\gamma_{00} + \gamma_{10}$ ($X_{ij} - \overline{X_{.j}}$) plus a random error having three components: $u_{0j}$ the random effect of unit $j$ on the mean; $u_{1j}$ ($X_{ij} - \overline{X_{.j}}$), where $u_{1j}$ is the random effect of unit $j$ on the slope $\beta_{1j}$; and the level-1 error, $r_{ij}$.

v. A model with nonrandomly varying slopes

In some cases, the research will prove quite successful in predicting the variability in the regression slopes, $\beta_{1j}$. For example, it might be found that the level-2 predictor, $W_j$ in Equation (3.38) does indeed predict the level-l slope $\beta_{1j}$. In fact, the analysis might find that after controlling for $W_j$ the residual variance of $\beta_{1j}$ (i.e., the variance of the residuals), very close to zero.

If the residuals $u_{1j}$ are indeed set to zero, the level-2 model for the slopes becomes,

$$\beta_{1j} = \gamma_{10} + \gamma_{11} W_j \tag{3.38}$$

and this model, when combined with Equations (3.37) and (3.38), the combined model is as below

$$Y_{1j} = \gamma_{00} + \gamma_{01} W_j + \gamma_{10}\left(X_{ij} - \overline{X_{.j}}\right) + \gamma_{11} W_j \left(X_{ij} - \overline{X_{.j}}\right) + r_{ij} + u_{0j} \tag{3.39}$$

In this model, the slopes do vary from group to group, but their variation is nonrandom. Specifically, as Equation shows, the slopes $\beta_{1j}$ vary strictly as a function of $W_j$.

We note that this equation can be viewed as another example of what we have called a random-intercept model, because $\beta_{0j}$ is the only component that varies randomly across level-2 units. In general, hierarchical linear models may involve multiple level-1 predictors where any combination of random, nonrandomly varying, and fixed slopes can be specified.

### 3.1.2.2.5 Estimation and hypothesis testing in HLM

One of the most common ways to estimate the parameters, regression coefficients, and intercept and slope variances is the maximum likelihood (ML) method. This part provides a non-technical explanation of the ML method, intended to aid readers' understanding and make informed decisions on the research estimation options displayed by the present software. Moreover, some alternatives concerned with the ML estimation method are briefly introduced and compared, involving generalized estimating equations, GLS, as well as Bayesian estimation methods such as Markov chain Monte Carlo. Bootstrapping methods are also briefly discussed in this part, which can be applied to improve the parameter estimates and the standard error. Finally, this part offers some basic procedures that can be applied to test hypotheses about specific parameters.

i. The ML method

The ML approach is a hierarchical linear modeling estimating procedure that gives population parameter values that maximize the probability of observing the data that are actually observed. Stiratelli et al. (1984), along with Wong and Mason (1985), were among the first to use a first-order approximation to the ML estimate to solve issues. Goldstein (1991) and Longford (1993) created software that enabled these methods to be used for a variety of discrete outcomes as well as two- and three-level models. On the other hand, under certain circumstances, as Breslow and Clayton (1993) showed, such approximations can be highly imprecise. A second-order approximation was also produced by Goldstein (1995). Accurate approximations to the ML estimate using Gauss–Hermite quadrature were created by Hedeker and Gibbons (2006) and Pinheiro and Bates (1995), and are presently implemented in the software packages Mixor and SAS Proc Mixed, respectively. A high-order Laplace transform (Raudenbush et al., 2000), which is implemented in the program HLM, provides an alternate approximation that is usually accurate and computationally convenient.

The ML estimation approach has the advantage of being generally resilient, with asymptotically efficient and consistent results. With large samples, ML estimates are usually resistant to minor assumption violations, such as non-normal errors. The likelihood function is maximized to get ML estimation. In hierarchical linear modeling, two likelihood functions are used. The first is full ML, which includes the regression coefficients as well as the variance components in the likelihood function. Another method, the restricted maximum likelihood (RML) estimation approach only considers the variance components, and the regression coefficients are computed in a subsequent stage. Both methods generate parameter estimates with accompanying standard errors as well as an overall model deviation that is a function of likelihood.

With respect to the full ML, when estimating the variable components, it concerns the regression coefficients as fixed unknowns but does not consider the degrees of freedom lost in estimating the fixed effects. RML estimates the variance component after excluding the fixed effect in this model. Therefore, the full ML estimation of the variance component is biased, although they are usually too small. By contrast, RML estimates have less bias. Moreover, RML has the attribute that if the group is balanced (with the same group size), RML estimates are equivalent to the analysis of variance (ANOVA) estimation, which is optimal.

Since the RML is more realistic, theoretically it could be more likely to provide accurate estimation, especially when the number of groups is small. In practice, the difference between the two methods is usually small. For example, if we compare the RML estimate of the intercept-only model of the popular data with the corresponding RML estimate, the only difference between the two decimals is level 2 intercept variance. The full ML is estimated to be 0.69 and the RML is estimated to be 0.70. The magnitude of this difference is absolutely insignificant. If important differences are found, the RML method usually performs better (Browne, 1998). The full ML method continues to be applied since it has two advantages over RML. First, it is usually easy to calculate. Secondly, since the regression coefficient is included in the likelihood function, the overall Chi square test based on likelihood could be applied to compare two different models in the fixed part, that is, regression coefficient. For RML, only the difference (variance component) of the random part can make a comparison with this test. Most of the tables in this book are generated by using the full ML estimation.

An iterative process is required to calculate the ML estimation. In the beginning, the computer program generates reasonable initial value parameters for various parameters. In the next step, a clever calculation program tries to refine the starting value to produce a better estimate. The second step is to iterate several times. Then, the program checks how much the estimate has changed from the previous iteration after each iteration. If the difference is insignificant, the program decides that the estimator has converged and is correctly completed. While using the multilevel program, we typically take the nuances of computing for granted. However, computational problems do sometimes arise. The iterative procedure is not always guaranteed to stop in systems that use iterative ML. For some models and data sets, the program may run indefinitely, with the only way to end it being to stop the program. As a result, most programs are limited to a certain number of iterations. The calculation can be redone with a higher limit if convergence is not reached within this time limit. If the calculation does not come to a conclusion. We believe they will never converge after a significant number of iterations. The issue is determining how to interpret non-convergent models. The most prevalent interpretation is that a model that does not converge is a bad model, based on the fundamental premise that if no estimate is found, the model is disqualified. The issue could, however, be with the data itself. The estimating procedure may fail, even though the model is valid, especially for tiny samples. Furthermore, we may be able to find acceptable estimations if we have superior computer techniques or beginning values. However, experience has shown that if a program fails to converge to a reasonably sized data set, the problem is often serious model errors. In multilevel analysis, when we try, we tend to have non-convergence by estimating too many random components that are actually hit or equal to zero. One of the solutions is to equivalent simplify the model by omitting some random components. In general, estimates from non-convergent solutions provide an indication of which random components can be ignored.

ii. Generalized least squares

GLS is an extension of the standard estimator OLS, which takes into account for heterogeneity and different observations. In terms of sampling variance, the GLS estimate is similar to the ML estimate, and they are generally equivalent. Asymptotic equivalence means that on a very large sample, they are virtually indistinguishable. Goldstein (2003) demonstrates that by limiting the number of iterations to one, the "expected GLS" estimate can be obtained by the ML method. Because GLS estimates are significantly faster to compute than that of full ML estimates, they can be used as an alternative to ML estimates when computing intensive processes (such as large data sets) or when using lifts. They can also be used when ML programs fail to converge; Checking GLS results may help diagnose the problem. Furthermore, since GLS estimates are respectable statistical estimates in themselves, GLS estimates, rather than the more common ML estimates, can be reported in this case. However, simulation studies have shown that, in general, GLS estimates are inefficient and the standard errors derived from GLS are inefficient. Therefore, ML estimates should be preferred.

The generalized estimation equation method estimates the variance and covariance of the random part of the multistage model directly from the residual, which makes their calculation faster than the full ML estimate. Typically, dependencies in multilevel data are explained by a very simple model, represented by a work-related correlation matrix. For individuals in a group, the simplest assumption is that respondents in the same group are all equally relevant. For repeated measurements, a simple autocorrelation structure is usually assumed. After an estimate of the variance component is obtained, GLS is generated to estimate the fixed regression coefficient. Robust standard errors are usually used to offset approximate estimates of random structures. For non-normal data, this results in a population average model where the emphasis is on estimating and mating average population effects rather than modeling individual and population differences. Raudenbush and Bryk (2002) describe the multilevel unity-specific model, which is mostly based on ML estimates, as a model designed to model the effects of predictive variables while providing statistical control for other predictive variables at different levels as well as for random effects in the model. In contrast, population-average models, mostly based on GEE estimation, control for other predictive variables but do not control for random effects. When estimating nonlinear models, GEE estimates are different from ML estimates. For example, in an interception-only LR model, the population mean probability of the repeating class can be estimated from the population mean of the intercepts. The unit-specific intercept is not normally used to calculate this probability. If the concern is group level change, for example, a unit-specific model is appropriate when modeling a level 1 effect difference using a level 2 variable. If we are interested only in population estimates of the average effect of a level 1 variable, such as national differences between boys and girls in the probability of resuming school, then the population average model is appropriate. According to Goldstein (2003), GEE estimates are less efficient than full ML estimates, but their assumptions are weaker regarding the structure of the random parts of the multistage model. If the random part of the model is correctly specified, ML estimates are more efficient, and model-based (ML) standard error is usually less than the robust standard error based on GEE. If the model for the random part is incorrect, the GEE-based estimates are still aligning with the robust standard errors. Therefore, if the sample size is quite large, GEE estimates are robust to error designations in the random part of the model, including violations of the normality hypothesis. One disadvantage of GEE method is that it only approximates the random effects structure, so it cannot analyze the random effects in detail. Therefore, most software will estimate the unstructured covariance matrix of a complete random part, which makes it impossible to estimate the random effects of intercept or slope. Given the general robustness of ML methods, it is best to use ML methods when they are available and to use robust estimates or bootstrapped corrections when there is serious doubt about the assumptions of ML methods. It is also worth stressing that robust estimates are closely related to GEE estimates (Burton et al., 1998).

iii. Bootstrapping

In the bootstrapping process, random samples were repeatedly selected and observed data were replaced. In each random sample, the estimated model parameters, FML or RML estimation is usually used. This process is repeated b times. This results in a set of B parameter estimates for each model parameter. The variance of these B estimates is used as an indicator of the sampling variance associated with the parameter estimates obtained from the full sample. Since the bootstrap sample is obtained from resampling the total sample, bootstrap belongs to the general term for resampling methods. Bootstrap can be used to improve point estimation and standard error. In general, at least 1,000 boot samples are required to obtain sufficient accuracy. This makes the method computationally demanding, but less demanding than the Bayesian method discussed in the next part.

iv. Bayesian methods

By attributing the distribution of potential values to the overall value of model parameters in Bayesian statistics, some uncertainty regarding the overall value of model parameters can be explained. Because it is set independently of the data, this distribution is known as a prior distribution. A posterior distribution is created when a prior distribution is paired with the possibility of data, and it represents the researchers' uncertainty about the total value after studying the data.

In general, the posterior distribution's variance is lower than the prior distribution's variance, implying that the observed data reduces our uncertainty about the population's probable values. We have two options for prior distribution: information prior or non-information prior. A peak distribution with modest variations that implies a strong conviction in unknown population parameters is known as information prior. Informative past knowledge will, of course, have a significant impact on the posterior distribution and, as a result, on our findings. As a result, many statisticians prefer non-informative or diffuse priors, which have no effect on the posterior and are simply employed to generate it. The uniform distribution is an example of a non-information prior, which essentially asserts that the unknown parameter value is an integer between positive and negative infinity and that all values are equally likely.

A posterior distribution can be used to construct confidence intervals for point estimates and population parameters if it has a mathematically simple shape, such as a normal distribution. However, in complex multivariate models, the posterior distribution is frequently a complex multivariate distribution, making it challenging to produce parameter estimation and confidence intervals directly from the posterior distribution. As a result, random samples from the location distribution are generated using simulation technology. After that, the simulated posterior distribution is utilized to provide point estimates, such as patterns or median values of simulated values, as well as confidence intervals.

In conclusion, Bayesian approach provides a sensible alternative approach, accurate parameter estimates, and are able to predict the uncertainties associated with them (Goldstein, 2003). In these cases. Standard errors will tend to be more realistic than under ML. In any case, they are computationally requesting, and the recreation must be checked to create beyond any doubt it works appropriately.

### 3.1.2.3 The advantages of HLM in PISA reading studies

HLM was developed to solve the limitations of traditional statistical methods such as regression analysis in processing multilayer nested data. It is a set of advanced theories and methods of social science data analysis around the world at present. Its advantages are mainly embodied in two aspects: first, it can be used to solve the problem of data nesting and second, it introduces a new method for follow-up study or repeated measurement study.

Traditional linear models, such as ANOVA or regression analysis, can analyze issues including one level of information, but cannot analyze issues including two or more levels of information comprehensively. The traditional linear regression model assumes that there is a linear relationship between different variables, and the variables are generally homogeneity of variance, normal distribution, as well as independent of random errors among individuals. Basically, traditional linear models have two disadvantages:

First, in terms of individual-level analysis, that is, traditional linear models may directly merge the data from different groups and analyze it at the individual level to obtain a general understanding of the social circumstance of the individual. All higher-level variables are regarded as the first-level variables, and the data are analyzed directly at the individual level of students. However, there may arise an issue that class variables have the same impact on students in the same class. Students in different classes correspond to different class variables without distinguishing the impact of classes on students. It is unreasonable to assume that students in the same class are independent of each other. Similarly, it is unreasonable to make the same assumption about students in different classes and students in the same class. This method basically spurns the consideration of the differences among different groups, therefore, numerous contrasts initially brought by gathering are translated as individual differences.

Second, with regard to the group level analysis, the individual data are put into the analysis of higher-level variables in the form of mean or other forms, that is, the measurement of the first level variable is directly combined into the estimation measurement of the second level variable, and only the influence of group-level factors on dependent variables is considered, without considering the effect of individual difference factors. For example, in educational research, the class level data of the second level are directly analyzed without considering the influence of students' individual factors. The main problem of this method is to lose the information on the differences between students in the class, and this part of the variation may account for a large part of the total variation. Although the traditional regression analysis method can reflect the role of group factors to a certain extent, it gives up the explanation of individual differences, which makes many conclusions unconvincing.

Obviously, such obliviousness may lead to outlandish or indeed off-base translation of information comes about, which is an unavoidable restriction of conventional regression method when analyzing stratified characteristics information. However, based on the discussion of the above methods, the two traditional regression data analysis methods have one thing in common: they do not take into consideration the characteristics of data stratification, so they may cause some unreasonable interpretation of the data results, which is the limitation of traditional regression analysis method in analyzing hierarchy structure data. The advantages of the multilayer linear model are mainly reflected in two aspects: one is to solve the limitations of traditional regression analysis methods in analyzing multilayer data nesting; second, it introduces new methods for diachronic research or repeated measurement research.

Hierarchical linear models provide effective statistical methods for solving these problems. The parameter estimation method of multilayer linear model is similar to the method of two regression in concept, but the statistical estimation and verification methods of the two are different, and the parameter estimation method of multilayer linear model is more stable. Therefore, the application range of multilayer model is also quite wide, compared with the traditional methods used to deal with multiple repeated measurements, the HLM has the characteristics of low requirements on data, and can clearly express the changes of individuals at the first level as well as explain the complex changes of individuals over time by defining random variation at the first and second levels. In addition, it also considers the influence of variables at higher levels on the growth of individuals.

Additionally, HLM can explicitly analyze the nested nature of data by simultaneously estimating the influence of predictors of different levels on the outcome variable at the individual level and meanwhile keeping these predictors in the appropriate analysis level, which will contribute to the development of multilevel theories since researchers must keep in mind which level the particular variable belongs to as well as its relationships with other variables in carrying out the analysis (Kozlowski & Klein, 2000; Raudenbush & Bryk, 2002).

Moreover, HLM enables analysts to take advantage of the overall data to improve the coefficient estimates of lower-level variables by generating Empirical Bayesian estimates, which are of substantial significance to the estimation of the fixed effects of higher-level variables (Raudenbush et al., 2004). In estimating the fixed effects of higher-level variables using HLM, GLS, instead of OLS, HLM is employed to give greater weight to the more reliable and accurate lower-level estimates. HLM also utilizes the interactive computing of unbalanced data to give valid estimates of variance–covariance components, which cannot be achieved by traditional regression methods such as the ANCOVA. Moreover, HLM provides robust estimates of standard error, which can be a very useful way to circumvent pesky heteroscedasticity problem. As for the assumption of homogeneity of regression slopes, HLM explicitly models the variability of the relationship between covariates and the outcome variable, thus overcoming possible problems relevant to this assumption. Again, as mentioned above, the assumption of independence can be cast aside since HLM is especially designed to take into consideration the variation between groups (Raudenbush & Bryk, 2002).

Furthermore, the HLM can define the complex covariance structure among repeated observed variables, conduct the significance test for different covariance structures, and clearly explain the complex situation of individuals changing with time by defining random differences at different levels of data. In terms of differences between individuals, for example, HLM model assumes that the object of study at different times of observation is related with the individual heterogeneity between measuring factors, so the set of random regression coefficients in the model, such as with random intercept reflect different initial levels of measurement value of individual results, with time variable random slope reflect the difference of the individual results observed overtime rate of change, Thus, individual specific effects are introduced to deal with the problem of interindividual heterogeneity. From the perspective of intra-individual differences, an appropriate residual variance–covariance structure can be set up at the beginning of the model to deal with the sequential correlation of data.

### 3.1.2.4 Literature review of the application of HLM in PISA reading

Reading literacy is a necessary skill for human survival development and lifelong learning, economic participation, and citizenship. Achievement in reading literacy is not just a primary way for other subjects' improvement within the educational system, but also a precondition of successfully taking part in most fields in this knowledge-based society (Cunningham & Stanovich, 1997). Thus, reading literacy in PISA evaluates the basic skills including "understanding, using, reflecting on and engaging with written texts, to achieve one's goals, to develop one's knowledge and potential, and to participate in society" (OECD, 2009, p. 23).

Some researchers point out that students' reading literacy can be affected by different factors, coming from both individual and contextual factors. Based on the previous literature, PISA reading studies can be divided into four categories: student individual factors, school factors, family factors as well as sociocultural factors. Student individual factors mainly focus on students' gender difference, metacognitive awareness of reading strategies, reading motivation, reading engagement, learning time, and so on. School factors consider school environment, such as the quality and quantity of teachers, qualification of teachers, education resources, and support.

In the field of PISA reading studies, researchers have made substantial efforts in this area. However, most of the existing studies, are conducted from a single linear perspective, only explore the influence of personal factors or school environmental factors on students' reading literacy, but fail to effectively combine and comprehensively evaluated the interactions between individual and environmental factors, and investigate the influence of various factors across levels on students' reading literacy. Therefore, it is necessary to explore and deeply analyze the influential factors as well as their specific effects on reading literacy from a multilevel and diversified perspective. Considering that the selected data structure is in the relationship of multilayer nesting, that is, student-level variables are nested in school-level variables, the hierarchical linear model is suitable and effective to be used for data analysis. Compared with the traditional regression analysis method, the multilevel linear model has better robustness, and can more accurately deal with the interaction relationship between variables at different levels, effectively avoid the convergence bias caused by the traditional regression analysis method, and improve the accuracy of data analysis results.

In this part, a brief overview of the application of hierarchical linear model in PISA reading studies in recent years will be illustrated, to further explore the varying impact of both student factors, school factors, family factors, as well as sociocultural factors on students' reading literacy performance.

### 3.1.2.4.1 Student Individual factors

In terms of students' gender difference, Mak et al. (2017) sought to explore the impact of gender difference on Macao students' reading performance by considering the underlying student- and across-level mediation mechanisms. Hierarchical linear models (HLM) were used as a method of data analysis and to analyze the extracted data from PISA 2009. Two findings of this research were indicated from both theoretical and pedagogical interests. First, three facets of students' engagement in reading, for instance, students' motivation of reading, a wide range of reading strategies from the nurture perspective elucidates substantially the gender gap in school-level. Second, there are gender-specific peer influences on student reading performance across levels in a coeducational setting where kids read cheerfully and skillfully.

Similarly, Rodríguez-Planas and Nollenberger (2018) examine the relationship between beliefs on gender social norms and students' reading, math, and science performance. By analyzing PISA data set from 11,527 second-generation immigrants across 35 countries or regions of ancestry, the research evidence elaborates that the country-of-ancestry gender factors have a positive impact on girls' math achievement, and this effect has significant correlation with boys. The correlation between general gender stereotypes and mathematical gender gap indicated that parents' ender factors affect teenagers' test scores by transmitting their specific preferences for cognitive skills. Furthermore, second-generation immigrant girls outperform boys in reading, and these immigrant girls whose place of descent is more gender equal tend to have higher reading achievements than boys, extending the females' literacy advantage in reading. Their findings, taken collectively, shed insight on the impact of general gender stereotypes on students' math gender gap, suggesting that parents' gender social norms influence their children's academic performance through conveying their preferences for cognitive talents.

In addition, Lau and Ho (2016) employ HLM to analyze the extracted data from PISA 2009, exploring the relationship between self-regulated learning (SRL) within the student-level and students' reading performance on the large-scale international assessments PISA. The results in this research suggested that compared to other OECD countries or regions: Hong Kong students showed higher levels of reading engagement and a more favorable classroom disciplinary climate in their reading lessons, but they utilized fewer reading control tactics, which are considered the most important SRL components for improving students' reading performance. Furthermore, the researchers look into some of the cultural and contextual aspects that may influence Hong Kong students' SRL and reading performance, as well as providing insights on the Chinese learner paradox and how to improve instructional techniques in Chinese classes.

Areepattamannil (2014) uses multilevel modeling to investigate factors that may affect Indian teenagers' reading, mathematics, and science literacy. To probe into these potential reasons, this study analyzed data from the fourth cycle of PISA to further examine the impact of student- and school-level factors on their reading, mathematics, and science literacy. A total of 4,826 students from 213 schools in India were examined. Moreover, Indian adolescents' reading, mathematics, and science literacy scores were considerably lower than other participating countries. The findings indicated that students' gender, metacognitive learning strategies, students' attitudes, as well as students' perceptions of classroom climate were found to be significantly correlated with their academic achievement on the PISA assessment.

David and Sonia (2012) apply a two-level HLM to explore gender differences in cognitive abilities, the magnitude of these differences, and whether these differences have realistic significance in the educational outcomes of girls and boys. Second, the researchers tend to investigate the interrelationship across different levels on the basis of PISA 2009 data set, for example, how did student-level variables influence students reading achievement, and what were the differences in reading literacy amongst the countries? Third, they also explore the influence of school-level variables on students' reading achievement scores and what were the differences in reading literacy amongst the countries. Additionally, when gender gaps in reading, science, and mathematics literacy are existing, they are more likely attributed to internal biological differences instead of social and cultural factors. Based on this international assessment, the results indicated that girls outperform boys in reading outcomes. By contrast, boys outperform girls in mathematics performance in the USA. With regard to science literacy, although the USA displayed the largest gender discrepancy across all countries in OECD gender differences across OECD nations were non-significant, and a small female advantage was found for non-OECD nations. Among reading, science and mathematics literacy, these discrepancies were more pronounced at both tails of the distribution for low- and high-achievers. And this national gender differences can account for gender equity measures, economic prosperity, as well as Hofstede's cultural dimension of power distance. This research also addresses some educational and societal implications as well as the mechanisms by which gender differences in cognitive abilities are culturally mediated.

### 3.1.2.4.2 School environment factors

Since the publication of the Coleman report in 1966, there has been a lot of attention and debate about the role of schools in influencing student achievement in comparison to the influence of family background. A significant amount of international and comparative research has also been done on the effects of schools on student accomplishment.

Based on the PISA 2009 database, Ning et al. (2015) use a two-level HLM to investigate the reading achievement difference between the Flemish and French communities in Belgium. Four factors from students' backgrounds, two from school composition, four from school resources, five from school atmosphere, and four from school governance were utilized as predictors. The results indicated that the impact of each predictor may differ depending on the community. The mean score discrepancy at the community level was decomposed using the Oaxaca-Blinder method, which demonstrated that different predictors' endowments and/or returns may benefit different communities more. The Juhn–Murphy–Pierce decomposition of the community level percentile score gap revealed that some factors may be explanatory for differences between communities among lesser achievers, while others may be explanatory for differences between communities among higher achievers. It also includes some helpful recommendations for school growth.

To explore the impact of officially recognized languages on 15-year-old students' reading performance, Arya et al. (2016) evaluated PISA 2009 database of reading literacy. Participants are from nations with only two official languages (e.g., Canada and Israel), and they speak only one of them at home. This study demonstrated that unless the minority language indicated a language internationally regarded and revered by local stakeholders, the dominant official language has a significant impact on students' reading achievement. This study also provides some implications that educational programs should consider the historical context of country-specific language ideologies and related stereotyped beliefs that favor the dominant language in the classroom.

Ning et al. (2020) employ HLM to explore the similarities and differences in educational effectiveness between two higher grade countries, Finland and Shanghai from student and school levels. Fourteen predictors representing student background such as students' gender, school characteristics, for example, school location and school educational resources were extracted from the PISA 2009 database. The findings showed that the Finnish educational system is more effective at converting given inputs, particularly student individual background factors, which have a significant correlation with their reading performance, whereas the general state of the school environment in Shanghai, for example, the value and effect size of the predictors, is conducive to the city's comparative strength in students' reading performance.

### 3.1.2.4.3 Family factors

Ho (2010) looked at the relationship between family factors and adolescents' scientific literacy performance in Hong Kong, which is a city that consistently excelled in science in PISA 2006 database. The researcher uses multilevel analysis, HLM, to examine the influence of parental participation as well as their investment on students' scientific literacy achievement. After controlling for student and school background factors, it was discovered that students' scientific literacy performance, as evaluated by science accomplishment and self-efficacy in science, was strongly associated with particular types of parental participation and involvement. Students' scientific literacy performance was revealed to be substantially associated with a parental investment in cultural resources as well as parental support in enriching science learning activities. This study also suggested that activities should be provided at an early age, for instance, watching science-related TV shows, reading science-related books, or listening.

### 3.1.2.4.4 The mixed factors across levels

Skryabin et al. (2015) study how students' reading, mathematics, and scientific literacy scores are influenced by national ICT development and individual ICT usage for fourth and eighth grade students. They examined country- and individual-level factors from the TIMSS 2011, PIRLS 2011, and PISA 2012 data set using hierarchical linear models (HLM). Their findings indicated that national ICT development was significantly positive related to students' educational outcomes in reading, science, and mathematics for both 4th and 8th-grade pupils in all three data sets. Furthermore, after controlling for students' gender and socioeconomic background, students' ICT use is a significant predictor; while, the importance of ICT varies between student groups and fields, depending on the sort of ICT usage.

HU et al. (2018) took a similar approach, which examined the impact of ICT-related factors on the mathematics, reading, and scientific literacy performance of students across 44 countries using a three-level HLM approach.

National ICT abilities, rather than national ICT access and use, were found to have a greater favorable impact on student academic attainment. Furthermore, students' access to ICT at school is linked to academic success, whereas access to ICT at home is linked to academic failure. This research also revealed some fresh insights, such as the possibility that student attitudes toward ICT have a mixed impact on academic attainment. Student enthusiasm, competency, and autonomy in using ICT, for example, exhibited favorable associations with student academic attainment.

Similarly, HU and Yu (2022) investigate the impact of ICT use on students' digital reading proficiency. This study used data from the PISA 2009, PISA 2012, PISA 2015, and PISA 2018 reading assessment along with student background data to explore 15-year-old Asian students. The data analysis of the input of school information resources was conducted using estimates of hierarchical linear modeling, which had a considerable favorable impact on digital reading achievement. Using social media, on the other hand, had a considerable detrimental impact on pupils' digital reading results. Furthermore, this study reveals that students who spend more time on recreational use of social media out of school are more likely to have better digital reading scores.

In conclusion, these studies shed light on the application of HLM in PISA reading and prove that HLM is effective in detecting nested data sets structure in PISA reading, thus gaining mass popularity from numerous scholars. Compare to traditional regression methods, HLM has better robustness, so as to effectively avoid aggregation bias and improve the accuracy of data analysis results. It can not only process hierarchical data set through parameter estimation precisely but is also able to analyze the effects of microscopic and macroscopic variables and cross-level interactions.

### 3.1.3 Structural equation model (SEM)

#### 3.1.3.1 The definition of SEM

Regression analysis investigates the connections between manifest variables, which are variables that can be measured directly and are hence referred to as observable variables. It is necessary to develop numerous questions to measure the latent variable indirectly if the study object cannot be assessed directly. This is referred to as the latent variable problem. These elements are referred to be indicators of the latent variable that corresponds to them. As a starting point for studying the relationship between latent variables through regression analysis, the simplest approach is to "transform latent variables into observed variables", which means first generating latent variables from the observed values of indicators and then using the generated latent variables as the obvious variables in the regression analysis. It is possible to construct latent variables in a variety of methods. The most straightforward and often used is the average of the indicators, which is also sometimes referred to as the weighted average of the indicators. In most cases, the weights are chosen by the researcher based on his or her previous experience. When doing factor analysis, some researchers favor factor scores over basic averages since they are theoretically determined and hence more objective than simple averages. Factor scores, which are often utilized, are essentially some form of weighted average of the indications. Using latent variables as observable variables has the drawback of ignoring the measurement error associated with the latent variables. If the measurement reliability is low, the findings of the regression analysis generated by "transforming latent variables into observable variables" may be insufficiently accurate, if not completely incorrect, in certain cases.

Using structural equation modeling (SEM), you may combine a confirmatory factor model with a (possible) causal model to solve a problem. The measurement model is a component of the factor model, and the equation that represents the link between latent variables and indicators is referred to as the measurement equation. The structural model is the portion of the causal model that represents the connection between the underlying variables, and the structural equation is the equation that describes the relationship between the underlying variables.

### 3.1.3.2 The mechanism and nature of SEM: What can it do and what is it used for?

The basic formula of SEM is covariance, and continuous observation variables $X$ and $Y$ are defined as:

$$\text{cov}_{XY} = r_{XY} + SD_X + SD_Y \tag{3.40}$$

where $r_{XY}$ is the Pearson correlation, $SD_X$ and $SD_Y$ are standard deviations. The covariance represents the strength of the association between $X$ and $Y$ and its variables. In any case, $cov_{XY}$ conveys more information than $r_{XY}$, only represents an association in a standardized measure.

It is accurate to say that covariance is the fundamental statistic of structural equation modeling (SEM) because the analysis has two primary goals: (1) to understand the covariance pattern between a set of observed variables and (2) to use the researcher's explanation to explain the greatest amount of variance in the observed variables. Model. The covariance structure is a part of the structural equation model that represents the assumptions of variance and covariance in the form of a graph.

The standard error of the mean (SEM) is not only connected to the covariance, but also to the mean. The actual difference between mean analysis and SEM, on the other hand, is that the mean of the latent variables may now be calculated. Analysis of variance, on the other hand, just considers the average of the variables that have been observed. A number of the effects normally associated with the analysis of variance may also be investigated with SEM, including the ability to make average comparisons between and within groups (e.g., repeated measures). Consider the following example: In SEM, you can calculate and estimate the amount of the group mean difference of latent variables, which is not really practical when using ANOVA.

### 3.1.3.2.1 Observed and latent variables

In structural equation modeling, there are two types of variables: observable variables and latent variables. The variables of the scores that have been gathered are represented by the classes that have been observed. Observable variables are sometimes referred to as explicit variables in certain cases. Although observed variables may be classified as categorical, continuous, and continuous-continuous, all latent variables in SEM are continuous-continuous-continuous.

Latent variables in structural equation modeling (SEM) are hypothetical structures or factors that are supposed to represent the continuum of explanatory variables rather than directly observable variables, and they correspond to hypothetical structures or factors in SEM. Indicators are variables that are observed and serve as an indirect assessment of structural complexity. Because of the clear disparities between variables and indicators in SEM, the test may make a variety of assumptions about the measurement throughout the analysis. Suppose the researcher thinks that variables $X_1$, $X_2$, and $X_3$ touch a different common domain than the one evaluated by $X_4$ and $X_5$. In SEM, it is relatively easy to specify a model, where $X_1$–$X_3$ is the index of one factor and $X_4$–$X_6$ is the index of another factor. If the model just described does not fit the data well, reject the measurement hypothesis. The ability of SEM to analyze and observe variables and latent variables sets it apart from more standard statistical techniques, such as analysis of variance and MR, which only analyze the observed variables.

The result variable, often known as the dependent variable, is another variable in SEM. It is possible for these variables to have matching residuals or error terms, which may be either observable or latent variables. The residual term in the case of the dependent variable indicates the unexplained variation of the component to be assessed in relation to the appropriate indicator, and it is defined as the cause of certain unexplained disparities that may be traced back to random measurement mistakes or unreliability of scores. The clear depiction of measurement error is a distinguishing feature of the SEM method.

As previously stated, a large number of latent variables or observable variables (or any mix of the two) may be employed as outcome variables for analysis in structural equation modeling. Typically, each variable contains an error term, which indicates the variation that the predictor variable is unable to explain in the absence of the predictor variable. In addition, observations or latent variables (or a mix of the two) may be used to forecast the SEM. As a result of this capacity, the sorts of hypotheses that may be investigated in the SEM can be quite diverse. In SEM, the model does not must include a significant number of latent variables. To put it another way, it is certainly feasible to assess models in SEM that are only concerned with the interactions between the observed variables.

### 3.1.3.2.2 SEM requires large samples

Due to the fact that some statistical estimations (such as standard errors) of scanning electron microscopy may be erroneous when the sample size is small, scanning electron microscopy is considered a big sample method in research. There is also a larger likelihood of technical difficulties throughout the analysis. On the link between sample size and model complexity, Jackson (2003) noted an excellent rule of thumb, the N:Q rule, which has some empirical validity as well as some practical use. Jackson (2003) suggested that researchers consider the minimum sample size in terms of the ratio of the case ($N$) to the number of model parameters ($q$) required for statistical estimation. The ideal sample size to parameter ratio is 20:1. For example, if $q = 10$ model parameters are required for statistical estimation, then the ideal minimum sample size would be 20×10, or $N = 200$. Less desirable is that the ratio of $N$ to $q$ is 10:1, and for the example just given with $q = 10$, the minimum sample size is 10×10, or $N = 100$. The reliability of the results is also reduced when the ratio of $N:q$ is lower than 10:1 (e.g., the ratio of $N = 50$ and $q = 10$ is 5:1).

### 3.1.3.3 Symbols for SEM model diagram

The McDonald Network Motion Model (RAM) is used to notate the SEM model image, which is used to notate the SEM model picture (McArdle & McDonald, 1984). The variables that can be observed are represented by squares or rectangles (e.g., ☐, ☐), whilst the variables that can be observed are represented by circles or ellipses (e.g., ◯, ◯). A single arrow indicates the hypothetical influence of one variable on another variable (also called exogenous variables in SEM). The curve with two arrows illustrates the connection between two separate exogenous factors that have not been investigated (e.g., →). This is left unexplored since it is hard to foresee why the two exogenous variables are covariant in the first place. Apart from that, exogenous variables' variance is represented by a curve with two arrows (e.g., ↔). Due to the absence of components relating to exogenous variables in the model diagram, the exit and re-entry arrows of the same variable imply that exogenous variables may be freely modified and covaried (e.g., ↶).

Endogenous variables, as contrast to exogenous variables, are explicitly mentioned in the model as hypothetical explanations for their existence. As a result, endogenous variables can neither change freely nor change in concert with one another. As a result, the symbol for unanalyzed correlation, or not directly connecting two separate endogenous variables, is utilized in the model diagram, and the sign of variance does not start and stop with any endogenous variable. Contrary to this, the complete model serves as the researchers' explanation for why endogenous factors and exogenous variables covary. During the course of the investigation, this model-based "interpretation" is compared to the sample covariance distribution (data). It is assumed that the model is fitting the data if the covariances of the prediction group and the observation group are comparable. If this is not the case, the "explanation" will be disregarded.

### 3.1.3.4 Steps of SEM

Most SEM investigations consist of six fundamental phases and two optional steps, which are as follows: (1) model specification; (2) model identification and evaluation (if a model cannot be discovered, return to step 1); (3) model selection; and (4) model assessment; (5) Selection of measurement methods (operations of construction); (6) Estimation of model parameters; (7) Re-establish the model's standardization; (8) Results should be reported. The following two optional procedures are included: (1) Results replication; and (2) Results implementation (Kline, 2011).

#### 3.1.3.4.1 Model specification

The assumptions given in the form of SEM are referred to as normative assumptions. Model diagrams may be used to accomplish the specification, or they can be expressed by a sequence of equations that specify the model parameters can be used. When a computer estimates latent variables from sample data, these equations relate to a hypothetical link between the observable variables and latent variables that were previously assumed. The specification phase is the most crucial since the outcomes of succeeding steps are predicated on the assumption that the model is fundamentally valid. As a consequence of theoretical or empirical findings, it is advisable to make a list of the potential modifications to the original model parameters. This is because the model is almost always re-designed (Step 5), and the re-designation should adhere to the same principles as the specification.

#### 3.1.3.4.2 Evaluation for model identification

A model is identified when it is theoretically possible for a computer to make a unique estimate of the parameters of each model. Otherwise, the model cannot be identified. Unrecognized models should be respecified (return to Step 1); Otherwise, trying to analyze them may be futile.

There are three general requirements for identifying basic SEM, which are necessary, but not sufficient:

1. The degrees of freedom of the model must be at least zero ($df_M \geq 0$).
2. Each latent variable (including the residual items) must be assigned a scale or metric.
3. Every factor has at least three indicators.

The identification of non-recursive structural models or non-standard measurement models, on the other hand, is not always straightforward. Because a non-recursive model may not include all conceivable interference dependencies or may not be block recursive, it may be difficult to apply recognition heuristics when the model is not recursive. Even if there are error-related heuristic measurement models or indicators with numerous elements, it is possible that these principles will not apply to more complicated models that have the two characteristics previously discussed.

### 3.1.3.4.3 Measures selection and data collection, preparation, and screening

Before making an official estimate of SEM, it is required to choose appropriate measuring standards, gather data, and review the results. The following are the reasons behind this: First and foremost, it is essential to choose a measuring technique with strong psychometric properties, and a written report summarizing these features is very important, since if the measured value or psychometric qualities with bad scores, the findings may be less significant. As a result, while measuring, it is necessary to ensure the reliability or validity of the score obtained. Second, the most generally used estimate strategy in SEM is to establish certain distribution assumptions about the data before doing the estimation. These assumptions must be treated seriously, since failing to adhere to them might result in discrimination towards a group of people. In the third instance, data-related difficulties prohibit SEM computer programs from producing logical answers. It is possible that researchers who do not adequately prepare and filter their data may come to feel that the model is incorrect.

### 3.1.3.4.4 Model estimation

This stage necessitates the employment of SEM computer tools for the purpose of data analysis. It is necessary to complete the following tasks in this step: To begin, assess model fit, or how effectively the model understands the data; this is done by measuring the degree to which the model is accurate. The original model developed by the researcher does not always correspond to the actual facts. When this occurs, the researcher must skip the next phases and go to the next step, which is to re-specify the model and then re-analyze it using the same data. (2) Provide an explanation for the parameter estimates, assuming that the model fits well. Following that, (3) explore models that are identical or nearly equivalent. However, although the equivalent model may describe the data as well as the researcher's chosen model, there are variances in the hypothetical relationship arrangement between the same variables across the models. The number of equivalent variations of a particular model may be many (and in some situations infinite). Consequently, researchers must provide an explanation as to why their chosen model should not be discarded in favor of a statistically equivalent model.

In the specific application of SEM, model fit has two different categories: the first is absolute fit and the second is incremental fit. Absolute fit reflects the fitting situation between the covariance matrix derived from the model and the actual observed covariance matrix. The numerical value of the fitting degree represents the difference between the model-derived number and the actual observed number. Incremental fit refers to how much the fitting degree of one model increases or decreases compared with that of another alternative model. The two concepts of fit degree apply to different model fit indices. However, all SEM analyses should first report chi-square statistic and chi-square ($x^2$) statistic calculation of the relevant information (degree of freedom, sample, significant data), when no statistic 0.05 significant level said hypothesis model is an acceptable model, this model can well represent the phenomenon of the real world, non-normal data after the correction. Scaled values should also be reported in addition to the traditional chi-squared values. The test statistics will deviate from the distribution in the case of small samples or when the distribution of sample data violates the assumption of multivariable normality. Therefore, the test statistics are not a completely reliable measurement value when evaluating model fit. Researchers should comprehensively evaluate the absolute fit index (e.g., GFI), residual analysis index (e.g., RMSEA), value-added fit index (e.g., CFI) and reduced fit index (e.g., PNFI, PGFI, AIC). The property of GFI index is similar to R of regression analysis. The larger the value is, the higher the percentage of the actual observed covariance matrix can be explained by the hypothesis model, and the better the model fitting degree is. GFI index can be said to reflect the best absolute fit index. The evaluation of incremental fit can use NNFI, IFI, and other indices. These indices are based on chi-square differences between models. NNFI or TLI index is the more commonly used index if the researcher uses the ML estimation procedure, but it is not recommended when the sample size is small (e.g., less than 150) and IFI index can be used instead. If the researcher uses the GLS method, the performance of IFI index is better. The important criteria for judging the fitness of the above different models are as follows: RMSEA <0.06, TLI >0.95, CFI >0.95, SRMR <0.08.

### 3.1.3.4.5 Model respecification

The majority of the time, researchers get to this step because their original model does not fit. With respect to model creation, the moment has come for academics in the field to refer to a series of theoretically feasible alterations that they may make while establishing their initial model. Rather than being led only by statistical reasons, the re-standardization of the model should be guided by logical concerns.

### 3.1.3.4.6 Reporting the results

The last phase in the SEM process is to write a report that properly and totally describes the findings of the investigation.

It is possible to do SEM in two different ways: by replicating results or by applying results. Furthermore, SEM is seldom assessed between separate samples by the same researcher who collected the original data (internal copy) or by other researchers who did not collect the original data (external copy) (external copy). Due to the enormous number of samples required by SEM, replication becomes difficult. To depict anything more than pure statistical practice, the SEM must be reproduced in its entirety at the end of the simulation process.

### 3.1.3.5 SEM family

The term structural equation modeling (SEM), also known as covariance structure analysis, covariance structure modeling, or covariance structure analysis, does not refer to a single statistical technique, but rather to a series of related procedures. Because different SEM models can solve different research problems, the term structural equation modeling (SEM) is often used interchangeably with covariance structure analysis.

#### 3.1.3.5.1 Path analysis

Path analysis (PA) is the oldest member of the SEM family, having been developed over a century ago. PA is a single-index approach that may be used to measure the structural properties of observations. Using structural models, researchers may test assumptions about the relationships and effects of observable variables that have been made before. A solid grasp of route analysis serves as the basis for a more comprehensive SEM.

#### 3.1.3.5.2 Structural Regression Models

The structural regression model is one of the most often used fundamental structural equation models (SR). The SR model is a hybrid of two models: the structural model and the measuring model. The specification of the SR model, like that of the PA model, allows for the testing of assumptions regarding direct and indirect causal effects. Although these effects may contain latent variables, unlike PA, they are not guaranteed to do so since the SR model also includes a measuring component that, like confirmatory factor analysis (CFA), employs seen variables as markers of hidden variables. The ability to evaluate assumptions about structure and measurement linkages in a single model allows for a significant deal of flexibility in modeling.

#### 3.1.3.5.3 Confirmatory factor analysis

It is possible to use CFA to test hypotheses regarding the connection between indicators and factors.

Technology based on CFA analyzes a priori measurement model that describes the number of components and their associated interactions with indicators in detail.

The following properties may be found in the conventional CFA model:

1. Each indicator is a continuous variable, represented by two reasons: a single factor that the indicator should measure, and all other unique sources of influence (ignoring the cause), represented by an error term.
2. The measurement errors are independent of one another and are not influenced by any other variables or circumstances.
3. There has been no investigation into the relationship between all of these variables (assuming these factors are covariant).

Using arrows, the line connects a factor to an indicator, demonstrating the supposed causal impact of the factor on the observed score. Factor loadings or model coefficients are statistical estimates of these direct impacts that are used to construct the model. They are often referred to as regression coefficients, and they may be found in both non-standardized and standardized forms of expression. Effect indicators and reflection indicators are terms used to describe indications that are believed to be caused by hidden causes. In this sense, the indicators in the typical CFA model are endogenous variables, while factors are exogenous variables that may vary freely and covariate with the indicators. This also explains the measurements of reflections. One of the indicators is represented by the number 1 in the diagram, which is located near the route connecting these elements and the indicator. Essentially, it is a proportionality constant, with each element having its own set of metrics, which allows the computer to estimate the variance and covariance of the factors. Each measurement error term represents a distinct variation, and the variance term of the analysis index of a factor cannot be explained by the component in which the measurement error term appears.

Other techniques mentioned by CFA include exploratory factor analysis (EFA), which is a method that is not typically recognized to be a part of the structural equation modeling family. EFA is a general term that refers to a group of processes that includes centroid, principal components, and main (public) factor analysis. They vary in terms of the statistical criteria used to calculate derived factors, among other things. It is not necessary to assume the factor-indicator correspondence or the number of factors to use this strategy. For example, it permits all indicators to be put on each factor; EFA evaluates factor models that are not constrained in any way. It is possible to do EFA in a more deterministic fashion, for example, by asking the computer to extract a specified number of components from the theory, although EFA does not need any specific assumptions to be applied.

### 3.1.3.5.4 Exploratory SEM

The measurement model is not constrained in specific areas during exploratory SEM (ESEM); however, certain sections of the measurement model are not restricted. To put it another way, the features of EFA and SEM are combined in this study. Depending on the researcher's organizational structure, this form of study may be appropriate, in which several indicators assess weak assumptions, which are often described in CFA or SR models.

### 3.1.3.6 Multilevel SEM

A multilevel data structure is created when there is a layered hierarchical structure between the data elements. When doing large-scale testing, it is common practice to employ multistage data for stratified sampling. Researchers in the domains of education, psychology, and management are sometimes confronted with data that has nested hierarchical patterns. Workers are nested inside institutions, patients are nested within hospitals, residents are nested within communities, and so on; all of these are two-level nesting systems. Sometimes researchers may come across nesting systems that include more than two tiers, such as students nesting inside a class, classes nesting within a school, and so on. In multilevel data, smaller units are measured at lower levels than larger units. For example, students nested in schools are measured at the first-level level while second-level schools are measured at the lowest level. When evaluating the nested structure of the data, the multistage model decomposes the source of residual error into numerous pieces at various levels, which is more in accordance with the real situation in terms of model assumptions than the single-stage model. More significantly, the data acquired via this approach may be used to expose the link between variables in a more reasonable and precise manner. Known variously as hierarchical linear modeling, random coefficient modeling, and other variants, the term multilevel modeling (MLM) refers to a collection of statistical techniques used to analyze hierarchical (nested) data in which (1) scores are nested into larger units and (2) the scores of each level are not independent of one another. Multilayer SEM, which is a combination of scanning electron microscopy and multilayer modeling, gives the following capabilities: (1) in the hierarchical data set, calculate the correct standard error for each level; (2) in the same analysis, calculate the correct standard error for each level from the individual level and the group level (situational impact); (3) When latent variables are assessed by several indicators, the unreliability of the data is taken into consideration; (4) The direct and indirect impacts of structural model analysis are calculated. As more and more SEM computer programs directly allow multilevel analysis in complicated sample designs, researchers will find it simpler to reap the benefits of these prospective advantages in their study.

### 3.1.3.7 The strengths and weaknesses of SEM

First and foremost, structural equation modeling (SEM) allows for the evaluation of the entire model, which provides a higher level of perspective to the analysis, whereas statistical tests, such as analysis of variance and MR, demonstrate the individual effects represented in the model. Second, when it comes to big sample sizes, statistical tests are not as successful as structural equation modeling (SEM). All effects are statistically significant when the sample size is big, which is the case in this case.

### 3.1.4 Mediation

Throughout the remainder of this chapter, we will explain the basics of mediation analysis, with a particular emphasis on the most fundamental mediation model, which links causal antecedents with subsequent variables via the use of mediation variables or mediations. A popular and widely estimated simple mediation model, this one is used to introduce the mechanism of PA and demonstrate how the impact of variables on the results can be divided into direct and indirect impacts, which can be quantified using OLS regression, is used to demonstrate how the impact of variables on the results can be divided into direct and indirect impacts. The reasoning exam of direct and indirect impact will be taught at the beginning of the course.

#### 3.1.4.1 The definitions of mediation

In the context of mediation analysis, it is used to measure and investigate the direct and indirect ways in which the pre-dependent variable X influences the pre-dependent variable Y via one or more mediators. Intermediary analysis, which identifies and investigates the processes by which interventions produce their effects, may find alternative and more successful intervention tactics while also providing insight into the mechanism of action.

#### 3.1.4.2 Mediation and its development

The first step of the study required us to attempt to create a link between the two variables X and Y, as well as to determine whether or not this relationship was causal in nature. Establishing a link between two variables is an essential component of science, and it is the issue of "if" or "if" that serves as the beginning point for comprehending the influence of your environment. It's true that almost every scientific area has a substantial quantity of research in the literature that gives answers to queries like "yes" or "if". However, as research has progressed and matured, the emphasis has switched from demonstrating the presence of an impact to understanding the mechanisms that cause it to occur. Grasp how an effect happens and respond to inquiries about it may help you get a better understanding of the research process, as well as providing insights and practical ideas on how to put that understanding into practice. The use of intermediary analysis is a common method of answering the "how" issue. In mediation analysis, the goal is to examine the link between a cause and effect variable X and an outcome variable Y by examining the relationship between one or more mediation variables. A form of statistical analysis known as mediation analysis is one of the most extensively used statistical methods in a broad range of subjects such as society, behavior, health science, business, medicine, and a variety of other professions. Mediation has been the subject of some of the most highly referenced publications in social scientific methods in the 21st century. Researchers and readers alike must be familiar with the notion of mediation and how to conduct an analysis of it.

#### 3.1.4.2.1 Definition

To establish or test how $X$ affects $Y$, researchers usually assume a model in which one or more intervention variables $M$ have a causal relationship between $X$ and $Y$. Figure 3.13 illustrates this model in its simplest form. These intervention variables, often referred to as mediation variables, are defined as the mechanisms by which $X$ influences $Y$. In other words, a change in $X$ causes a change in one or more intermediary variables $M$, and a change in $M$ causes a change in $Y$.

The researcher is interested in the research mechanism through process modeling to empirically evaluate and test the hypothesis that the influence of two paths through $X$ is affected as shown in Figure 3.13, one directly from $X$ to $Y$ and the other indirectly through $M$. Often referred to as mediation analysis, this type of analysis is common in almost all disciplines. Some of the most cited journal articles on methodology (e.g., Baron & Kenny, 1986) and more recently (Preacher & Hayes, 2004, 2008) used mediation analysis and various statistical methods to quantify and test hypotheses about the direct and indirect effects of $X$ on $Y$ are discussed.

#### 3.1.4.2.2 Simple mediation model

The most basic mediation model (the simple mediation model) is represented in Figure 3.13 in the form of a conceptual diagram. It can be seen that this model contains two subsequent variables $(M)$ and $(Y)$ and two antecedent variables $(X)$ and $(M)$. $X$ has a causal effect on $Y$ and $M$. A simple mediation model is any causal system in which at least one causal antecedent variable $X$ affects $Y$ through a single mediator variable $M$. In this model, $X$ can affect $Y$ through two paths. These paths can be found by tracing the path from $X$ to $Y$, but never in the opposite

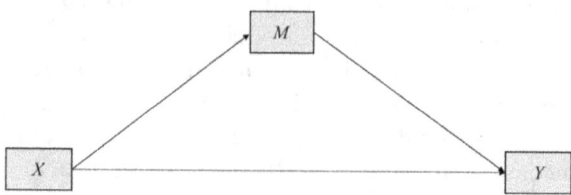

**FIGURE 3.13** A conceptual diagram of a simple mediation model with a single mediator variable M causally located between $X$ and $Y$.

direction from the arrow. One path from $X$ to $Y$ has no direct effect through $M$ and the second path is called the direct effect from $X$ to $Y$ and $Y$ equals $X$ and $Y$ has an indirect effect through $M$. It goes first from antecedent $X$ to consequent $M$ and then from consequent $M$ to consequent $Y$ and the indirect effect represents how $X$ and $Y$ affect through a causal sequence where $X$ affects $M$ and $M$ affects $Y$.

In mediation models, $M$ is often referred to as a mediator variable, and it represents a possible or proposed mechanism—the content of the "black box"—through which the message framework influences behavior. Once $X$ has an effect on $M$, then the causal effect of $M$ on $Y$ produces a variation in $Y$.

For causal processes that include an intermediate component, the major focus is on estimating and explaining direct and indirect effects, as well as conducting reasoning tests, while conducting empirical testing. It is necessary to estimate the components of indirect effects, that is, the influence of $X$ on $M$ as well as the effect of $Y$ on $M$, to arrive at these effects.

Using a basic statistical graph, Figure 3.14 illustrates how a mediation model may be implemented. There is no difference between the conceptual diagram and the statistical diagram of the basic mediation model when comparing Figures 3.13 and 3.14, as shown in the comparison. An analogy may be drawn between a statistical diagram and a route diagram in that they both graphically show a collection of equations that correlate to a conceptual diagram According to the statistical diagram, the influence indicated in the conceptual diagram is really calculated by a mathematical model, as opposed to the conceptual diagram (such as a linear regression model). According to the statistical graph, the box indicates a clearly measured or observed variable, and the solid one-way arrow represents a predictor or predictor variable from that variable, depending on whether the arrow points to the variable or originates from the variable. The variable pointed to by the arrow in a statistical chart is referred to as the outcome variable, and the variable pointed to by the arrow is referred to as the antecedent variable in statistical charts. It is synonymous with the predictor variable or independent variable to refer to the former dependent variable, and the post-dependent variable may be used to refer to either the dependent or the post-dependent variables. By definition, if a variable in the image has an arrow pointing to it, it is the outcome variable predicted by the antecedents of all the arrows pointing to it. Similarly, the number of following variables in the statistical graph corresponds to the number of equations shown in the graph. Using a statistical model, each variable that emerges as a consequence is regarded to have been anticipated by its antecedents, with a given amount of uncertainty. It is depicted as a statistical graph with the letter E in the center and a dotted line connecting the letter E to the relevant outcome variable. The incorrect index will be the same as the label that is assigned to the next variable in the chain. Instead of a solid line connecting the related result variables, a dashed line should be used to indicate that the estimated error is not the expected value of the outcome variable (represented by the solid arrow). Each of the arrows in Figure 3.14 has a label attached to it. The labels on the arrows between the variables reflect the regression coefficients of the variables that came before them in the statistical model that was developed as a consequence of the analysis. They may be numbers or other symbols, such as letters in the alphabet, depending on whether the graph depicts the model before the coefficient is calculated or communicates the outcome after the coefficient is computed. The graph can be described as follows: While using graphs to explain the predicted outcomes of your model, you may utilize the available data to figure out what your real regression coefficients are. Alternatives include using labels in the chart while putting their estimations in the table that corresponds to the graphic. In most cases, the linear regression model given by Equation (3.1) has a regression constant or intercept, which is indicated by I in this case. In rare cases, data manipulations such as mean centering or normalization may result in the constant being set to zero. However, just because it is not explicitly mentioned in the equation does not rule out the possibility that it exists. According to whether or not the outcome variable is the same as the premise variable, the result variable may or may not be the premise variable. According to certain models, variables may be classified as either pre-dependent variables or post-dependent variables, which implies that the same variable can be the outcome or dependent variable of one equation while simultaneously serving as the predictor or independent variable of another equation. The antecedent and result variables in SEM are comparable to, but distinct from, the exogenous and endogenous variables in other studies. When using SEM, endogenous variables are characterized as post-variables; however, endogenous variables cannot be both exogenous variables and post-variables simultaneously. The result variable, if it contains an arrow that points to another variable, may likewise serve as a precondition variable. Figure 3.14 depicts a graph with two outcome variables, and two linear models are needed for each of the two result variables in the graph. Two equations are represented in the figure:

$$M = i_M + aX + e_M \qquad (3.41)$$
$$Y = i_Y + c'X + bM + e_Y \qquad (3.42)$$

where $i_M$ and $i_Y$ are regression constants, $e_M$ and $e_Y$ are estimated errors of $M$ and $Y$, respectively, $c'$ quantifies the relative direct influence of $X$ on $Y$ when controlling the influence of $M$ on $Y$, $a$ quantifies the relative direct influence of $X$ on $M$, and $b$ quantifies the direct effect of $X$ on $M$ when controlling for other variables.

The direct and indirect effects perfectly partition how differences in $X$ map on to differences in $Y$, the total effect of $X$ is denoted as $c$. The total impact of $c$ quantifies how much two cases that differ by one unit on $X$ are estimated to differ on $Y$. In a simple mediation model, $c$ can be derived by estimating $Y$ from $X$ alone:

$$Y = i_{Y\star} + cX + e_{Y\star} \qquad (3.43)$$

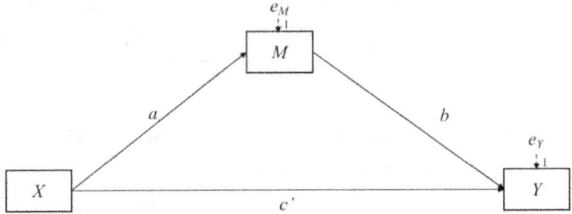

**FIGURE 3.14** A statistical diagram of simple mediation model with a single mediator variable $M$ causally located between $X$ and $Y$.

The total effect of $X$ on $Y$ is equal to the sum of the direct and indirect effects of $X$:

$$c = c' + ab \tag{3.44}$$

This relationship can be rewritten as $ab = c-'$, which provides an alternative definition of indirect effects. The indirect effect is the difference between the total effect of $X$ on $Y$ and the effect of $X$ on $Y$ controlling for $M$, namely, the direct effect.

In a simple mediation model, the total effect of $X$ on $Y$ is the sum of the direct effect of $X$ on $Y$ and indirect effect of $X$ on $Y$ through $M$ while there are many options for inferring the indirect effects, the total effect of the inference is simple and clear. Although the total effect is the sum of the two paths of influence, $X$ can be estimated by regression $Y$, and $M$ is not included in the model.

$M$ has two examples in which the quantitative assessment of the direct effect of distinct $Y$ is identical, but the quantitative estimation of the direct influence of $X$ and $Y$ varies by one unit between the two cases. In the regression model, the inference in the intermediate analysis is often employed in conjunction with the conventional inference approach. The correlation coefficient between two variables. There are two ways to do this: by testing the null hypothesis about $Tc'$ against alternative hypotheses or by creating a confidence interval for $Tc'$. Unless there were exceptional situations, researchers concentrated on evaluating if $Tc'$ is greater than zero based on the available information. Assuming that this is the case, it lends weight to the claim that $X$ is tied to $Y$ and has nothing to do with the mechanism represented by $M$. If this is not the case, it might be argued that when $X$ and $Y$ are explained using the mechanism of $M$, there is no proof that there is a connection between the two variables. In other words, the effect of $X$ on $Y$ is unrelated to the influence of $M$ on $Y$ in the same way.

The indirect effect quantifies the influence of two different units on $Y$ due to the influence of $X$ on $M$. Conversely, whether the indirect effect that affects $Y$ and the effect of $X$ can be said to be the propagation mechanism of the $X{\rightarrow}M{\rightarrow}Y$ event in the causal chain. As with direct effects, researchers usually want to know whether the data allows claims that the difference in $Y$ estimates caused by this mechanism can be said to be non-zero. If so, you can claim that $M$ is the intermediary of $X$'s influence on $Y$. For the inference of direct influence, the inference can be expressed by testing the null hypothesis of TaTb or by constructing interval estimation.

Generally speaking, model coefficients are viewed as estimations of the posited causal effect of each variable in a system on the other variables in the system. The purpose of the analysis is to estimate these coefficients, put them together, and provide explanations for them. It is possible to estimate these coefficients by using programs in statistical software packages such as Statistical Product Service Solutions (SPSS) and SAS as well as R and other statistical software packages, by using SEM programs (such as the LISREL, AMOS, Mplus, or EQS), or by using the Process in SPSS to perform two OLS regression analyses.

i. The causal steps approach

The causal stages technique has been around since the 1950s, but it was popularized in the 1980s by a very significant paper by Baron and Kenny (1986) in the Journal of Personality and Social Psychology that helped to promote the method. It is for this reason that the causal steps technique is sometimes referred to as the Baron and Kenny method by many people. Historically, the causal stages technique has been used in the great majority of published mediation studies, and this has continued to be the case today. Its popularity, on the other hand, is waning. It is necessary to apply the causal steps technique to determine if a particular variable $M$'s function functions as a mediator in the connection between $X$ and $Y$ when the modeling process is being carried out. The causal step technique focuses only on a set of tests that examine the significance of the findings for each route of the causal system, as opposed to other approaches. If $M$ is to be viewed as a mediator of the impact of $X$ on $Y$, it is required to first prove the presence of a mediated effect, which indicates that $X$ and $Y$ are correlated, according to the causal stages approach. Rejecting the null hypothesis, which states that the total impact $Tc$, is zero, is the litmus test for determining if $X$ has an influence on $Y$. If this is the case, the conditions have been satisfied, and the researchers may go on to step 2. If this is not the case, all testing will be terminated. Taking into consideration that the first condition has been satisfied, the impact of $X$ on $M$ is calculated in the second step. It is statistically significant if an is greater than one, which meets the second condition of the causal steps method, which states that $X$ must have an effect on $M$. An inability to reject the null hypothesis that $Ta = 0$ terminates the procedure and suggests that $M$ is not a mediator of the relationship between $X$ and $Y$. The third criterion is then tested to see whether $M$ has an effect on $Y$ while controlling for the first two. If the second and third criteria are both met, the test for the third criterion is carried out. When testing the null hypothesis that $Tb = 0$ is used to construct this standard, equation (3.42) is utilized for regression of $Y$ against $X$ and $M$ to establish this standard. This approach comes to an end if the null hypothesis cannot be rejected since $M$ is not acting as a mediator of the interaction between two variables. As long as, however, the third condition is met, then the direct influence of the variable $X$ ($c'$) is evaluated in relation to the overall effect of the variable ($c$). The effect of $X$ on $Y$ is said to be totally mediated if $c'$ is closer to zero than c and $c'$ is not statistically significant. In other words, the effect of $X$ on $Y$ is said to be wholly explained by the influence of $M$. However, if $c'$ is closer to zero than $c$, but $c'$ is statistically different from zero, then $M$ mediates a portion of the influence of $X$ on $Y$ in some way. Only a portion of the influence of $X$ on $Y$ is passed over to $M$ in this case.

This strategy may be popular since it is straightforward to comprehend, straightforward to convey, and straightforward to teach. It may be summed up in a few phrases and does not need the use of specialized tools or significant knowledge in statistics or data analysis to complete. As a result, even researchers who do not adhere to the suggested technique literature continue to advocate the approach.

However, people are becoming more aware that this strategy is neither statistically nor philosophically optimal. For the following reasons, the days of middlemen being required to satisfy these requirements are over: As a starting point, according to the causal step method, the presence of indirect effects may be deduced logically from the findings of a null hypothesis test that has not been quantified as indirect effects from First and foremost, the capacity to assert that $M$ is an intermediate is contingent on the ability to correctly reject three erroneous assumptions. Thought-provoking questions are a human creation, and they are prone to mistakes. They are predicated on assumptions that may or may not be satisfied, which has an impact on their performance. Although these assumptions are satisfied, hypothesis testing may still be unable to reject the false null hypothesis or may incorrectly reject the genuine null hypothesis if the actual null hypothesis is rejected. The greater the number of hypothesis tests that a person does to establish or support a claim, the greater the likelihood that the assertion is incorrect. Aim to reduce the number of inference programs that must be employed to support the assertion to the absolute minimum. For indirect effects, we merely need to do a straightforward logic test. In the third phase, before moving on to the causative step, researchers often conduct hypothesis testing to see if $X$ has an effect on $Tc$ $Y$. The null hypothesis cannot be rejected because of the entire impact of $X$. As a result, $Tc = 0$ indicates that the major criteria created by $M$ is no longer important as an intermediate, and so the causal step is terminated. According to this argument, because non-existent effects cannot be modified, it is pointless to attempt to describe the process that causes such non-existent effects to manifest themselves. However, this reasoning is faulty. It is conceivable for $X$ to have an indirect influence on $Y$ via $M$, even if the hypothesis test is unable to demonstrate that the overall effect is not more than zero. Neither the size of the total impact nor the size of the indirect effect is limited or determined by the magnitude of the total effect. Even though the overall impact is more than zero, the indirect effect is greater than zero as well. The overall impact is equal to the sum of the direct and indirect effects, minus the direct effect. The addition of these two effects may produce values that are near zero, if the signs of the two effects are different from one another. The indirect effect may be different from zero, and the uncertainty is fairly significant (that is, the confidence interval is tight), but when a tiny result is added, it is predicted that there is a considerable amount of variability in the indirect impacts (e.g., the confidence interval is large). It is possible that the impact contains such sampling error that it is impossible to identify a zero change. If there are any subgroups in which $X$ has the opposite influence on $Y$, this is another circumstance in which the overall impact is close to zero.

The difficulty is that it is incorrect to confine the examination of indirect effects to evidence of the overall influence of $X$, and there is widespread agreement among those who are contemplating this approach for mediation analysis that this is incorrect. It is certain that data analysis will take place for researchers that use a causal step method and insist on a statistically significant overall impact of $X$ prior to calculating and assessing indirect effects. Consequently, they will be unable to recognize the indirect influence, leading to a distortion of the process that resulted in the data's collection and analysis. In the long term, if this method is abandoned, there will be less mistakes in thinking.

Some researchers utilize joint significance tests to analyze mediators that have little (or no) evidence of having an overall influence on the study's outcome. This test requires that A and B be statistically significant to support mediation claims, but it does not need that C be statistically significant. However, this approach does not yield interval estimates of indirect uncertainty or any other kind of uncertainty measure, and it needs two tests rather than just one. As a result, the common sense test is in violation of the second and third principles of common sense, respectively. Others use a variation of this approach in which indirect effects may only be obtained if a causal step process (e.g., using a bootstrap confidence interval) is used to demonstrate the statistical significance of a single route comprising the whole effect before carrying out the testing. In other words, an acceptable causal step criterion is employed as a gatekeeper for the more relevant indirect effect test, which is performed after the satisfactory causal step criterion. As a result, the statistical ability of the detecting agent is reduced as a result of the redundant data processing. There is no longer a difficulty with "establishing mediation standards". The test of indirect effects is more relevant than the test of a single route in the model, which is less important.

Lastly, since the causal step technique is not predicated on the measurement of indirect effects, it encourages researchers to think about indirect and mediating effects in terms of their qualitative nature rather than quantitative ones. The specifics of the testing process, such as whether the indirect influence created by one intermediary is different in magnitude from the indirect impact produced by another intermediary, are difficult to assess from these viewpoints, making it difficult to analyze the nuances of the testing process. Because of this qualitative way of thinking, it is also hard to identify the process as being regulated.

ii. The normal theory approach

Known by several names, including the coefficient method of inference, the Sobel product test, and the delta method among others, the normal theory method is based on the same inference theory that is described in basic statistics textbooks on total and direct effects, as well as many other inference tests. Make an estimate of $ab$'s standard error and make an assumption that the sample distribution of $ab$ is normally distributed. Given a certain null hypothesis value of $TaTb$, it is possible to calculate the $p$-value of $ab$ or to construct an interval estimate.

The conventional theoretical techniques are flawed in two ways, making them impossible to suggest. First and foremost, the technique is predicated on the assumption that the sample distribution of AB is normally distributed. In contrast, an examination of the data and simulations reveals that the distribution of sample size is not regular. It is preferable to use tests that do not necessitate making such assumptions because, given the characteristics of the problem, it is never possible to know with certainty whether the sampling distribution is sufficiently close to normal to apply the method of assuming normality without risking a false positive. The second point to mention is that simulation studies in which this method is compared to various competitive reasoning methods reveal that it is one of the weakest methods and frequently produces confidence intervals that are not as accurate as some of the methods described below (e.g., Hayes & Scharkow, 2013). If $X$ does have an indirect effect on $Y$ via $M$, then conventional theoretical approaches are less likely to uncover it than alternative ways.

iii. Bootstrap confidence interval

The practice of bootstrapping has been around for decades as a resampling strategy. This is made feasible by the development of high-speed computers. Self-direction is becoming increasingly common in current statistical software as computer capabilities improve and the cost of acquiring these skills drops. It is a broad strategy that may be used to a wide range of reasoning difficulties that researchers may come into in their study. If the statistical behavior of repeated sampling is unknown, too complicated to be deduced, or strongly reliant on context, this method is very beneficial.

However, complex the reasoning issue, the nature of the bootloader remains consistent across applications. As a result, the original sample of size $N$ is viewed as a microcosm of the original population of the original sample. Once this sample has been "resampled" through replacement, certain statistics of interest are computed in a new sample of size $N$ as a result of this replacement procedure, which results in a new sample of size $N$. An empirical representation of statistics is produced after millions of ideal repetitions, and this empirical representation is then used for the reasoning job at hand.

In mediation analysis, the bootstrap technique is used to establish an empirically generated representation that indirectly impacts the sampling distribution, and the empirical representation is then used to build a confidence interval for $TaTb$ using the sample distribution as a reference point. There are no assumptions made regarding the form of the sample distribution of $ab$, in contrast to the conventional theoretical technique. Because the bootstrap confidence interval takes into account the irregularity of the sample distribution of $ab$, the conclusions drawn from it are more likely to be correct than those drawn from conventional theoretical approaches. When applied to hypotheses, the outcome is a stronger test than is possible using conventional theoretical approaches.

There are six steps to construct a bootstrap confidence interval for $T_a T_b$:

1. Randomly select $n$ cases from the original sample and perform substitution sampling for these cases, where n is the size of the original sample, which is called a bootstrap sample.
2. Estimate the indirect effect $ab^\star$ in the bootstrap sample, where $ab^\star$ is the product of $a$ and $b$ from equations (3.41) and (3.42).
3. Repeat (1) and (2) for a total of $k$ times, where $k$ is a large number, and save the value of $ab^\star$ each time. In general, $k$ is at least a few thousand. It can be seen that, with the increase in the number of bootstrap samples, the change of the confidence interval limit estimation is significantly and rapidly reduced. In general, 5,000 to 10,000 bootstrap examples are sufficient in most applications. There is relatively little added value in raising it above 10,000, because the accuracy gain above that is quite small.
4. Sort the $k$ indirect effects $ab^\star$ estimated by steps (1), (2), and (3) from low to high.
5. For the $ci$ % confidence interval, find the $ab^\star$ value in the $k$ estimated distribution that defines the $0.5(100-ci)$ percentile of the distribution. This is the lower limit of the $ci$% confidence interval. It will be the value of $ab^\star$ at $0.005k(100-ci)$ in the sorted distribution.
6. Find the value of $ab^\star$ in the $k$ estimate distribution of the $[100-0.5(100-ci)]$ percentile that defines the distribution. This is the upper bound on the confidence interval of $ci$ %. It will be the value of $ab^\star$ in ordinal position $k[1-0.005(100-CI)] + 1$ in the sorted distribution.

Thus, the random resampling procedure is analogous to the process of repeating the research time and time again, but utilizing data from individuals who previously participated in the study, rather than gathering data from a large number of new people. Despite the fact that it seems to be thus, it has absolutely nothing to do with cheating, fabricating data, or artificially expanding the sample size. Instead of repeated sampling from the original population, this is a creative method of determining the AB change between samples simply by repeating the sampling procedure while utilizing the original sample as a representative of the population.

In this technique, the value of $ab\star$ is fully dependent on the value of $ab\star$, which splits the upper and bottom (100 $ci$)/2% of the estimated distribution of k bootstrap for indirect effects into two halves, which is referred to as the percentile bootstrap confidence interval. Alternative ways of creating the bootstrap confidence interval include bias correction and acceleration, as well as bias correction and acceleration and correction and acceleration. When bias correction is performed, the bootstrap confidence interval is identical to the percentile position confidence interval; however, the endpoints are changed based on the $k$ values of $ab\star$, where $ab$ is the point estimate data of the indirect impact in the original computation. With this ratio, the endpoints are shifted up or down to various degrees, depending on their relative positions. For the acceleration component, extra changes are applied to the distribution skew obtained using the k bootstrap estimate to account for the acceleration component.

Percentile bootstrap confidence intervals are not without their limitations and objections as a means of deducing information. Before anyone can have sufficient confidence in bootstrap-based reasoning, it is obvious that they must have a certain confidence in the quality of their samples, which must be representative of the overall distribution of the measured variables to have sufficient confidence in the bootstrap-based reasoning. To recreate the original sampling process, bootstrapping is based on the concept of sampling from a person's sample replacement and re-sampling from that sample replacement. In contrast, if the sample used does not appropriately reflect the population of the source, the introduction string may generate findings that are difficult to interpret and hence difficult to trust. It is not required to choose the initial sample from the population in a random manner as long as the distribution of the measured variable closely resembles the distribution of the population in general. Of course, random sampling helps in the depiction of this information, but it is not essential. Second, when compared to the normal theory method, the bootstrap method is particularly useful in small samples, because the sampling distribution of AB is likely to be the most non-normal in a small sample, whereas the asymptotic behavior of the normal theory method is more important in a large sample, as previously mentioned. Although it is difficult to trust the sample, the distinctive benefits of the bootstrap method are much more apparent. However, if the original sample is relatively tiny, at the very least in concept, one or two irregularities may cause the guided analysis to be distorted in some manner, maybe even more so than the conventional reasoning process itself. Because the Bootstrap confidence interval is based on random resampling of the data, its endpoints are not a set number of points. Every time a leading confidence interval is formed from the same data, the resulting confidence interval is somewhat different from the previous confidence interval. Some individuals find this to be problematic since, in an ideal world, two persons studying the same data in the same manner should come up with precisely the same findings. The practice of repeating self-initiated analyses until they achieve the answers they desire may also lead to unethical investigators engaging in unethical behavior.

iv. Distribution of the product

The product distribution technique is based on a mathematical estimate of the product sample distribution and is used to distribute products. This complicated procedure does not take into account non-mathematical descriptions. It is necessary to convert ab to a standardized indicator, find the value of the standardized indicator, use these values to define the upper and lower bounds of the confidence interval indirectly affected by the standardized indicator, and then convert the endpoints of the confidence interval back to the original indicator. In the same way as the Monte Carlo technique is implemented, all that is required to implement this approach is the variables a, b, sea, and seb in the intermediate analysis. There is no need for raw data.

### 3.1.4.2.3 Confounding and epiphenomenal association

Through $M$, $X$ may have an indirect impact on $Y$. In reality, another variable is the mechanism variable, which is the variable via which $X$ operates indirectly. Epigenetic association is the term used to describe this. As a result, the connection between $M$ and $Y$ may be described as follows: $X$ influences the behavior of other variables, and other variables influence the contingency of $Y$, but since $M$ is influenced by other factors, $M$ seems to be a variable that influences $X$ via $Y$. The efficiency of causal reasoning is discussed in detail below. The findings of the intermediate analysis are substantially jeopardized as a consequence of the statistically significant association. It is also possible for confusion or incorrect connections to constitute a major danger to efficacy. Confusion will undermine the causal statements about the relationship if the link between variables can be reduced to a third variable that has causal effects on both variables.

Fortunately, the phenomenon associations and obfuscations that threaten the validity of causal claims can be managed at least in part by statistical controls. If two variables $M$ and $Y$ are related or confused due to the relationship between them and some variables $C$, $M$, and $Y$, there should be no person equal to $C$. In general, we cannot just arbitrarily hold $C$ constant by research design in this way. However, if we measure $C$, we can mathematically eliminate the effect of $C$ on the quantification of putative causal associations in a mediation model. In the mediation analysis, by using $C$ as a predictor in $M$ and $Y$ models, confusion and tabulated associations caused by $C$ can be excluded, as shown in Figure 3.15. Conveniently, adding $C$ to the model of $M$ and $Y$ would also remove $C$ as a threat of contingency or confounding claims about causality between $X$ and $M$, $X$ and $Y$, and $M$ and $Y$.

Controlling $C$ does not exclude the possibility of other types of misunderstanding or phenomenological connections. It is possible that a variable other than C causes the connection in the mediation model to become confused, or that C causes another variable to become confused. It is not an issue if additional variables are assessed in addition to the one being tested for multiple confusion. They may be used as additional predictors in the mediation analysis by including them in the M and Y models.

In practice, researchers often think of more than one potential confounding variable, and they wish to statistically partially exclude associations between variables in a simple mediation model. Denoting C as the set of $q$ variables ($q \geq 1$, frequently called covariates in this context) that may threaten a claim of causality due to confounding or epiphenomenal association, their effects on the paths in a mediation model (i.e., $a$, $b$, and $c'$) can be statistically removed by estimating the coefficients in the following models of M and Y:

$$M = i_M + aX + \sum_{i=1}^{q} f_i C_i + e_M \tag{3.45}$$

$$Y = i_Y + c'X + bM + \sum_{i=1}^{q} g_i C_i + e_Y \tag{3.46}$$

As you can see, the only change in equations (3.45) and (3.46) with respect to equations (3.41) and (3.42) is the addition of the $q$ covariable to the model for M and Y. The resulting estimates for $a$, $b$, and $c'$ can now be said to "purify" the influence of covariates on their values, excluding C from the model. In estimating other effects in the model, covariates are held mathematically or statistically constant. In this model, $c'$ is still the direct influence of X on Y, $ab$ is still the indirect influence of X on Y through M, and the total effect of X on Y is the sum of the direct and indirect effects, $c' + ab$. The total effect will be equal to $c$ in a model of Y without M but including the $q$ covariates:

$$Y = i_{Y\star} + cX + \sum_{i=1}^{q} h_i C_i + e_{Y\star} \tag{3.47}$$

The understanding of the direct, indirect, and total impacts stays the same, but the addition of "equal on C," "keeping C constant, "or" statistically controlling

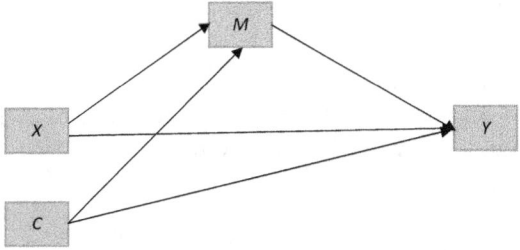

**FIGURE 3.15** A conceptual diagram of a simple mediation model with statistical controls.

for C" has changed the meaning of the words (terms that have the same meaning and can be used interchangeably). To put it another way, when two examples vary by one unit on X, it is expected that they will differ on Y while M and C are held constant. A measure of the indirect effect, ab, is the amount by which two cases that differ by one unit on X but are equal on covariates C are estimated to differ on Y as a result of the effect of X on M, which in turn has an effect on Y. The indirect effect, ab, can be expressed as a percentage of the difference between two cases that are equal on covariates C. Furthermore, the total impact of X, denoted by the letter c, estimates how much two instances that vary by a unit on X are projected to differ on Y, after statistically adjusting for the letter C.

### 3.1.4.2.4 Effect size

When it comes to the interpretation of direct and indirect impacts, X and Y measurements are used to convey it in quantitative terms. The direct and indirect processes of $c'$ and AB units, respectively, are used to estimate the two scenarios in which X varies by one unit. Due to the fact that these consequences are quantified in terms of X and Y indicators, their magnitude is constrained and will thus be determined by judgments concerning the indicators themselves. So the absolute amount of direct and indirect affects does not tell us whether these impacts are great or little from a practical or theoretical standpoint. X and Y may be multiplied or divided by a constant to get values that are arbitrarily big or tiny, for example. As a result, standardization should be used to measure the impact size in a way that is consistent across research. The next sections discuss two effect size metrics that may be used to analyze direct, indirect, and total effects in the mediation model, as well as their applications.

## 3.2 The partially standardized effect

The partially standardized effect size (MacKinnon, 2008) is a transformation of an effect that expresses it relative to the standard deviation of Y rather than in the original metric of Y, thereby giving it context relative to variability in the outcome. The formulas for the partially standardized direct and indirect effects are simple:

$$c'_{ps} = c' + \frac{c'}{SD_Y} \tag{3.48}$$

$$ab_{ps} = \frac{ab}{SD_Y} \tag{3.49}$$

As already discussed many times, the sum of the direct and indirect effects yields the total effect of X. So too do the partially standardized direct and indirect effects add to yield the partially standardized total effect. That is,

$$c_{ps} = \frac{c}{SD_Y} = c'_{ps} + ab_{ps} \tag{3.50}$$

## 3.3 The completely standardized effect

The partial standardization effect changes the values of $c'$ and $ab$ to correspond to the standard deviation of $Y$, but it does not change the value of $X$. Due to their scale-limited nature, the impacts of partial standardization are only noticeable at a small scale. Their magnitude, therefore, will depend on the scale of $X$. In most cases, the change in one unit of $X$ has little or no relevance in terms of substance. The direct and indirect impacts are represented by the scale that is used to exclude $X$ from the partial standardized effects. This is the difference in the standard deviations of $Y$ in the two situations, expressed as a percentage. The two scenarios vary by one standard deviation in terms of $X$. This produces the following completely standardized effect:

$$c'_{cs} = \frac{SD_X(c')}{SD_Y} = SD_X(c'_{ps}) \tag{3.51}$$

$$ab_{cs} = \frac{SD_X(ab)}{SD_Y} = SD_X(ab_{ps}) \tag{3.52}$$

When direct and indirect effects are calculated using standardized regression coefficients (or when standardized $X$, $M$, and $Y$ are used in the model rather than $X$, $M$, and $Y$ in their original metric), these two measures are identical to the direct and indirect effects calculated using standardized regression coefficients (e.g., Cheung, 2009; Preacher & Hayes, 2008).

Just like with the partly standardized effect, the totally standardized direct and indirect effects combine to produce the completely standardized total effect, which is expressed as follows:

$$c_{cs} = \frac{SD_X(c)}{SD_Y} = c'_{cs} + ab_{cs} \tag{3.53}$$

## 3.4 Multiple $X$ variables

Modifications to the technique now being presented are not required for the computation of direct and indirect effects in a model with numerous $X$ variables. For each outcome, the factors in the model that may have contributed to it are regressed, and the resulting coefficients are either cobbled together or directly explained by the variables in the model.

If we consider a basic intermediate model, there are only $k$ $X$ variables, each of which transmits its effects to a single $Y$ variable and indirectly to another via a single $M$ variable. A total of $k$ direct and indirect effects are present, one for each of the $X$ variables. Due to the fact that there are two follow-up variables in the model, there are two variables for which a linear model is required to assess the effect. The two models are as follows:

$$M = i_M + a_1 X_1 + a_2 X_2 + \cdots + a_k X_k + e_M \tag{3.54}$$
$$Y = i_Y + c'_1 X_1 + c'_2 X_2 + \cdots + c'_k X_k + bM + e_Y \tag{3.55}$$

and they can be estimated as a set of separate OLS regressions. The indirect effect of $X_i$ on $Y$ through $M$ is $a_i b$, and the direct effect is $c'_i$. The total effect of $X_i$ is the sum of its direct and indirect effects: $c_i = c'_i + a_i b$. The total effect of $X_i$ on $Y$ could also be estimated by predicting $Y$ from all $k$ $X$s but not $M$:

$$Y = i_{Y\star} + c_1 X_1 + c_2 X_2 + \cdots + c_k X_k + e_{Y\star} \qquad (3.56)$$

As a result of the presence of all $k$ $X$s in the model at the same time, the direct and indirect effects of $Xi$ are expressed as the estimated difference in $Y$ between two instances that vary by one unit in $Xi$ but are equal in the other $k-1$ $Xi$ variables (or, rewritten as, keep the remaining $k-1$ $X$ variables unchanged, or control these variables). In other words, they indicate the direct and indirect effect of $Xi$ on $Y$, which is unique to $Xi$ and cannot be represented by any other factor. Consequently, when the remaining $k-1$ $X$ variables are conceived of as statistical controls rather than variables whose effects are particularly intriguing, the effects are interpreted in the manner in which they are conceived of.

The overall, direct, and indirect impacts of $Xi$ in a model with $K$ $X$ variables may be the same as or different from the equivalent effects in a basic mediation model that excludes all other $K-1$ $X$ variables. Each individual difference is determined by the correlation between Xi and the other $K-1$ $X$ and the correlation between other $X$ and the two other variables.

When many $X$s are included in an intermediate model, there is a risk that the highly linked $X$s will cancel each other out when statistical control is incorporated. This is a classic issue requiring linear models of predictors that are connected to one another. $X$ variables that are significantly associated with each other (or two $X$ variables and one control variable) may be connected to $M$ or $Y$, and therefore when they are both included in the mediation model as predictors of $M$ or $Y$, they will be different from attempting to explain Changes in $M$ and $Y$. Its regression coefficients quantify the unique relationship that it has with model intermediate variables as well as with outcome variables. As a result, we can observe that when each variable is viewed as a separate $X$, each variable has a direct and/or indirect influence on $Y$ to $M$, but when all of the variables are evaluated together, none of the variables seems to have any effect.

## 3.5 Multiple *Y* variables

When investigating the direct and indirect impacts of a putative causal antecedent on several outcome variables, investigators may be interested in both direct and indirect effects. In fact, when you look at it in terms of k *Y* variables, it turns out to be merely $k$ basic mediation models that share a common $X$ and $M$. Because $Yi$ is determined solely by $X$ and $M$, the direct and indirect effects of $X$ on $Yi$ will be the same regardless of whether they are estimated simultaneously with the other $k-1$ $Y$ variables in the model analytically (which would necessitate the use of a structural equation modeling program) or separately for each Y variable using k separate analyses.

## 3.6 Multiple mediators

This section presents the mediation model with numerous mediations, which is used throughout the rest of the chapter. According to this paradigm, the impact of one variable may be conveyed to another variable at the same time via a number of different methods. It is proposed two different types of numerous intermediary models. If intermediates function in parallel with one another without impacting one another or whether they operate serially, with intermediaries connected together in a causal chain, is the difference between them. By integrating several intermediate elements in the model, the indirect effects of various theoretical processes may be represented by statistical comparisons, allowing theories to compete with one another in a more realistic setting than before.

## 3.7 The parallel multiple mediator model

In a parallel multiple mediator models, antecedent variable $X$ is modeled as impacting subsequent variable $Y$ both directly and indirectly via two or more mediators, with the constraint that no mediator effects another causally. Figure 3.16 illustrates a statistical diagram of parallel multiple mediator models with $k$ mediators.

As seen in Figure 3.16, parallel multiple mediator models with k mediators contains $k + 1$ subsequent variables (one for each of the $k$ mediators $M$ and one for $Y$), and hence requires $k + 1$ equations to predict all of $X$'s effects on $Y$. These are the equations:

$$M_i = i_{M_i} + a_1 X + e_{M_i} \quad \text{for all } i = 1 \text{ to } k \quad (3.57)$$

$$Y = i_Y + c'X + \sum_{i=1}^{k} b_i M_i + e_Y \quad (3.58)$$

In this set of equations, $a_i$ estimates the effect of $X$ on $M_i$, $b_i$ estimates the influence of $M_i$ on $Y$ when $X$ and the other $k-1$ $M$ variables are held constant, and $c'$ estimates the effect of $X$ on $Y$ when all $k$ $M$ variables are held constant.

As illustrated in Figure 3.16, $X$ is modeled to exert its effect on $Y$ via $k+1$ pathways. One road is direct, flowing directly from $X$ to $Y$ without involving any of the hypothesized mediators, while the remaining k channels are indirect, each involving a single mediator. In a model with many mediators, the indirect effects are referred to as specific indirect effects. Thus, a model with k mediators has k distinct indirect effects, one via M1 (X (M1 (Y), another via M2 (X (M2 (Y), and so on, all the way up to Mk (X (lM$_k$ (lY). As with a straightforward mediation model, the indirect influence of $X$ on $Y$ via a specific mediator $M_i$ is

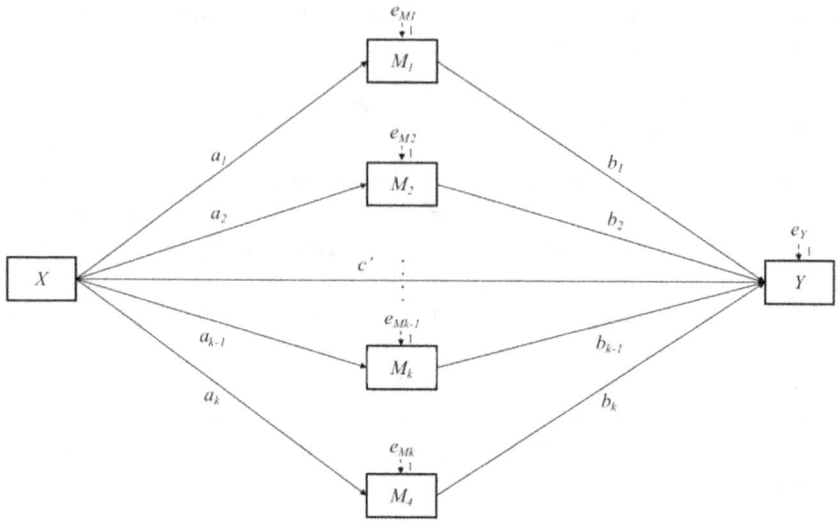

**FIGURE 3.16** A statistical diagram representing a parallel multiple mediator model with *k* mediators.

quantified as the product of the pathways connecting $X$ and $Y$ via $M_i$. Only two pathways connect $X$ to $Y$ via $M_i$ in a simultaneous multiple mediator architecture. The first of these paths corresponds to the influence of $X$ on $M_i$, while the second corresponds to the path between $M_i$ and $Y$. When the regression coefficients for various pathways are put together, the precise indirect influence of $X$ on $Y$ via $M_i$ is obtained. A specific indirect impact is interpreted similarly to the simple mediation model, except that "all other mediators in the model are controlled". Thus, the particular indirect effect of $X$ on $Y$ via $Mi$ is the estimated amount by which two cases that differ by one unit on $X$ are estimated to differ on $Y$ as a result of $X$'s effect on $M_i$, which affects $Y$. When the specific indirect effects are summed together, the overall indirect effect of $X$ on $Y$ via all mediators in the model is obtained. In a model with k mediators, the following is true:

$$\text{Total indirect effect of } X \text{ on } Y = \sum_{i=1}^{k} a_i b_i \tag{3.59}$$

The direct effect of $X$ estimates the estimated difference in $Y$ between two examples that differ by one unit on $X$. As previously stated, this is $c'$ in the model of $Y$ as a result of $X$ and all mediators.

As with the simple mediation model, the overall effect of $X$ is the sum of the direct and indirect effects. From the coefficients in equations (3.47) and (3.48), in a model with $k$ mediators.

$$c = c' + \sum_{i=1}^{k} a_i b_i \tag{3.60}$$

Methodology 133

where $c$ denotes the cumulative effect of X. Additionally, the entire influence can be determined by regressing Y on X. In equation (3.61), the total indirect effect is equal to the difference between the total and direct effects of X:

$$\sum_{i=1}^{k} a_i b_i = c - c' \tag{3.61}$$

## 3.8 The serial multiple mediator model

With the researcher's estimate of the sequential multimediation model, the researcher is able to explore both the direct and indirect impacts of $X$ on the outcome of $Y$, while modeling a process in which $X$ results in $M1$, $M1$ results in $M2$, and so on, with $Y$ as the final outcome.

The complexity of the serial multimediation model grows fast as the number of mediations increases. This is because the number of mediations increases the number of routes between cause and effect. For the sake of this section, sequence mediation is defined as a kind of mediation in which variables presumed to represent causal priors are modeled to have an impact on all following variables in a causal sequence. The fact that this is the most complicated serial mediation model possible is due to the fact that it maximizes the number of pathways that must be estimated.

Figure 3.17 depicts two serial multiple mediator models in the form of statistical diagrams, which may be found in the text. An example of a two-mediator model is shown in Figure 3.17, in which $X$ is represented as having an effect on $Y$ via four paths. There are three types of indirect pathways: one that travels from $X$ to $Y$ via $M1$ exclusively, a second that runs through $M2$ solely, and a third that passes through both $M1$ and M2 in serial, with $M1$ impacting $M2$. The remainder of $X$'s influence is sent directly from $X$ to $Y$, bypassing either $M1$ or $M2$ completely.

This statistical model translates into three equations, because the model contains three consequent variables:

$$M_1 = i_{M_1} + a_1 X + e_{M_1} \tag{3.62}$$
$$M_2 = i_{M_2} + a_2 X + d_{21} M_1 + e_{M_2} \tag{3.63}$$
$$Y = i_Y + c'X + b_1 M_1 + b_2 M_2 + e_Y \tag{3.64}$$

It is important to note that in this set of equations, each consequent contains as antecedents all variables that are supposed to be causally previous. As a result, $M1$ is estimated alone from $X$, $M2$ is calculated solely from $X$ and $M1$, and $Y$ is estimated solely from $X$, $M1$, and $M2$, and $Y$ is estimated solely from $X$, $M1$, and $M2$.

According to the most common scenario, a serial multiple mediator models with k mediators needs the estimation of $k+1$ equations since there are only $k+1$ consequent variables (one for each of the $k$ mediators plus one for $Y$):

$$M_1 = i_{M_1} + a_1 X + e_{M_1} \tag{3.65}$$

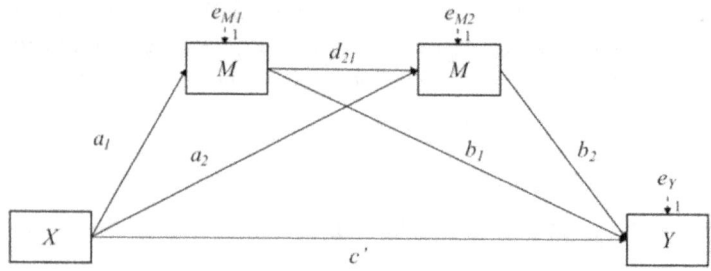

**FIGURE 3.17** A serial multiple mediator models in statistical diagram form with two mediators.

$$M_i = i_{M_i} + a_i X + \sum_{j=1}^{i-1} d_{ij} M_j + e_{M_i} \quad \text{for all } i = 2 \text{ to } k \quad (3.66)$$

$$Y = i_Y + c'X + \sum_{i=1}^{k} b_i M_i + e_Y \quad (3.67)$$

Similarly to the basic and parallel multiple mediation models, the entire influence of X on Y is split into direct and indirect components, which are then combined to form the serial multiple mediation model. There is no change in the direct influence of Y depending on the number of media in the model, and it is always understood as-in both situations that the estimated difference of Y varies by one unit in X but is equal across all media in the model. Direct effects, which are produced by multiplying the regression weights associated with each step in the indirect route, may have a large number of indirect effects, depending on the number of model media in use. The disparity between various units in the two situations may be explained by their assessment of Y in each case. The causal chain from X to the intermediate is represented by the letter X (s). Regardless of how many indirect impacts there are, Y is the sum of all of the indirect effects combined (X). Here's an example of a continuous mediation model with two or more mediations, and the process sequence may have any number of different mediation models in it.

Consider the following scenario: a serial multiple mediator models with two mediators is considered. Three unique indirect impacts and one direct effect are included in the model. Using regression weights that connect X and Y via at least one M, the three unique indirect effects are each calculated as the product of regression weights linking X and Y. The particular indirect impact of X on Y via M1 alone is 1b1, the specific indirect effect through M2 alone is 2b2, and the specific indirect effect through the series connection of M1 and M2 is a1d21b2, as shown in Figure 3.17. If you add up these three indirect affects of X, you obtain the overall indirect influence of X, which is as follows: 1+ 2 + 1+ 1+ 1d21b2. c is the entire indirect impact of X when it is added to the direct effect of X. This is the overall effect of X, which can be determined by merely calculating the regression of Y from the direct effect of X:

$$c = c' + a_1 b_1 + a_2 b_2 + a_1 d_{21} b_2 \quad (3.68)$$

As in the simple and parallel multiple mediator models, the total indirect effect of $X$ on $Y$ in the serial multiple mediator models is the difference between the total effect of $X$ on $Y$ and direct effect of $X$ on $Y$:

$$c - c' = a_1 b_1 + a_2 b_2 + a_1 d_{21} b_2 \tag{3.69}$$

The sole distinction between the serial and parallel multiintermediary models in a model with two intermediaries is the addition of a causal channel from $M1$ to $M2$, which is not present in the serial multiintermediary model. The serial model makes an estimate of this impact, but the parallel model makes the assumption that it is zero, which is akin to altogether eliminating it from consideration. The model may be a combination of parallel and serial intermediary processes when there are more than three intermediates, depending on which pathways between the intermediaries are estimated and which paths are set to zero by being eliminated from the model. For more introduction to the models with parallel and serial mediation, please refer to *Mediation, Moderation, and Conditional Process Analysis* (Hayes, 2013).

## 3.9 Mediation analysis with a multicategorical antecedent

A multicategorical antecedent variable is a categorical antecedent variable that has three or more categories yet is fundamentally categorical. In some circumstances, antecedent variable $X$ is neither dichotomous nor continuous, necessitating the use of a mediation analysis with a multicategorical antecedent. It is possible to use an antecedent variable with $g$ categories as an antecedent variable in a regression model if the antecedent variable is dummy coded and transformed into $g$-1 variables. By utilizing dummy coding, $g$-1 indicator variables can be used to indicate which of the $g$ groups a case belongs to. These indicator variables are then used as antecedents in a regression model to ascertain the group to which a case belongs. When establishing the indicator codes, create $g$-1 variables $D_i$ for each instance and set each variable to one if the case belongs to group 1, and to zero otherwise. Due to the fact that only $g$-1 variables are generated, no group will acquire its own indicator variable. On the other hand, the group that does not obtain its own indicator obtains a zero for all $g$-1 $D_i$ indicator variables. The reference group or baseline group is referred to as this group.

The statistical diagram illustrates a mediation model with a multicategorical $X$ and a single mediator $M$. The model is composed of a single mediator, $M$, and a multicategorical variable, $X$. In equation form, the model is as follows:

$$M = i_M + a_1 D_1 + a_2 D_2 + \cdots + a_{g-1} D_{g-1} + e_M \tag{3.70}$$
$$Y = i_Y + c'_1 D_1 + c'_2 D_2 + \cdots + c'_{g-1} D_{g-1} + c'^{D_1} + e_Y \tag{3.71}$$

When the relative direct and indirect impacts of $X$ are summed together, the relative total effects are obtained.

There are now $g-1$ paths from $X$ to $M$ in Figure 3.18, one for each of the $g-1$ variables representing $X$. In equation (3.70), these are the $g-1$ $a$ coefficients. Each of them corresponds to a portion of $X$'s effect on $M$. Their values and interpretation will be determined by the representation mechanism for the g groups. For example, if $X$ classified three groups and utilized indicator coding with group 3 as the reference, $a_1$ would be the mean difference in $M$ between those in group 1 and those in group 3. That is, $a_1 = \bar{M}_1 - \bar{M}_3$. Similarly, $a_2$ is the mean difference in M between groups 2 and 3, $a_2 = \bar{M}_2 - \bar{M}_3$. When the pattern of values on the $g$-1 D variables is replaced into equation (3.71) for each group, the outcome is M. Thus, once estimated using available data, equation (3.71) generates the $g$ group means on $M$.

It is worth noting that even though the M model contains $g-1$ regression coefficients, the Y model only has a single $M$ regression coefficient. This is represented by the letter b in Equation (3.31). When the two instances vary by one unit on $M$, but are equal in $X$ and predicted to be different in $Y$, it quantifies the degree to which the two cases differ by one unit on $M$. This meaning of "equal on $X$" refers to being a member of the same group. As a result, when $X$ is controlled, b represents an estimate of the effect of $M$ on $Y$. It will be unaffected by $X$'s virtual encoding, for example.

The path from $X$ to $Y$ to $M$ in Figure 3.18 is made up of $g-1$ possible routes. In each technique, the process begins with one of the $Dj$ variables representing the group, then moves on to $M$, and finally to Y. The collection and multiplication of pathways from $X$ to $M$ to $Y$ results in a relative indirect impact of $g-1$, which is denoted by the symbol ajb. Using these methods, each of them measured a portion of the difference in $Y$ across groups that was produced by the interaction of $X$ on $Y$ and the interaction of $X$ on $M$. No single indirect impact exists, although $g-1$ has a significant relative indirect influence on the other variables. The interpretation of the group will be dependent on how the group is coded, just as it is with a route. To determine if $M$ mediates the impact of $X$ on $Y$, one must first determine whether the influence of $X$ on $Y$ is mediated by $M$ by checking whether at least one of the relative indirect effects of $g-1$ is greater than zero in the case of X.

XY is quantified by the direct impact equation (3.71) of the $g-1$ regression coefficient level $g-1$ variable, where $X$ represents each C level and $Y$ represents the total amount of $XY$ in the equation. It is a reasonably direct impact, measured by the $XY$ portion, and it is controlled directly, without the need of $M$. Consider the case when $g = 3$, and in the index coding scheme, the third group is referred to as the reference group. $C'1$ denotes the relative direct effect of the first group on $Y$ as opposed to the third group, and $C'2$ denotes the relative direct influence of the second group on $Y$ as opposed to the third group. $C'1$ denotes the relative direct influence of the first group on $Y$ as opposed to the third group. Instead of using the $M$ attribution mechanism to quantify the difference between groups on Y, these components measure the difference between groups on Y. Determine whether or not the null hypothesis is correct on the basis of the confidence interval or $p$-value, which indicates that the relatively direct impact is zero.

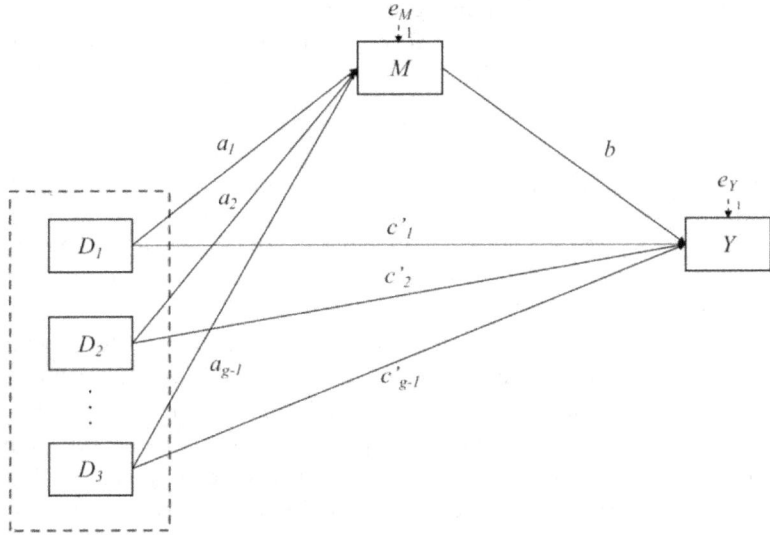

**FIGURE 3.18** A statistical diagram of the simple mediation model with a multicategorical antecedent X with g categories.

It is possible to apply Equation (3.71) to create the adjusted mean that has been determined from the examination of the covariance literature. When the covariate is set to its sample mean, the adjusted Y mean is the estimated Y for each group. In the mediation model, the mediation function behaves mathematically in the same way as a covariate would behave. After controlling M, it is possible to evaluate the effect of X on Y. The difference between these adjusted averages has a relatively direct influence, and this is represented by the relatively direct impact.

The direct and indirect effects of X are added together to obtain the total effect of X in a mediation study. When X is a multicategorical antecedent, both direct and indirect effects are $g-1$ relative. When the relative direct and indirect effects associated with each of the $g-1$ variable coding groups are summed together, a relative total effect is obtained. Thus, the entire relative effect of Dj is $c_j = c'_j + a_j b$. The interpretation of the relative total effects, like the relative direct and indirect effects, is dependent on how the g groups are represented using the $g-1$ variables coding groups.

To quantify the relative impacts of the whole first estimate of the respective direct and indirect effects using 30 and 31-year-old equations, and then add, or conversely, regression on the G1 of the Y variable encoding group, leaving the model with the following parameters:

$$Y = i_Y + c_1 D_1 + c_2 D_2 + \cdots + c_{g-1} D_{g-1} + e_Y \tag{3.72}$$

Equation (3.72) may be estimated by using inferences about the relative total effect, which can be expressed as the confidence interval for each regression coefficient in the g-1 variable coding group, or as the *p*-value equal to zero when the regression coefficient is zero. Equation (3.72) replaces the mean value of each group of variables $g-1$ $D$ into the equation to get the mean value of each group of variables.

## 3.10 Multilevel mediation

When data has a layered structure, researchers are often interested in the complicated interaction between variables, and multilayer mediating effect analysis may be used in a similar way to multilayer SEM.

The notion of multilevel mediation was introduced by Kenny, Kash, and Bolger (Kenny et al., 1998) for the first time. The most basic version of the model consists of three variables: a premise variable $X$, an intermediate variable, and an outcome variable $Y$. The model is composed of three variables. For example, if we consider the secondary intermediary model, there are theoretically eight possible intermediary models based on the different levels of $X$ and $Y$ and $M$, which are as follows: the 1-2-2, 1-2-1, 1-1-2, and 1-1-1 models. The secondary intermediary model is a type of intermediary model in which the $X$ and $Y$ and $M$ levels are different. The model is designated as 1-1-1 if all three variables are at Level-1; the model is designated as 2-1-1 if the pre-dependent variable is at Level-2, while the intermediate and outcome variables are both at Level-1. When both the pre-dependent variable and the intermediate variable are assessed at level 2 and the outcome variable is measured at level 1, they are referred to as the 2-2-1 conditional distribution.

Low-level variables, on the other hand, seldom have an impact on high-level variables, which leads to the existence of four frequent ones in practice. The 2-2-2, 2-2-1, 2-1-1, and 1-1-1 models, in particular, are used to examine the mediating effects of the same-level variables or high-level factors on low-level variables, among other things. The 2-2-2 approach allows you to completely abandon the multilevel model's analytical framework, integrate the data from the first level into the second level, and conduct the standard single-level intermediate variable analysis. As a result, there are only three regularly used models in research considering multilevel mediation effects, namely the 2-2-1, 2-1-1, and 1-1-1 models, which are all derived from the 2-2-1 model (Zhang et al., 2008).

### 3.10.1 The application of mediation

The short version is that structural equation modeling (SEM) is a diverse and powerful multivariate technique that uses conceptual models, route diagrams, and relational regression equation systems to demonstrate the complex and dynamic interactions between observable and unobserved variables. Despite the fact that SEM and regression models seem to be quite similar, the distinction is that in regression models, the dependent variables and independent variables are clearly distinct from one another. These principles are only applicable to relative situations in SEM since the dependent variables in a model equation may become independent variables in other SEM models as a result of this transformation (Bollen, 1989; Kowalski & Tu, 2007). It is the combination of factors that allows SEM to infer possible causation in a given situation.

The causal link and temporal sequence between the variables are represented by the intermediate hypothesis variable. While Baron and Kenny (1986) utilized regression equations to assess the intermediate process in their first analysis of intermediary analysis, Baron and Kenny (Baron & Kenny, 1986) employed a set of regression equations in their second study of intermediary analysis. For this reason, the traditional regression paradigm is not appropriate for modeling causal connections since it pre-designates each variable as having a causal link at the outset of the interaction (Kraemer et al., 2001; MacKinnon & Fairchild, 2009; Rothman & Greenland, 1986). The opposite is true: SEM offers a more appropriate reasoning framework for intermediate analysis and other sorts of causal analysis than other approaches.

There are several benefits of using SEM in the context of intermediate analysis, as previously stated. When there are latent variables in the model, SEM provides for straightforward interpretation and estimate. As a result of its architecture, SEM makes the confirmation of the mediation hypothesis easier to demonstrate since it tests these more sophisticated mediation models in a single study (MacKinnon, 2008). When the mediation process is expanded to include many independent factors, mediation variables, or outcome variables, structural equation modeling (SEM) may be employed. This is in contrast to ordinary regression, which requires the employment of specific techniques to estimate indirect and total effects, among other things (Baron & Kenny, 1986; Clogg et al., 1992; Sobel, 1982). These unique approaches, to obtain the asymptotic variance, depend on the combination of the solutions of two or more equations. Especially difficult is the situation in which the several regression equations describing the intermediate phase each have a different amount of data available.

In addition to providing model information, which indicates the coherence and reasonableness of the causal hypothesis when compared to normal regression techniques, SEM has another significant benefit over these approaches (Bollen & Pearl, 2013; Imai et al., 2010). A possible intermediate model is shown below. Barron and Kenny's conventional regression approach, which they initially suggested, was likewise shown to be less successful. For a final issue, Bollen and Pearl (Bollen & Pearl, 2013) noted that even if the same equation is used in both SEM and regression analysis, the results would vary since the assumptions utilized in each are considerably different. Statistical regression analysis is used to describe the statistical connection based on conditional expectations, while structural equation modeling (SEM) is used to describe the functional relationship stated using conceptual models, route diagrams, and mathematical equations. As a consequence, SEM is more accurate than ordinary regression analysis at expressing the dual role of causality, the simultaneity of indirect and direct impact, the source of the outcome, and the effect of intervention in the hypothetical mediation process.

Intermediary analysis may be performed using SEM programs and associated software packages. Furthermore, in addition to particular software products such as LISREL and MPlus and EQS and Amos, SEM may also be implemented in common statistical software packages such as R, SAS, and STATA as well as the statistical software package Statistica. These packages give inference based on ML, extended least squares, and weighted least squares methods, among other methods.

### 3.10.2 Literature review of the application of mediation and SEM in PISA reading

PISA is characterized by its policy orientation, that is, PISA-related research links data on student learning outcomes with data on other key factors that may affect student learning inside and outside the school (OECD, 2019). Therefore, the probability of causality should be reliably analyzed. Mediation analysis is considered to be a powerful tool to explore the underlying mechanism of independent variables and dependent variables and provides more reliable evidence for their possible causality. Therefore, intermediary analysis has always been a useful technique for exploring PISA data (such as Chen & HU, 2020) and inferring possible outcomes of policy implications (Grek, 2009).

In most PISA-related mediation studies, significant results with teaching significance have been produced (Xie & Ma, 2019; Yildirim, 2012), while a few studies have proven that there are no significant mediation results. For example, there is no evidence that in any country, the impact of household income is regulated by cultural resources, wealth (using household assets as indicators), or educational resources (Marks & Pokropek, 2019), and the Big-Fish-Little-Pond effect. In particular, the close relationship between the Pond effect and the clear school-level tracking duration is not affected by the size of the difference in performance between schools (Salchegger, 2016).

PISA is characterized by its data hierarchy, that is, student-level data is nested at the school level, and then further nested at the country level (OECD, 2009). Whether multilevel modeling is required is proved by calculating the intra-class correlation coefficient (ICC). As a general rule of thumb, an ICC value greater than 0.1 indicates that a multilevel analysis is required, because it means that the total variance greater than 0.1 is explained by the variance between levels (Snijders & Bosker, 2012). Due to the hierarchical characteristics of PISA data, most studies use multilevel modeling (Wu et al., 2020; Yi & Kim, 2019). The number of studies using single-level meditation is limited, because even if PISA has data Hierarchical characteristics, not all selected variances meet the standard of ICC greater than 0.1. For example, after proving that ICC is less than 0.1, use a single-level intermediary to explore family and school factors such as SES, parents' education-related beliefs, and school performance levels are related to

Turkish students' mathematics scores, and this association Is it regulated by students' math-specific motivational beliefs (Niehues et al., 2020). Three first-level regressions were used to explore the mediating role of online reading activities and ICT use in explaining gender differences in digital reading performance (Cheung et al., 2013).

A linear regression model that does not consider the data level will not be able to identify the variance within and between the layers. The use of multilevel models, also known as hierarchical linear models (HLM) (Bryk & Raudenbush, 1992), recognizes the fact that students are nested in schools and countries. The results measure the relative differences between students and schools in the same school, so it can be evaluated. Two-level intermediary analysis shows that teaching support and reading participation can mediate the relationship between gender differences in reading performance (student level) and gender composition differences (school level) and students' digital reading performance (Mak et al., 2017); five strategies to adjust the relationship between student SES (level 1), school SES (level 2) and student reading, math and science scores (Callan et al., 2017); and solve The ability to question plays a mediating role between immigration status and student academic performance (Martin et al., 2012). The three-level multilevel multiple intermediary regression model is also used to explore PISA data, with students at the first level, schools at the second level, and countries at the third level (Callan et al., 2017).

Although HLM has its advantages in using hierarchical features to analyze data, it also has obvious disadvantages. HLM is essentially regression-based, so it is difficult to analyze multilevel models with latent variables. PISA has multiple data types. In addition to measuring students' academic performance, PISA also collects relevant data on students' backgrounds, learning attitudes, and behavior patterns. So we have collected different types of data, which can be roughly divided into two categories, continuous data, and categorical data. For continuous data, students' academic performance falls into this category, including students' performance in reading, mathematics, and science. In addition, the variables derived from considering several issues in specific aspects of the assessment are also continuous. The PISA 2018 Student Questionnaire provides 39 derivative variables based on the IRT scale, such as Joy/Like Reading derivative variables (JOYREAD), which are derived from five project parameters. Using a five-item scale (ST160), students are required to rate their attitudes towards reading pleasure on a four-level scale ranging from "strongly disagree", "disagree", "agree" to "strongly agree". In terms of categorical data, the data collected based on the Likert scale items are also categorical data, and student gender information is a typical categorical data. Considering the different types of PISA data, factor analysis is needed to explore the relationship between different types of data. Compared with SEM, HLM has a poorer ability to handle different variables and relationships between variables. The mediation analysis implemented by SEM allows various data types to be processed in PISA, and there are many mediation analysis studies related to PISA that deal with different types of variables. In Pisa-related research, students' academic performance is usually used as a dependent variable to explore the factors that affect students' reading (Hahnel et al., 2016; Lee & Wu, 2013; Lenkeit et al., 2020; Notten & Becker, 2017; Schoor, 2016; Torppa et al., 2018; Wu, 2014), mathematics (Kriegbaum & Spinath, 2016; Marks & Pokropek, 2019; Martin et al., 2012; Niehues et al., 2020) and scientific performance (Kang & Keinonen, 2017; Liou, 2021; Martin et al., 2012; Nagengast & Marsh, 2012; Wu et al., 2020; Yi & Kim, 2019).

Through the SEM analysis of the underlying variables or the factors derived from the observational variables, the first-level intermediary analysis explored the influence of teacher-led teaching practice on scientific achievement mediated by students' attitudes towards science (Liou, 2021). The mediating role of motivation in the relationship between parental SES and children's standardized test scores in mathematics (Kriegbaum & Spinath, 2016); the impact of art-related ICT use on problem-solving skills (Liem et al., 2014); to what extent does the immigration status mediated by psychological characteristics affect academic performance (Xu & Wu, 2017); whether the learning experience based on inquiry has a positive predictive effect on students' career aspirations, and its impact whether it is regulated by the expected result (Kang & Keinonen, 2017).

The intermediary analysis performed by SEM also supports multilevel modeling. ICC first proved the need for multilevel modeling in the second-level intermediary analysis. Rasmusson and Aberg-Bengtsson (2015) found that the ICC is between 0.17 and 0.20, indicating the need for multilevel modeling, and the selected variables are all at the individual level. Therefore, the author decided to calculate a two-level model and isolate the school-level variance by simply allowing covariance of the dominant variable at the second level. Similar solutions can be found when exploring whether intrinsic value plays a mediating role between growth feedback and achievement (Niehues et al., 2020). Although all the leading variables are at the student level, to explain the school-level differences, we included school-level covariates such as school location, type, scale, average school ESCS, gender composition, and science teacher education background. The other two levels of intermediary analysis explored variables at the student and school levels to analyze whether the negative environmental impact of academic self-concept on career aspirations is regulated by the academic self-concept of average secondary school grades (Nagengast & Marsh, 2012). The mediating role of scientific interest and self-efficacy between informal science learning and scientific performance, school average SES and school science education resources (Tang & Zhang, 2020). In addition, a three-level multilevel SEM with latent variables is used to study the relationship between students' perceptual inquiry teaching practice and teacher-led teaching practice (level 1), teacher self-efficacy (level 2), and cultural values (level 3) (Bonneville-Roussy et al., 2019).

## *3.10.3 The weakness of mediation analysis in PISA-related studies*

Some researchers suspect that the causal step approach actually leads to correlation rather than causality (Maxwell et al., 2011; Trafimow, 2015). The nature of PISA data collection makes it almost impossible to clearly prove cause and effect. At best, it establishes covariance between variables in a causal system. But this is the problem with all statistical methods: they cannot prove causality. In fact, even simple regression analysis has the same problem. Establishing causality is not so much data analysis as it is research design and logical analysis. Statistical methods are simple mathematical tools that allow researchers to identify the order in chaos, or deal with noise signals in random backgrounds, or other processed signals that have not yet been incorporated into the model. Researchers' inferences about causality are not a mathematical product of the modeling process. Rather, reasoning is the product of how the researcher interprets the observed correlation, that is, the signal extracted from the noise. Therefore, researchers should strive to design rigorous studies so that they can make clear causal inferences when possible. Recognizing the limitations of the data collected, researchers should interpret the results with due care. Before establishing the model, it is necessary to propose the causal relationship with the hypothetical variables. The causal relationship represented by each arrow in the mediation model includes "$X{\rightarrow}Y$", "$X{\rightarrow}M$" and "$M{\rightarrow}a$". All causality should be based on rational evidence, or supported by some theory, literature or empirical knowledge. In summary, every relationship in the causal chain must be supported to make assumptions and models; otherwise, there is no basis for assumptions. If there are only "$X{\rightarrow}M$" and "$M{\rightarrow}Y$", we can also infer "$X{\rightarrow}Y$" and make assumptions.

To solve the limitations of one-time experimental research, a series of experimental research can be helpful to a certain extent (Stone-Romero & Rosopa, 2010). First, the researchers tried to determine that after the experimental study of $M$ and $Y$ in $X$ was successful, the cause of $M$ could be established in the second experimental study, instead of $Y$ causing $M$. From such an analysis (which may include moderate components) can be pieced together to establish indirect attributes (conditions). Second, collecting data on the same variables over time has some advantages as an alternative method of studying causal processes, and more and more literature focuses on longitudinal mediation analysis (Bauer et al., 2006; Cole & Maxwell, 2003; Selig & Preacher, 2009). Cook and Campbell (1979) also proposed three criteria for establishing causality, namely covariance, chronological order, and elimination of competing explanations. Based on these standards, social science research can analyze causality from the following aspects: (1) theoretical analysis and causal reasoning; (2) inference from experimental design; and (3) follow-up study design.

For theoretical analysis and causal reasoning methods, please consider the following reasoning. For the two related variables $X$ and $Y$, the following theoretical analysis can be used to improve the confidence that "$X$ leads to $Y$": (1) Observe the properties of variables $X$ and $Y$, and judge that $X$ is a more basic (or more durable and stable) Attributes are better than general $Y$ attributes, basic attributes affect state attributes, long-term attributes affect temporary attributes, and stable attributes affect unstable attributes. Take students' intelligence and academic performance as examples. The former is more important. Therefore, it is intelligence that affects academic performance. Another example is the relationship between adult height and weight. Height is more stable than weight, so in most cases, height affects weight. As for sex, it is biologically determined by chromosomes. Over time, the gender variable is more important and stable than any other variable in the social sciences. Therefore, all gender-related variables in social sciences can be said to be affected by gender, that is, gender is the "cause" of these variables. (2) When the causal order of $X$ is reversed, the result is difficult to interpret. In other words, "$Y{\rightarrow}X$" is not as easy to explain as "$X{\rightarrow}Y$". For example, we found that the average grades of students who participated in the cram school were not as good as those of the students who participated in the cram school. Some people might think that the cram school did not improve their grades. What is obviously overlooked here is that poor performance is the reason for participating in the remedial class, not the result. (3) Try to eliminate the influence caused by general causes. For example, the age of marriage is positively correlated with annual medical expenses. Marriage age and annual medical expenses are not the reasons, because these two variables have a common cause: age.

The second suggested method is to infer causality from the experimental design. The key to experimental design is to control the external factors that have nothing to do with the purpose of the experiment but may affect the dependent variable, and to see whether the change of the independent variable causes the change of the dependent variable. Pizza research, research doping research is based on second-hand data, which means that it is unrealistic for researchers to participate in the initial research design, but the inspiration for this method is that researchers consider and control factors that may affect the final result. As a result, a more concentrated causal relationship can be preliminarily inferred.

The third method is to design follow-up studies. Follow-up research refers to the repeated measurement (twice or more) of the independent variables, intermediate variables, and dependent variables of the research object over a period of time to obtain diachronic data. Subsequent mediation analysis is used to test whether the independent variables will affect the intermediate variables of subsequent observations, and whether the intermediate variables will affect the dependent variables of subsequent observations. Since the effects of certain variables may take a period of time to be observed, follow-up research is needed, which is called the lag effect. For example, changes in academic performance may have a direct impact on confidence, but over time, changes in confidence may have an impact on academic performance. In this case, cross-sectional experimental data cannot be used for causal inference, while longitudinal data need to be obtained through follow-up research (Cole & Maxwell, 2003).

In summary, whether the intermediary analysis is only a correlation analysis depends on the content. Correlation cannot prove causality. The causality in regression or mediation analysis depends on theories other than statistics (including theoretical analysis, experiments, and follow-up investigations). Researchers should not lightly assume that mediation analysis necessarily implies causality or simple correlation. The combination of solid theoretical analysis and statistical verification has strengthened researchers' confidence in causal reasoning. All methods can only prove causality to a certain extent, and experimental design is the most reliable method. However, none of these methods can ultimately prove causality, but can only refute it. The establishment of causality ultimately needs to be tested in practice.

### *3.10.4 The main software and environments for DM*

#### *3.10.4.1 WEKA*

Waikato Environment for Knowledge Analysis (WEKA) is a free, non-commercial (as opposed to Clementine, SPSS's commercial data mining product), open source machine learning, and data mining software suit based on JAVA environment. It implements a great number of machine learning algorithms for performing different DM tasks such as data preprocessing, classification, clustering, association rule mining, and visualization. WEKA supports a series of document types (e.g., arff, xrff, and csv).

#### *3.10.4.2 SPSS*

SPSS is a statistical product and service solution software launched by IBM for statistical analysis operations, data mining, predictive analysis, and decision support tasks. SPSS has a variety of practical analysis methods from basic statistical feature descriptions to various high-level analysis such as non-parametric test and survival analysis. In addition, SPSS also has a powerful drawing function, easy to learn and use, simple operation; compatible with a variety of data file formats, according to the needs of users, select the required module. SPSS comes with SaxBasic built in, which is mixed with the syntax command language for efficiency and ease of use by advanced users.

#### *3.10.4.3 Python*

Python differs from other major compiled languages like C and C++ because the code for Python doesn't need to be built and linked like code in those languages. Although Python is a very popular programming language, it also has its own flaws. One of the most important limitations it suffers from is execution speed. As an interpreted language, it is slow compared to an assembled language. This limit can be a bit restrictive in situations where extremely high-performance code is required. This is a major area of improvement for future implementations of Python, and each subsequent Python release will address it. While we must admit that it will never be as fast as assembly language, it makes up for it by being efficient in other ways.

### 3.10.4.4 Mplus

Mplus is a statistical modeling software allowing for cross-sectional and longitudinal data to be analyzed together, single- and multilayer data, data from different mothers, with or without visible heterogeneity. The variables that can be analyzed and visible are continuous (continuous data), censored (censored data), binary (two-category data), ordered categorical (ordinal), unordered categorical (nominal), counts (count variable) or a combination of these variable types. Mplus also has special functions for missing values, complex survey data, and multilevel data. In addition, Mplus is powerful for any model that can generate and analyze data in a Monte Carlo simulation study.

Mplus was developed by the Muthen couple (Muthén & Muthén, 1998), both of whom are also very accomplished in psychology. The main functions of Mplus include regression analysis and PA, exploratory factor analysis, CFA, structural equation modeling, growth modeling and survival analysis, mixed modeling, multilevel mixed modeling, etc. It is different from other statistical analysis software in the following aspects: first, different models and analysis methods can be selected according to different processing requirements. Second, it can handle cross-sectional and longitudinal data, single-layer and multilayer data. Third, it can be well analyzed for the combination of various data types, such as observation variables as categorical variables, latent category analysis, exploratory structural equation model (ESEM), etc.

### 3.10.4.5 R language

R language could be regarded as an implementation of the S language. As a statistical analysis software, R could run on different operating systems such as UNIX, Windows and Macintosh, and embeds a very convenient and practical system. As a programmable language and an open statistical programming environment, the syntax is easy to understand, and it is easy to learn and master the syntax of the language (R Core Team, 2019). Except that the graphic output is in another window, its input and output windows are all performed in the same window. The output graphics can be directly saved as a series of image formats.

### *3.10.5 The rationale for using ML in this study*

The difference between machine learning methods and the conventional statistical methods (i.e., HLM and SEM) is that the former intends to build effective models which could predict the outcome variables, while the latter is suited for the examination of the model estimation (Shmueli, 2010). Compared with conventional methods, machine learning algorithms enjoy the hard-wired virtue of conducting analysis using large database. Regarding data set consisting of complex variables, conventional methods are often dwarfed by SVM (Chen et al., 2021a). They are powerful in clarifying the complex interactions between these factors, and in solving the problem of high-dimensionality (Alzahrani & Abdullah, 2019). Recent years have witnessed the wide application of machine learning methods to the analysis of international educational data sets for a better understanding of students' academic performance (e.g., Chen et al., 2022; HU et al., 2021, 2022). These studies have provided a solid basis for future investigations using the trending machine learning methods. Additionally, the rapid development of educational data mining also calls for a further invitation of novel methods into this promising field, especially in reading education.

The selection of the ML methods is both theory-driven and data-driven. The triennial global assessment, namely, PISA, upgrades at a fast updating speed. The main areas of each round of the assessment appear similar but run with a different focus every three years. This research intends to investigate the collective impacts of factors of different levels from a great number of variables for a deeper analysis of the individual characteristics and external factors that may shape the students reading outcomes. Echoing the numerous variables both in the dynamic model of educational effectiveness and in the PISA data set, the machine learning methods are thus selected in this analysis to address the questions proposed in this study. Of all the machine learning algorithms, the SVM is selected due to its effectiveness and high accuracy in detecting latent variables as well as the collective effects of the feature set (HU et al., 2021).

## 3.11 Data extraction and pre-processing for the PISA data set

### 3.11.1 The domains of data pre-processing

Data pre-processing technology is created to increase the quality of data mining. Data preparation can be done in a variety of ways, including data cleansing, data integration, data transformation, data reduction, and so on. These data processing methods are utilized before data mining, which dramatically increases the quality of data mining patterns and cuts down on the time spent mining. Before categorizing or grouping the gathered data, it is important to do processing such as review, screening, and sorting.

#### 3.11.1.1 Data evaluation

In terms of audit content and methodology, statistical data received through various sources differ. The original data will be scrutinized primarily for completeness and correctness. The purpose of an integrity audit is to see if there are any omissions in the units or persons being examined, and if all investigation items or indications are filled in completely. The two basic features of accuracy auditing are: First, determine if the data accurately reflect the objective current condition and whether the content is accurate; second, determine whether the data is incorrect, whether the calculation is proper, and so on. Logic and calculation checks are the most common approaches for verifying data correctness. The purpose of a logic check is to see if the data follows logic, if the content is acceptable, and if there are any inconsistencies between distinct items or figures. This strategy is best for auditing qualitative (high-quality) data. The purpose of the calculation check is to see whether any of the data in the questionnaire has any problems in the calculation results or techniques. It's mostly utilized to look over numerical (quantitative) data.

In the case of second-hand data collected through other means, we should examine its applicability and timeliness in addition to its integrity and correctness. Secondary data might originate from a number of different sources. Some data may have been collected through a particular inquiry for a specific reason or processed to meet the demands of that purpose. Users should first evaluate the source of data, data quality, and important background information, to assess whether these data satisfy the demands of their own analysis and research, whether they need to be reprocessed and rearranged, and whether they can be applied mechanically. In addition, the data's timeliness should be examined. Because of various issues with strong timeliness, if the gathered data arrives too late, the research's relevance may be lost. In general, wherever feasible, the most recent statistics should be utilized. It is required to filter and sort the data after it has been evaluated and confirmed to be acceptable for real purposes.

### *3.11.1.2 Data filtering*

Errors discovered during the audit will be remedied to the greatest extent practicable. After the investigation, if the data inaccuracies cannot be fixed, or if certain data does not satisfy the inquiry's standards and cannot be made up, the data must be screened. Data filtering has two aspects: the first is to eliminate unqualified data or data with evident faults, and the second is to filter out data that satisfies particular criteria and delete data that does not. In market research, economic analysis, and managerial decision-making, data screening is critical.

### *3.11.1.3 Data sorting*

Data sorting is the process of arranging data in a certain order so that researchers may browse the data for clear traits or patterns, as well as hints to solve issues. Sorting also aids in the verification and correction of data, as well as providing a foundation for categorization or grouping. In certain circumstances, one of the goals of analysis is to rank things. Sorting may be done quickly and easily with the aid of a computer. There are only two ways to categorize numerical data: growing and decreasing. Order statistics refers to the sorted data.

## 3.11.2 Missing data handling

There may be some erroneous and missing values in the data as a result of survey, coding, and input problems, which must be addressed accordingly. Although we aim to obtain entire sets of data as researchers, we frequently encounter missing data. Estimation, entire case deletion, variable deletion, and paired deletion are all common processing methods.

1. Prediction. The easiest method is to use the sample mean, median, or mode of a variable to replace the erroneous and missing values. This approach is straightforward; however, it fails to take into account all of the data's existing information, resulting in a significant mistake. Another method is to use correlation analysis or logical inference between variables to estimate the responses of respondents to other questions. For example, product ownership may be linked to family income. The likelihood of having this product may be computed based on the respondents' household income.
2. To delete samples with missing values, use casewise deletion. Due to the possibility of missing values in many surveys, this method may result in a considerable reduction in the effective sample size and the inability to fully utilize the data gathered. As a result, it's only appropriate when critical variables are absent or the fraction of samples with incorrect or missing values is very low.
3. Variable deletion: If a variable has a lot of incorrect and missing values, and the variable isn't critical to the problem being examined, you might want to consider eliminating it. This method decreases the number of variables to be analyzed while maintaining the same sample size.
4. Pairwise deletion retains all variables and samples in the data set while using a specific code (typically 9,99,999, etc.) to denote incorrect and missing values. However, because only samples with complete responses are employed in the specified computation, the effective sample size of various analyses will vary owing to the many factors involved. This is a conservative processing approach that preserves as much information in the data collection as possible.

Different processing methods might affect the analysis findings, especially if the missing data are not random and the variables are highly connected. In maintaining the data's integrity, invalid and missing values should be avoided in the inquiry.

Interpolating missing values with plausible values (PVs) is a frequent method in addition to removing missing data. Its inspiration comes from the fact that interpolating the missing value with the highest feasible value results in less information loss than removing all incomplete samples. When it comes to data mining, we're generally dealing with a vast database containing dozens, if not hundreds, of properties. We lose a big number of other attribute values due to the lack of one attribute value. Because this loss is a significant waste of data, the concept and method of interpolating missing values with PVs is developed. The methods listed below are widely utilized.

1. Imputation based on the mean. Fixed distance type and non-fixed distance type attributes are the two types of data attributes. If the missing value is of fixed distance type, it is interpolated with the average value of the existing value of the attribute; if the missing value is of non-fixed distance type, the mode of the attribute (i.e., the value with the highest frequency) is used to supplement the missing value, according to the mode principle in statistics.
2. Use the same mean imputation method. Single value imputation uses the same mean imputation procedure. The distinction is that it uses a hierarchical clustering model to forecast the kind of missing variables before employing this method of mean imputation. Assuming $x = ()$ is a complete variable and $Y$ is a variable with missing values, cluster $X$ or its subset first, and then interpolate the mean value of distinct classes based on the class of missing cases. If the inserted explanatory variables and y are to be studied in a future statistical analysis, this imputation procedure will introduce autocorrelation into the model, causing analysis problems.
3. Estimation of ML. Under the assumption that the model is valid for the whole sample and that the deletion type is random deletion, the unknown parameters may be approximated using the marginal distribution of the observed data (little and Rubin). ML estimate with missing data is another name for this approach. The computational approach usually employed in practice for ML parameter estimate is expectation maximization (EM). This strategy is more appealing than eliminating cases and imputation of a single value. It is built on a key premise: it can handle big samples. There are enough effective samples to ensure that the ML estimate is asymptotically unbiased and follows the normal distribution. However, this approach has the potential to slip into a local extremum, the convergence speed is slow, and the computation is complicated.
4. Imputation with several variables (MI). Bayesian estimate inspired the concept of multivalued imputation. The value to be interpolated is thought to be random, and its value is derived from the observed value. In reality, the interpolated values are normally calculated first, and then various noises are added to provide many groups of potential imputation values. Using a selection basis, choose the most appropriate imputation value. The three phases of the multiple imputation approach are as follows: (1) For each null value, develop a set of alternative imputation values that reflect the unresponsive model's uncertainty; each value may be used to interpolate missing values in the data set to produce many full data sets. (2) The statistical procedure for the entire data set is used to examine each interpolated data set. (3) To obtain the final imputation value, the scoring algorithm selects the results from each imputation data set.

Multiple imputation and Bayesian estimate are similar in concept, but multiple imputation compensates for some of the Bayesian estimation's flaws. The greatest likelihood approach is used to estimate Bayesian estimates first. The greatest likelihood technique necessitates the accuracy of the model's shape. If the parameter form is erroneous, we will arrive at the incorrect conclusion, i.e., the prior distribution will influence the posterior distribution's correctness. Multiple imputation is based on the principle of asymptotically full data for large samples. Because the quantity of data in data mining is so huge, the previous distribution will have little effect on the outcome, hence prior distribution will have little effect on the outcome. Second, the Bayesian estimate does not employ the connection between parameters and simply requires knowledge of the prior distribution of unknown parameters. Multiple imputation uses the link between parameters to estimate the joint distribution of parameters.

At the same time, MI retains the two primary benefits of single imputation, namely, the capacity to use a comprehensive data analysis strategy and incorporate data collector expertise. When compared to single imputation, multiple imputation offers three major advantages: To begin with, random sample imputation improves the accuracy of estimation by representing the data distribution. Second, when multiple MI is random sampling under a given model, it may simply fuse complete data inference in a straightforward method to provide effective inference, that is, it represents the additional variance caused by missing values. Third, utilizing the whole data technique, the sensitivity of inference under alternative models without answers may be directly evaluated. MI also has the following drawbacks: (1) multiple imputation needs more effort than single imputation; (2) multiple imputation data sets demand more storage space; and (3) evaluating multiple imputation data sets requires more effort than single imputation.

The aforementioned four imputation strategies have a favorable effect on random missing value imputation. The two mean imputation methods are the easiest to use and have been in the past, but they contain a lot of sample interference. The estimated value of the parameter deviates substantially from the true value, especially when the imputed value is employed as an explanatory variable in regression. ML estimation and multiple imputation, on the other hand, are two superior imputation approaches. ML lacks the uncertainty of multiple imputation; hence, multivalued imputation approaches are becoming more popular.

In the field of EDM and large-scale educational assessments, there are also a series of emerging and commonly-used imputation algorithms in previous research. Some software also provides insightful methods for missing data imputation. For instance, in WEKA, for numeric attributes, the software can help replace missing values with the mean, and for nominal attributes, it can replace missing values with its mode (the most occurring value). For instance, the C4.5 algorithm aims to manage missing data with a probabilistic approach. Different from the main imputation methods (e.g., Mean, hot/cold deck, regression, and interpolation), this approach seems to perform better in large databases with a great percentage of missing values (Grzymala-Busse & HU, 2001). In addition, J48 helps to manage missing data in any predictor variable selected in a node by assigning to each derived branch "a weight proportional to the number of training instances going down that branch, normalized by the total number of

**152** Methodology

training instances" (Witten et al., 2016, p. 230). In R language, the md pattern of mice package could form a missing table, while the central Imputation() function of the DMwR package uses the central trend value of the data to fill in the missing values. In SPSS, in addition to the pair-wise deletion, the MI is the most advanced data imputation method. These tools have provided efficient ways for researchers to deal with a large number of missing data.

### 3.11.3 Data

Data were drawn from the PISA 2018 data set (URL: http://www.oecd.org/pisa/data/2018database/). The two compulsory questionnaires, the student questionnaire and the school questionnaire, were selected in this study and cover the majority of factors in other optional questionnaires (e.g., the questionnaires for parents and teachers), thus providing sufficient data for research. Overall, the detailed descriptions for the original 146 variables were provided below in the **Appendix** for ease of reference.

Students from OECD countries were selected in our analysis because of their relatively social and economic similarities, the great proportion of academic resilient students in OECD countries, and the high scale reliabilities of variables in OECD countries (see Figure 3.19). First, OECD countries boast similar social (i.e., the upholding of market value and market economy) and economic (i.e., developed countries with a relatively high living standard) development statuses. Considering that country-level factors play an important role in students' science performance, the cultural and economic homogeneity of OECD countries could to a large extent cushion the distinguished social and economic differences among countries. In this regard, within OECD countries, students characterized as high

**FIGURE 3.19** The 38 OECD countries selected in this study.

performers and low performers in reading were extracted. The upshot is that except for samples with a large proportion of missing values, 38 OECD participating countries with 84,660 students in total were selected for this study (Table 3.2).

**TABLE 3.2** Demographic information of samples

| Country/Region | Observation | Female (percentage) | High Performers (percentage) | Low Performers (percentage) |
| --- | --- | --- | --- | --- |
| Australia | 4,027 | 1,844(45.8%) | 1,675(41.6%) | 2,348(58.4%) |
| Austria | 1,901 | 829(43.6%) | 518(27.2%) | 1,383(72.8%) |
| Belgium | 2,236 | 1,063(47.5%) | 769(34.4%) | 1,467(65.6%) |
| Canada | 5,826 | 2,720(46.7%) | 2,744(47.1%) | 3,082(52.9%) |
| Chile | 1,892 | 849(44.9%) | 273(14.4%) | 1,619(85.6%) |
| Colombia | 3,429 | 1,709(49.8%) | 99(2.9%) | 3,330(97.1%) |
| Costa Rica | 2,756 | 1,302(47.1%) | 41(1.4%) | 2,715(98.5%) |
| Czech Republic | 1,961 | 901(45.9%) | 803(40.9%) | 1,158(59.1%) |
| Denmark | 1,473 | 670(45.5%) | 426(28.9%) | 1,047(71.1%) |
| Estonia | 1,310 | 635(48.5%) | 737(56.3%) | 573(43.7%) |
| Finland | 1,536 | 734(47.8%) | 796(51.8%) | 740(48.2%) |
| France | 1,701 | 723(42.5%) | 510(30%) | 1,191(70%) |
| Germany | 1,350 | 588(43.6%) | 525(38.9%) | 825(61.1%) |
| Greece | 2,057 | 801(38.9%) | 250(12.2%) | 1,807(87.8%) |
| Hungary | 1,462 | 661(45.2%) | 317(21.7%) | 1,145(78.3%) |
| Iceland | 999 | 409(40.9%) | 201(20.1%) | 798(79.9%) |
| Ireland | 1,298 | 611(47.1%) | 641(49.4%) | 657(50.6%) |
| Israel | 2,599 | 1,173(45.1%) | 653(25.1%) | 1,946(74.9%) |
| Italy | 3,010 | 1,208(40.1%) | 598(19.9%) | 2,412(80.1%) |
| Japan | 1,642 | 743(45.2%) | 609(37.1%) | 1,033(62.9%) |
| Korea | 1,816 | 797(43.9%) | 855(47.1%) | 961(52.9%) |
| Latvia | 1,371 | 535(39.0%) | 207(15.1%) | 1,164(84.9) |
| Lithuania | 2,077 | 813(39.1%) | 311(15.0%) | 1,766(85.0%) |
| Luxembourg | 1,831 | 808(44.1%) | 375(20.5%) | 1456(79.5%) |
| Mexico | 2,832 | 1,416(50%) | 69(2.4%) | 2763(97.6%) |
| Netherlands | 1,476 | 656(44.4%) | 414(28.0%) | 1,062(72.0%) |
| New Zealand | 1,772 | 854(48.2%) | 771(43.5%) | 1,001(56.5%) |
| Norway | 1,611 | 705(43.8%) | 576(35.8%) | 1,035(64.2%) |
| Poland | 1,490 | 679(45.6%) | 693(46.5%) | 797(53.5%) |
| Portugal | 1,577 | 672(42.6%) | 418(26.5%) | 1159(73.5%) |
| Slovak Republic | 1,934 | 827(42.8%) | 280(14.5%) | 1,654(85.5%) |
| Slovenia | 1,690 | 639(37.8%) | 369(21.8%) | 1,321(78.2%) |
| Spain | 8,954 | 3,900(43.6%) | 1,880(21%) | 7,074(79%) |
| Sweden | 1,604 | 752(46.9%) | 697(43.5%) | 907(56.5%) |
| Switzerland | 1,714 | 696(40.6%) | 424(24.7%) | 1,290(75.3%) |
| Turkey | 2,047 | 828(40.4%) | 220(10.7%) | 1,827(89.3%) |
| United Kingdom | 2,994 | 1,382(46.2%) | 1,140(38.1%) | 1,854(61.9%) |
| United States | 1,409 | 671(47.6%) | 560(39.7%) | 849(60.3%) |
| Total | 84,660 | 37,803(44.9%) | 23,444(29.4%) | 61,216(71.8%) |

*Source:* PISA 2018 database.

## 3.11.4 Variables

The dependent variable of the study was dichotomous: high performance with science scores at Levels 5 and 6 and low-performance scores at Levels 1a and 1b. According to PISA 2015, 10 PVs were used to show participants' reading performance; however, "there are no significant differences between using one plausible value or five plausible values, due to the large number of the samples" (OECD, 2009, p. 48). Therefore, PV1READ (the first PV 1 in Reading) was randomly selected to represent each student's science score, which is a fair and accurate method for estimating their real reading literacy (Gorostiaga & Rojo-Álvarez, 2016). The independent factors/variables extracted from the student questionnaire and school questionnaire were analyzed at three levels, namely, at the school, classroom, and student levels. Some variables were directly extracted from the original questions, while others were derived variables that were developed by PISA 2018 from a combination of different questions.

## References

Alker H. (1969). A typology of ecological fallacies. In M. Dogan and S. Rokkan (Eds.), *Quantitative ecological analysis in the social sciences* (pp. 69–86). Cambridge: The MIT Press.

Alzahrani, N. A., & Abdullah, M. A. (2019). Student engagement effectiveness in E-learning system. *Bioscience Biotechnology Research Communications*, *12*(1), 208–218. https://doi.org/10.21786/bbrc/12.1/24

Areepattamannil, S. (2014). International note: What factors are associated with reading, mathematics, and science literacy of Indian adolescents? A multilevel examination. *Journal of Adolescence*, *37*(4), 367–372. https://doi.org/10.1016/j.adolescence.2014.02.007

Arya, D. J., McClung, N. A., Katznelson, N., & Scott, L. (2016). Language ideologies and literacy achievement: six multilingual countries and two international assessments, *International Journal of Multilingualism*, *13*(1), 40–60, https://doi.org/10.1080/14790718.2015.1021352

Baldi, P., Brunak, S., Chauvin, Y., Andersen, C. A., & Nielsen, H. (2000). Assessing the accuracy of prediction algorithms for classification: An overview. *Bioinformatics*, *16*, 412–424. https://doi.org/10.1093/bioinformatics/16.5.412

Baron, R. M., & Kenny, D. A. (1986). The moderator-mediator variable distinction in social psychological research: Conceptual, strategic, and statistical considerations. *Journal of Personality and Social Psychology*, *51*(6), 1173–1182. https://doi.org/10.1037/0022-3514.51.6.1173

Bauer, D. J., Preacher, K. J., & Gil, K. M. (2006). Conceptualizing and testing random indirect effects and moderated mediation in multilevel models: New procedures and recommendations. *Psychological Methods*, *11*(2), 142–163. https://doi.org/10.1037/1082-989X.11.2.142

Bollen, K., & Pearl, J. (2013). Eight myths about causality and structural equation models. In S. L. Morgan (Ed.), *Handbook of causal analysis for social research* (pp. 301–328). Dordrecht: Springer Netherlands. https://doi.org/10.1007/978-94-007-6094-3

Bollen, K. A. (1989). A new incremental fit index for general structural equation models. *Sociological Methods and Research*, *17*, 303–316. https://doi.org/10.1177/0049124189017003004

Bonneville-Roussy, A., Bouffard, T., Palikara, O., & Vezeau, C. (2019). The role of cultural values in teacher and student self-efficacy: Evidence from 16 nations. *Contemporary Educational Psychology, 59*, 101798. https://doi.org/10.1016/j.cedpsych.2019.101798

Boyd, L. H., & Iversen, G. R. (1979). *Contextual analysis: Concepts and statistical techniques.* Beverly, MA: Wadsworth Publishing Company.

Braun, H. I., Jones, D. H., Rubin, D. B., & Thayer, D. T. (1983). Empirical Bayes estimation of coefficients in the general linear model from data of deficient rank. *Psychometrika, 48*(2), 171–181. https://doi.org/10.1007/BF02294013[13]

Breiman, L., Friedman, J., Olshen, R. A., & Stone, C. J. (1984). *Classification and regression trees.* Boca Raton, FL: Chapman & Hall/CRC.

Breslow, N. E., & Clayton, D. G. (1993). Approximate inference in generalized linear mixed models. *Journal of the American Statistical Association, 88*, 9–25. https://doi.org/10.1080/02664763.2018.1506020

Browne, W. J. (1998). *Applying MCMC methods to multilevel models.* Bath: University of Bath. https://doi.org/10.1007/978-0-387-73186-5_2

Bryk, A. S., & Raudenbush, S. W. (1988). Toward a more appropriate conceptualization of research on school effects: A three-level hierarchical linear model. *American Journal of Education, 97*(1), 65–108. https://doi.org/10.1086/443913[17]

Bryk, A. S., & Raudenbush, S. W. (1992). *Hierarchical linear models for social and behavioural research: Applications and data analysis methods.* London: Sage Publications.

Burton, P., Gurrin, L., & Sly, P. (1998). Extending the simple linear regression model to account for correlated responses: An introduction to generalized estimating equations and multi-level mixed modeling. *Statistics in Medicine, 17*, 1261–1291. https://doi.org/10.1002/(SICI)1097-0258(19980615)17:11%3C1261::AID-SIM846%3E3.0.CO;2-Z

Callan, G. L., Marchant, G. J., Finch, W. H., & Flegge, L. (2017). Student and school SES, gender, strategy use, and achievement. *Psychology in the Schools, 54*(9), 1106–1122. https://doi.org/10.1002/pits.22049

Chang. C. C., & Lin. C. J. (2011). LIBSVM: A library for support vector machines. *ACM Transactions on Intelligent Systems and Technology, 2*(3), 1–27.https://doi.org/10.1145/1961189.1961199

Chen, F., Sakyi, A., & Cui, Y. (2022). Identifying key contextual factors of digital reading literacy through a machine learning approach. *Journal of Educational Computing Research.* Advanced online publication. https://doi.org/10.1177/07356331221083215

Chen, J., Zhang, Y., & HU, J. (2021a). Synergistic effects of instruction and affect factors on high- and low-ability disparities in elementary students' reading literacy. *Reading and Writing: An Interdisciplinary Journal, 34*(1), 199–230. https://doi.org/10.1007/s11145-020-10070-0

Chen, J., Zhang, Y., Wei, Y., & HU, J. (2021b). Discrimination of the contextual features of top performers in scientific literacy using a machine learning approach. *Research in Science Education, 51* (suppl. 1), 129–158. https://doi.org/10.1007/s11165-019-9835-y

Chen, T., & Guestrin, C. (2016). XGboost: A scalable tree boosting system. In *Proceedings of the 22nd ACM SIGKDD international conference on knowledge discovery and data mining* (pp. 785–794). New York: ACM. https://doi.org/10.1145/2939672.2939785

Chen, X., & HU, J. (2020). ICT-related behavioral factors mediate the relationship between adolescents' ICT interest and their ICT self-efficacy: Evidence from 30 countries. *Computers & Education, 159*, Article 104004. https://doi.org/10.1016/j.compedu.2020.104004

Cheung, K. C., Mak, S. K., & Sit, P. S. (2013). Online reading activities and ICT use as mediating variables in explaining the gender difference in digital reading literacy:

Comparing Hong Kong and Korea. *Asia-Pacific Education Researcher, 22*(4), 709–720. https://doi.org/10.1007/s40299-013-0077-x

Cheung, M. W. (2009). Comparison of methods for constructing confidence intervals of standardized indirect effects. *Behavior Research Methods, 41*(2), 425–438. https://doi.org/10.3758/BRM.41.2.425

Cios, K. J., Pedrycz, W., Swiniarski, R. W., & Kurgan, L. A. (2007). *Data mining: A knowledge discovery approach.* Berlin: Springer. https://doi.org/10.1007/978-0-387-36795-8

Clogg, C., Petkova, E., & Shihadeh, E. (1992). Statistical methods for analyzing collapsibility in regression models. *Journal of Educational and Behavioral Statistics, 17,* 51–74. https://doi.org/10.3102/10769986017001051[30]

Cole, D., & Maxwell, S. (2003). Testing mediational models with longitudinal data: Questions and tips in the use of structural equation modeling. *Journal of Abnormal Psychology, 112,* 558–577. https://doi.org/10.1037/0021-843X.112.4.558

Cook, T., & Campbell, D. (1979). *Quasi-experimentation: Design & analysis issue for field settings.* Boston: Houghton Mifflin.

Cortes, C., & Vapnik, V. (1995). Support-vector networks. *Machine Learning, 20*(3), 273–297. https://doi.org/10.1023/A:1022627411411

Cover, T. M. (1965). Geometrical and statistical properties of systems of linear inequalities with applications in pattern recognition. *IEEE Transactions on Electronic Computers, EC14*(3), 326. https://doi.org/10.1109/PGEC.1965.264137

Cristianini, N., & Shawe-Taylor, J. (2000). *An introduction to support vector machines and other kernel-based learning methods.* Cambridge: Cambridge University Press. https://doi.org/10.1017/cbo9780511801389

Cronbach, L. J., Gleser, G. C., Nanda, H., & Rajaratnam, N. (1972). *The dependability of behavioral measurements: Theory of generalizability for scores and profiles.* Hoboken, NJ: Wiley.

Cunningham, A. E., & Stanovich, K. E. (1997). Early reading acquisition and its relation to reading experience and ability 10 years later, *Developmental Psychology, 33*(6), 934–945. https://doi.org/10.1037/0012-1649.33.6.934

Dansereau, F., Alutto, J., & Yammarino, F. (1984). *Theory testing in organizational behavior.* Hoboken, NJ: Prentice-Hall.

David, R., & Sonia, B. (2012). Gender, culture, and sex-typed cognitive abilities. *PLoS One, 7*(7), Article e39904. https://doi.org/10.1371/journal.pone.0039904

Dempster, A. P., Laird, N. M., & Rubin, D. B. (1977). Maximum likelihood from incomplete data via the EM algorithm. *Journal of the Royal Statistical Society. Series B (Methodological), 39,* 1–38. https://doi.org/10.1111/j.2517-6161.1977.tb01600.x

Dempster, A. P., Rubin, D. B., & Tsutakawa, R. K. (1981). Estimation in covariance components models. *Journal of the American Statistical Association, 76*(374), 341–353. https://doi.org/10.2307/2287835

DiPrete, T. A., & Grusky, D. B. (1990). Structure and trend in the process of stratification for American men and women. *American Journal of Sociology, 96,* 107–143.

Dong, X. & HU, J. (2019). An exploration of impact factors influencing students' reading literacy in Singapore with machine learning approaches. *International Journal of English Linguistics, 9*(5), 52–65. https://doi.org/10.5539/ijel.v9n5p52

Fan, R. E., Chang, K. W., Hsieh, C. J., Wang, X. R., & Lin, C. J. (2008). Liblinear: A library for large linear classification. *Journal of Machine Learning Research, 9,* 1871–1874. Retrieved from: https://www.jmlr.org/papers/volume9/fan08a/fan08a.pdf

Galtung, J. (1967). *Theory and method of social research.* New York: Columbia University Press. https://doi.org/10.1080/00220612.1968.10671802

Goldstein, H. (1986). Multilevel mixed linear model analysis using iterative generalized least squares. *Biometrica, 78*(1), 43–56. https://doi.org/10.1093/BIOMET/73.1.43

Goldstein, H. (1991). Nonlinear multilevel models with an application to discrete response data. *Biometrika, 78*(1), 45–51. https://doi.org/10.1093/biomet/78.1.45
Goldstein, H. (1995). Hierarchical data modeling in the social sciences. *Journal of Educational and Behavioral Statistics, 20*(2), 201–204. https://doi.org/10.3102/10769986020002201
Goldstein, H. (2003). *Multilevel models in educational and social research* (3rd ed.). London: Edward Arnold.
Gordon, L. & Olshen, R. A. (1985). Tree-structured survival analysis. *Cancer Treatment Report, 69*(10), 1065–1069. https://pubmed.ncbi.nlm.nih.gov/4042086/
Gorostiaga, A., & Rojo-Álvarez, J. (2016). On the use of conventional and statistical-learning techniques for the analysis of PISA results in Spain. *Neurocomputing, 171*, 625–637. https://doi.org/10.1016/j.neucom.2015.07.001
Grek, S. (2009). Governing by numbers: The PISA 'effect' in Europe. *Journal of Education Policy, 24*(1), 23–37. http://doi.org/10.1080/02680930802412669
Grzymala-Busse, J. W., & HU, M. (2001). A comparison of several approaches to missing attribute values in data mining. In W. Ziarko & Y. Yao (Eds.), *Rough sets and current trends in computing* (pp. 378–385). Berlin: Springer. https://doi.org/10.1007/3-540-45554-X_46
Guyon, I., Weston, J., Barnhill, S., & Vapnik, V. (2002). Gene selection for cancer classification using support vector machines. *Machine Learning, 46*, 389–422. http://doi.org/10.1023/A:1012487302797
Hahnel, C., Goldhammer, F., Naumann, J., & Kroehne, U. (2016). Effects of linear reading, basic computer skills, evaluating online information, and navigation on reading digital text. *Computers in Human Behavior, 55*, 486–500. https://doi.org/10.1016/j.chb.2015.09.042
Hayes, A. F., & Scharkow, M. (2013). The relative trustworthiness of inferential tests of the indirect effect in statistical mediation analysis: Does method really matter? *Psychological Science, 24*(10), 1918–1927. https://doi.org/10.1177/0956797613480187
Hedeker, D., & Gibbons, R. D. (2006). *Longitudinal data analysis*. Hoboken, NJ: Wiley.
Ho, E. (2010). Family influences on science learning among Hong Kong adolescents: What we learned from PISA. *International Journal of Science & Mathematics Education, 8*(3), 409–428. https://doi.org/10.1007/s10763-010-9198-3
Hofmann, D. A. (1997). An overview of the logic and rationale of hierarchical linear models. *Journal of management, 23*(6), 723–744. https://doi.org/10.1177/014920639702300602
Homey, J., Osgood, D., & Marshall, I. (1995). Criminal careers in the short-term: Intra-individual variability in come and its relation to local life circumstances. *American Sociological Review, 60*, 655–673. Retrieved from https://www.jstor.org/stable/2096316?seq=2
Hox, J. J., Kreft, I. G. G., & Hermkens, P. L. J. (1991). The analysis of factorial surveys. *Sociological Methods & Research, 19*(4), 493–510. https://doi.org/10.1177/0049124191019004003
Hox, J. J., & Maas, C. (2006). Multilevel models for multimethod measurements. In M. Eid & E. Diener (Eds.), *Handbook of multimethod measurement in psychology* (pp. 269–281). Washington, DC: American Psychological Association. https://doi.org/10.1037/11383-019
HU, J., Dong, X. & Peng, Y (2021). Discovery of the key contextual factors relevant to the reading performance of elementary school students from 61 countries/regions: Insight from a machine learning-based approach. *Reading and Writing, 35*, 93–127. https://doi.org/10.1007/s11145-021-10176-z
HU, J., & Yu, R. (2021). The effects of ICT-based social media on adolescents' digital reading performance: A longitudinal study of PISA 2009, PISA 2012, PISA

2015 and PISA 2018. *Computers & Education, 175*, 1–20. https://doi.org/10.1016/j.compedu.2021.104342

Hu, X., Gong, Y., Lai, C. & Leung, F.K.S. (2018). The relationship between ICT and student literacy in mathematics, reading, and science across 44 countries: A multilevel analysis. *Computers & Education, 125*(1), 1–13. https://doi.org/10.1016/j.compedu.2018.05.021

Huttenlocher, J., Haight, W., Bryk, A., Seltzer, M., Lyons, T. (1991). Early vocabulary growth: Relation to language input and gender. *Developmental Psychology, 27*(2), 236–249. https://doi.org/10.1037/0012-1649.27.2.236

Imai, K., Keele, L., & Tingley, D. (2010). A general approach to causal mediation analysis. *Psychological Methods, 15*(4), 309–334. https://doi.org/10.1037/a0020761

Jackson, D. L. (2003). Revisiting sample size and number of parameter estimates: Some support for the N:q hypothesis. *Structural Equation Modeling: A Multidisciplinary Journal, 10*(1), 128–141. https://doi.org/10.1207/S15328007SEM1001_6

James, G., Witten, D., Hastie, T., & Tibshirani, R. (2013). *An introduction to statistical learning.* Berlin, Springer.

Joachims T. (1998). Text categorization with support vector machines: Learning with many relevant features. In C. Nédellec, & C. Rouveirol (Eds.), *Machine learning: ECML-98* (pp. 137–142). Berlin, Heidelberg: Springer. https://doi.org/10.1007/BFb0026683

Kang, J., & Keinonen, T. (2017). The effect of inquiry-based learning experiences on adolescents' science-related career aspiration in the Finnish context. *International Journal of Science Education, 39*(12), 1669–1689. https://doi.org/10.1080/09500693.2017.1350790

Kasgari, A. A., Divsalar, M., Javid, M. R., & Ebrahimian, S. J. (2013). Prediction of bankruptcy Iranian corporations through artificial neural network and probit-based analyses. *Neural Computing and Applications, 23*, 927–936. https://doi.org/10.1007/s00521-012-1017-z

Kenny, D. A., Kashy, D. A., & Bolger, N. (1998). Data analysis in social psychology. In D. T. Gilbert, S. T. Fiske, & G. Lindzey (Eds.), *The handbook of social psychology* (pp. 233–265). New York: McGraw-Hill.

Kline, R. B. (2011). *Principles and practice of structural equation modeling* (3rd ed.). New York: Guilford Press.

Kotsiantis, S. B. (2012). Use of machine learning techniques for educational proposes: A decision support system for forecasting students' grades. *Artificial Intelligence Review, 37*(4), 331–344. https://doi.org/10.1007/s10462-011-9234-x

Kowalski, J., & Tu, X. M. (2007). *Modern applied U statistics.* Hoboken, NJ: Wiley. https://doi.org/10.1002/9780470186466

Kozlowski, S. W. J., & Klein, K. J. (2000). *A multilevel approach to theory and research in organizations: Contextual, temporal, and emergent processes.* New York: Jossey-Bass.

Kraemer, H. C., Stice, E., Kazdin, A., Offord, D., & Kupfer, D. (2001). How do risk factors work together? Mediators, moderators, and independent, overlapping, and proxy risk factors. *American Journal of Psychiatry, 158*(6), 848–856. https://doi.org/10.1176/appi.ajp.158.6.848

Kriegbaum, K., & Spinath, B. (2016). Explaining social disparities in mathematical achievement: The role of motivation. *European Journal of Personality, 30*(1), 45–63. https://doi.org/10.1002/per.2042

Kruppa, J., Ziegler, A., & König, I. R. (2012). Risk estimation and risk prediction using machine-learning methods. *Human Genetics, 131*, 1639–1654. https://doi.org/10.1007/s00439-012-1194-y

Laird, N. M., & Ware, H. J. (1982). Random-effects models for longitudinal data. *Biometrics, 38*(4), 963–974. https://doi.org/10.2307/2529876

Lau, K., & Ho, E. (2016). Reading performance and self-regulated learning of Hong Kong students: What we learnt from PISA 2009. *The Asia-Pacific Education Researcher, 25*(1), 159–171. https://doi.org/10.1007/s40299-015-0246-1

Lazarsfeld, P. F., & Menzel, H. (1961). On the relation between individual and collective properties. In A. Etzioni (Ed.), *Complex organizations: A sociological reader* (pp. 422–440). New York: Holt, Rinehart and Winston.

Lee, Y. H., & Wu, J. Y. (2013). The indirect effects of online social entertainment and information seeking activities on reading literacy. *Computers & Education, 67*, 168–177. http://doi.org/10.1016/j.compedu.2013.03.001

Lenkeit, J., Schwippert, K., & Knigge, M. (2020). Configurations of multiple disparities in reading performance: Longitudinal observations across France, Germany, Sweden and the United Kingdom. *Assessment in Education-Principles Policy & Practice, 25*(1), 52–86. http://doi.org/10.1080/0969594X.2017.1309352

Leyland, A. H., & Goldstein, H. (2001). *Multilevel modelling of health statistics*. Hoboken, NJ: Wiley.

Liem, G. A. D., Martin, A. J., Anderson, M., Gibson, R., & Sudmalis, D. (2014). The role of arts-related information and communication technology use in problem solving and achievement: Findings from the programme for international student assessment. *Journal of Educational Psychology, 106*(2), 348–363. http://doi.org/10.1037/a0034398

Lin, H. F., Juo, S. H. H., & Cheng, R. (2005). Comparison of the power between microsatellite and single-nucleotide polymorphism markers for linkage and linkage disequilibrium mapping of an electrophysiological phenotype. *BMC Genetics, 6*(Suppl. 1), Article S7. https://doi.org/10.1186/1471-2156-6-S1-S7

Lindley, D., & Novick, M. R. (1981). The role of exchangeability in inference. *Annals of Statistics, 9*, 45–58. http://doi.org/10.1214/aos/1176345331

Lindley, D. V., & Smith, A. F. M. (1972). Bayes estimates for the linear model. *Journal of the Royal Statistical Society, Seires B, 34*, 1–41. https://doi.org/10.1111/j.2517-6161.1972.tb00885.x

Liou, P. Y. (2021). Students' attitudes toward science and science achievement: An analysis of the differential effects of science instructional practices. *Journal of Research in Science Teaching, 58*(3), 310–334. https://doi.org/10.1002/tea.21643

Littell, R. C., Milliken, G. A., Stroup, W. W., & Wolfinger, R. D. (1996). *SAS system for mixed models*. Cary, NC: SAS Institute, Inc.

Livieris, I., Drakopoulou, K., Kotsilieris, T., Tampakas, V., & Pintelas, P. (2017). *DSSP-SP—A decision support tool for evaluating students' performance*. Cham: Springer.

Loh, W. Y. (2011). Classification and regression trees. *Wiley Interdisciplinary Reviews: Data Mining and Knowledge Discovery, 1*(1), 14–23. https://doi.org/10.1002/widm.8

Longford, N. T. (1987). Fisher scoring algorithm for variance component analysis with hierarchically nested random effects. *ETS Research Report Series, 1987*(2), 1–20. https://doi.org/10.1002/j.2330-8516.1987.tb00236.x

Longford, N. T. (1993). Regression analysis of multilevel data with measurement error. *British Journal of Mathematical and Statistical Psychology, 46*(2), 301–311. https://doi.org/10.1111/j.2044-8317.1993.tb01018.x

Lu, O. H. T., Huang, A. Y. Q., Huang, J. C. H., Lin, A. J. Q., Ogata, H., & Yang, S. J. H. (2018). Applying learning analytics for the early prediction of students' academic performance in blended learning. *Educational Technology & Society, 21*(2), 220–232. Retrieved from: https://www.jstor.org/stable/26388400

MacKinnon, D., & Fairchild, A. (2009). Current directions in mediation analysis. *Current Directions in Psychological Science, 18*(1), 16–20. https://doi.org/10.1111/j.1467-8721.2009.01598.x

MacKinnon, D. P. (2008). *An introduction to statistical mediation analysis.* Routledge. https://doi.org/10.4324/9780203809556

Mak, S. K., Cheung, K. C., Soh, K., Sit, P. S., & Leong, M. K. (2017). An examination of student- and across-level mediation mechanisms accounting for gender differences in reading performance: A multilevel analysis of reading engagement. *Educational Psychology, 37*(10), 1206–1221. https://doi.org/10.1080/01443410.2016.1242712

Marks, G. N. (2005). Accounting for immigrant non-immigrant differences in reading and mathematics in twenty countries. *Ethnic and Racial Studies, 28*(5), 925–946. http://doi.org/10.1080/01419870500158943

Marks, G. N., & Pokropek, A. (2019). Family income effects on mathematics achievement: Their relative magnitude and causal pathways. *Oxford Review of Education, 45*(6), 769–785. http://doi.org/10.1080/03054985.2019.1620717

Martin, A. J., Liem, G. A. D., Mok, M. M. C., & Xu, J. (2012). Problem solving and immigrant student mathematics and science achievement: Multination findings from the Programme for International Student Assessment (PISA). *Journal of Educational Psychology, 104*(4), 1054–1073. https://doi.org/10.1037/a0029152

Mason, W. M., Wong, G. Y., & Entwisle, B. (1983). Contextual analysis through the multilevel linear model. *Sociological Methodology, 14,* 72–103. https://doi.org/10.2307/270903

Maxwell, J. A. (1998). Designing a qualitative study. In L. Bickman & D. J. Rog (Eds.), *Handbook of applied social research methods* (pp. 69–100). London: Sage Publications.

Maxwell, S. E., Cole, D. A., & Mitchell, M. A. (2011). Bias in cross-sectional analyses of longitudinal mediation: Partial and complete mediation under an autoregressive model. *Multivariate Behavioral Research, 46*(5), 816–841. https://doi.org/10.1080/00273171.2011.606716

McArdle, J. J., & McDonald, R. P. (1984). Some algebraic properties of the reticular action model for moment structures. *The British Journal of Mathematical and Statistical Psychology, 37,* 234–251. http://doi.org/10.1111/j.2044-8317.1984.tb00802.x

Meijer, R. J., & Goeman, J. J. (2013). Efficient approximate k-fold and leave-one-out cross-validation for ridge regression. *Biometrical Journal, 55*(2), 141–155. https://doi.org/10.1002/bimj.201200088

Mitchell, T. (1997). *Machine Learning.* New York: McGraw Hill.

Morris, C. N. (1983). Parametric empirical Bayes inference: Theory and applications. *Journal of the American Statistical Association, 78*(381), 47–55. https://doi.org/10.1080/01621459.1983.10477920

Müller, A. C., & Guido, S. (2016). *Introduction to machine learning with Python: A guide for data scientists.* Cambridge, MA: O'Reilly Media.

Muthén, L. K., & Muthén, B. O. (1998). *Mplus user's guide.* Los Angeles, CA: Muthen & Muthen

Nagengast, B., & Marsh, H. W. (2012). Big fish in little ponds aspire more: Mediation and cross-cultural generalizability of school-average ability effects on self-concept and career aspirations in science. *Journal of Educational Psychology, 104*(4), 1033–1053. https://doi.org/10.1037/a0027697

Niehues, W., Kisbu-Sakarya, Y., & Selcuk, B. (2020). Motivation and maths achievement in Turkish students: Are they linked with socio-economic status? *Educational Psychology, 40*(8), 981–1001. https://doi.org/10.1080/01443410.2020.1724887

Ning, B. (2020). What makes a difference in reading achievement? Comparisons between Finland and Shanghai. In B. Ning (Ed.), *School climate matters* (pp. 71–90). Routledge. https://doi.org/10.4324/9781003049821-4

Ning, B., Damme, J. V., Noortgate, W., Yang, X., & Gielen, S. (2015). The influence of classroom disciplinary climate of schools on reading achievement: A cross-country comparative study. *School Effectiveness and School Improvement, 26*(4), 586–611. https://doi.org/10.1080/09243453.2015.1025796

Notten, N., & Becker, B. (2017). Early home literacy and adolescents' online reading behavior in comparative perspective. *International Journal of Comparative Sociology, 58*(6), 475–493. https//doi.org/10.1177/0020715217735362

OECD. (2009). *PISA data analysis manual: SAS* (second edition). Paris: OECD Publishing. https://www.oecd.org/pisa/pisaproducts/pisadataanalysismanualspssandsasecondedition.htm

Oladokun, V. O., Adebanjo, A. T., & Charles-Owaba, O. E. (2008). Predicting students' academic performance using artificial neural network: A case study of an engineering course. *The Pacific Journal of Science and Technology, 9*(1), 72–79. Retrieved from: https://www.researchgate.net/profile/Victor-Oladokun/publication/228526441_Predicting_Students_Academic_Performance_using_Artificial_Neural_Network_A_Case_Study_of_an_Engineering_Course/links/00b495231c4f18aa26000000/Predicting-Students-Academic-Performance-using-Artificial-Neural-Network-A-Case-Study-of-an-Engineering-Course.pdf

O'Muircheartaigh, C., & Campanelli, P. (1999). A multilevel exploration of the role of interviewers in survey non-response. *Journal of the Royal Statistical Society: Series A (Statistics in Society), 162,* 437–446. https://doi.org/10.1111/1467-985X.00147

Pickery, J., & Loosveldt, G. (1998). The impact of respondent and interviewer characteristics on the number of "no opinion" answers. *Quality and Quantity, 32*(1), 31–45. https://doi.org/10.1023/A:1004268427793

Pickery, J., Loosveldt, G., & Carton, A. (2001). The effects of interviewer and respondent characteristics on response behaviour in panel surveys. *Sociological Methods & Research, 29,* 509–523. https://doi.org/10.1177/0049124101029004004

Pinheiro, J., & Bates, D. (1995). Approximations to the log-likelihood function in the nonlinear mixed-effects model. *Journal of Computational and Graphical Statistics, 4*(1), 12–35. https://doi.org/10.1080/10618600.1995.10474663

Preacher, K. J., & Hayes, A. F. (2004). SPSS and SAS procedures for estimating indirect effects in simple mediation models. *Behavior Research Methods, Instruments, & Computers, 36*(4), 717–731. https://doi:10.3758/bf03206553

Preacher, K. J., & Hayes, A. F. (2008). Asymptotic and resampling strategies for assessing and comparing indirect effects in multiple mediator models. *Behavior Research Methods, 40*(3), 879–891. https://doi.org/10.3758/brm.40.3.879

Qiao, X., & Jiao, H. (2018). Data mining techniques in analyzing process data: A didactic. *Frontiers in Psychology, 9,* 1–11. https://doi.org/10.3389/fpsyg.2018.02231

R Core Team (2019). R: A language and environment for statistical computing. R Foundation for Statistical Computing, Vienna, Austria. Available online at: https://www.R-project.org/.

Rasbash, J., & Goldstein, H. (1994). Efficient analysis of mixed hierarchical and cross-classified random structures using a multilevel model. *Journal of Educational and Behavioral Statistics, 19*(4), 337–350. https://doi.org/10.2307/1165397

Rasmusson, M., & Aberg-Bengtsson, L. (2015). Does performance in digital reading relate to computer game playing? A study of factor structure and gender patterns in

15-year-olds' reading literacy performance. *Scandinavian Journal of Educational Research, 59*(6), 691–709. https://doi.org/10.1080/00313831.2014.965795

Raudenbush, S. W., & Bryk, A. S. (2002). *Hierarchical linear models: Applications and data analysis methods.* London: Sage.

Raudenbush, S. W., Bryk, S., Cheong, Y. F., & Congdon, R. (2004). *HLM6: Hierarchical linear and nonlinear modeling.* Michigan: Scientific Software International.

Raudenbush, S. W., & Chan, W. S. (1993). Application of a hierarchical linear model to the study of adolescent deviance in an overlapping cohort design. *Journal of Consulting and Clinical Psychology, 61*(6), 941–951. https://doi.org/10.1037/0022-006X.61.6.941

Raudenbush, S. W., Yang, M. L., & Yosef, M. (2000). Maximum likelihood for generalized linear models with nested random effects via high-order, multivariate Laplace approximation. *Journal of Computational and Graphical Statistics, 9*, 141–157. https://doi.org/10.2307/1390617

Robinson, W. S. (1950). Ecological correlations and the behavior of individuals. *American Sociological Review, 15*, 351–357. https://doi.org/10.2307/2087176

Rodríguez-Planas, N., & Nollenberger, N. (2018). Let the girls learn! It is not only about math: It's about gender social norms. *Economics of Education Review, 62*, 230–253. https://doi.org/10.1016/j.econedurev.2017.11.006

Romero, C., Espejo, P. G., Zafra, A., Romero, J. R., & Ventura, S. (2013). Web usage mining for predicting final marks of students that use Moodle courses. *Computer Applications in Engineering Education, 21*(1), 135–146. https://doi.org/10.1002/cae.20456

Rothman, K. J., & Greenland, S. (1986). *Modern epidemiology.* Philadelphia, PA: Lippingcott Williams and Wilkins.

Rubin D. (1987). *Multiple imputation for non-response in surveys.* New York: John Wiley and Sons, Inc

Rumberger, R. W. (1995). Dropping out of middle school: A multilevel analysis of students and schools. *American Educational Research Journal, 32*(3), 583–625. https://doi.org/10.2307/1163325

Salchegger, S. (2016). Selective school systems and academic self-concept: How explicit and implicit school-level tracking relate to the big-fish-little-pond effect across cultures. *Journal of Educational Psychology, 108*(3), 405–423. https://doi.org/10.1037/edu0000063

Sampson, R. J., Raudenbush, S. W., & Earls, F. (1997). Neighborhoods and violent Crime: A multilevel study of collective efficacy. *Science, 277*, 918–924. http://dx.doi.org/10.1126/science.277.5328.918

Schoor, C. (2016). Utility of reading—Predictor of reading achievement? *Learning and Individual Differences, 45*, 151–158. https://doi.org/10.1016/j.lindif.2015.11.024

Selig, J. P., & Preacher, K. J. (2009). Mediation models for longitudinal data in developmental research. *Research in Human Development, 6*(2–3), 144–164. https://doi.org/10.1080/15427600902911247

Shmueli, G. (2010). To explain or to predict? *Statistical Science, 25*(3), 289–310. https://doi.org/10.1214/10-sts330.

Shoaib, M., Sayed, N., Amara, N., Latif, A., Azam, S., & Muhammad, S. (2022). Prediction of an educational institute learning environment using machine learning and data mining. *Education and Information Technologies*, 1–25. Advance online publication. https://doi.org/10.1007/s10639-022-10970-4

Skryabin, M., Zhang, J., Liu, L., & Zhang, D. (2015). How the ICT development level and usage influence student achievement in reading, mathematics, and science. *Computers & Education, 85*, 49–58. https://doi.org/10.1016/j.compedu.2015.02.004

Snijders, T. A. B., & Bosker, R. J. (2012). *Multilevel analysis: An introduction to basic and advanced multilevel modeling* (2nd Ed.). London: Sage Publications.

Sobel, M. E. (1982). Asymptotic intervals for indirect effects in structural equations models. In S. Leinhart (Ed.), *Sociological methodology* (pp. 290–312). New York: Jossey-Bass.

Stiratelli, R., Laird, N., & Ware, J. (1984). Random effects models for serial observations with binary response. *Biometrics, 40*(4), 961–971. https://doi.org/10.2307/2531147

Stone-Romero, E. F., & Rosopa, P. J. (2010). Research design options for testing mediation models and their implications for facets of validity. *Journal of Managerial Psychology, 25*(7), 697–712. https://doi.org/10.1108/02683941011075256

Tang, X., & Zhang, D. (2020). How informal science learning experience influences students' science performance: A cross-cultural study based on PISA 2015. *International Journal of Science Education, 42*(4), 598–616. https://doi.org/10.1080/09500693.2020.1719290

Tate, R. L., & Hokanson, J. E. (1993). Analyzing individual status and change with hierarchical linear models: Illustration with depression in college students. *Journal of Personality, 61*(2), 181–206. https://doi.org/10.1111/j.1467-6494.1993.tb01031.x

Torppa, M., Eklund, K., Sulkunen, S., Niemi, P., & Ahonen, T. (2018). Why do boys and girls perform differently on PISA Reading in Finland? The effects of reading fluency, achievement behaviour, leisure reading and homework activity. *Journal of Research in Reading, 41*(1), 122–139. https://doi.org/10.1111/1467-9817.12103

Trafimow, D. (2015). Introduction to the special issue on mediation analyses: What if planetary scientists used mediation analysis to infer causation? *Basic and Applied Social Psychology, 37*(4), 197–201. https://doi.org/10.1080/01973533.2015.1064290

van Duijn, M. A. J., van Busschbach, J. T., & Snijders, T. A. B. (1999). Multilevel analysis of personal networks as dependent variables. *Social Networks, 21*(2), 187–209. https://doi.org/10.1016/S0378-8733(99)00009-X

Witten, I. H., Frank, E., Hall, M. A., & Pal, C. J. (2016). *Data mining: Practical machine learning tools and techniques*. Burlington, MA: Morgan Kaufmann.

Wong, G., & Mason, W. (1985). The hierarchical logistic regression model for multilevel analysis. *Journal of the American Statistical Association, 80*(391), 513–524. https://doi.org/10.1080/01621459.1985.10478148

Wu, H., Shen, J., Zhang, Y., & Zheng, Y. (2020). Examining the effect of principal leadership on student science achievement. *International Journal of Science Education, 42*(6), 1017–1039. https://doi.org/10.1080/09500693.2020.1747664

Wu, J. Y. (2014). Gender differences in online reading engagement, metacognitive strategies, navigation skills and reading literacy. *Journal of Computer Assisted Learning, 30*(3), 252–271. https://doi.org/10.1111/jcal.12054

Xiao, Z., Wang, Y., Fu, K., & Wu, F. (2017). Identifying different transportation models from trajectory data using tree-based ensemble classifiers. *ISPRS International Journal of Geo-Information, 6*(2), Article 57. https://doi.org/10.3390/ijgi6020057

Xie, C., & Ma, Y. (2019). The mediating role of cultural capital in the relationship between socioeconomic status and student achievement in 14 economies. *British Educational Research Journal, 45*(4), 838–855. https://doi.org/10.1002/berj.3528

Xu, D., & Wu, X. (2017). The rise of the second generation: Aspirations, motivations and academic success of Chinese immigrants' children in Hong Kong. *Journal of Ethnic and Migration Studies, 43*(7), 1164–1189. https://doi.org/10.1080/1369183x.2016.1245132

Yi, P., & Kim, H. J. (2019). Exploring the relationship between external and internal accountability in education: A cross-country analysis with multi-level structural equation modeling. *International Journal of Educational Development, 65*, 1–9. https://doi.org/10.1016/j.ijedudev.2018.12.007

Yildirim, S. (2012). Teacher support, motivation, learning strategy use, and achievement: A multilevel mediation model. *Journal of Experimental Education, 80*(2), 150–172. https://doi.org/10.1080/00220973.2011.596855

Yoo, J., & Kim, J. (2014). Can online discussion participation predict group project performance? Investigating the roles of linguistic features and participation patterns. *International Journal of Artificial Intelligence in Education, 24*(1), 8–32. https://doi.org/10.1007/s40593-013-0010-8

Zhang, D., Qian, L., Mao, B., Huang, C., Huang, B., & Si, Y. (2018). A data-driven design for fault detection of wind turbines using random forests and XGboost. *IEEE Access, 6*, 21020–21031. https://doi.org/10.1109/ACCESS.2018.2818678

Zhang, Z., Zyphur, M. J., & Preacher, K. J. (2008). Testing multilevel mediation using hierarchical linear models: Problems and solutions. *Organizational Research Methods, 12*(4), 695–719. https://doi.org/10.1177/1094428108327450

Ziegler, A., & Konig, I. R. (2014). Mining data with random forests: Current options for real-world applications. *WIREs Data Mining Knowledge Discovery, 4*(1), 55–63. https://doi.org/10.1002/widm.1114

# 4
# RESULTS

## 4.1 The classification performance of the SVM model

Generally, when the performance indicators of the SVM model are above 0.7, it means that the model is fair. It is found that the three SVM models composed of 146 factors exhibit impressive performances in the binary classification, with all of the indicators above 0.89. Gorostiaga and Rojo-Álvarez (2016) found that the minimum number of factors in the optimal factor set was generally between 20 and 30. The optimal factor set in another study conducted by Chen et al. (2021) also included 20 factors, which confirmed the findings of Gorostiaga and Rojo-Álvarez (2016). It is noted that when the number of features reaches 20, the performance of the SVM model is stable at a high ACC score of 0.896 (see Table 4.1). We can also see that the five-fold CV presents on an increasing curve first with the accumulation of the features, then remain mild after the number of 20 (see Figure 4.1). In this regard, the optimal feature set composed of 20 features was selected.

**TABLE 4.1** The classification performance of the two SVM models

| Feature Number | ACC | AUC | F-Measure | SEN | Precision |
|---|---|---|---|---|---|
| 146 | 0.913 | 0.905 | 0.899 | 0.892 | 0.911 |
| 20 | 0.896 | 0.885 | 0.847 | 0.879 | 0.892 |

Source: ACC stands for the proportion of real findings in the selected population, encompassing both positive and negative results; AUC is a ranking-based classification performance metric that can identify a randomly selected positive example from a randomly selected negative example; F-measure is the harmonic mean of ACC and recall (another performance metric); SEN represents the proportion of genuine positives that are accurately identified; precision reflects the proportion of projected positive instances among the actual number of positive cases.

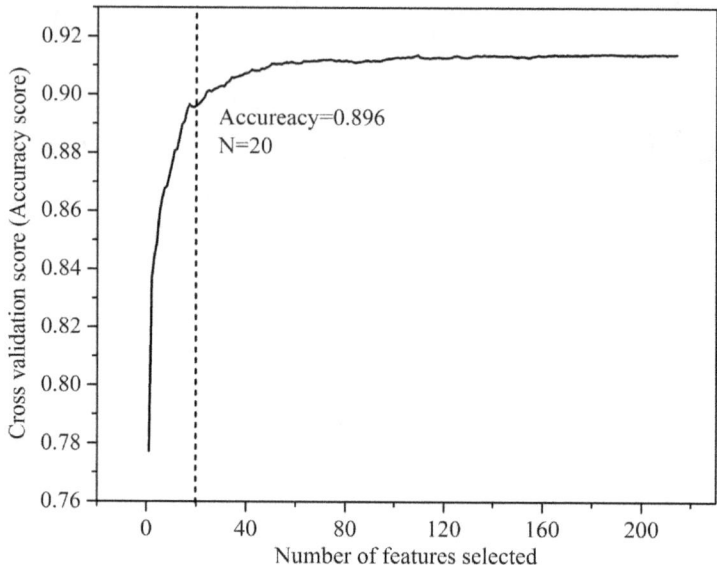

**FIGURE 4.1**  The five-fold cross-validation for the SVM model.

## 4.2 The detailed descriptions of the 20 key features

The detailed descriptions of the 20 key features are provided in Table 4.2 for ease of references. It can be seen that the top 20 features belong to three categories, namely, the student level, the classroom level, and the school level. These factors dynamically interact with each other, and collectively exert influences on students' digital reading performance. At the student level, affective factors play an important role. Students' interests in reading (JOY-READ) were identified as the most important feature of the classification, followed immediately by students' expected occupational status (BSMJ). At the classroom level, teachers' instructions are proven influential (e.g., whether they have incorporated the ICT resources in teaching and the instructional behaviors they used). At the school level, school extracurricular activities (CREATIV) and teacher certificates (PROATCE and PROAT5AB) are indispensable. The country-level factor (i.e., the GDP per capita) is not significant in the results.

**TABLE 4.2** The ranking and detailed description of the top 20 factors

| Rank | Key factor | Description | Value scale | Overall M (SD) | M (SD) of high-performing students | M (SD) of low-performing students |
|---|---|---|---|---|---|---|
| *Student-level factors* | | | | | | |
| 1 | JOYREAD | Joy/Like reading | ~3.2096~4.0128 | ~0.038 (1.084) | 0.734 (1.081) | ~0.348 (0.919) |
| 2 | BSMJ | Students expected occupational status | 11.01~88.96 | 63.136 (18.902) | 73.061 (12.449) | 59.166 (19.572) |
| 3 | SCREADCOMP | Self-concept of reading: Perception of competence | ~2.4403~1.9713 | ~0.090 (1.052) | 0.713 (0.910) | ~0.411 (0.926) |
| 12 | SCREADDIFF | Self-concept of reading: Perception of difficulty | ~1.8876~2.7752 | 0.126 (1.035) | ~0.505 (0.847) | 0.378 (0.995) |
| 13 | GFOFAIL | General fear of failure | ~1.8939~1.8905 | ~0.005 (0.927) | 0.208 (0.951) | ~0.090 (0.904) |
| 14 | ST176Q02IA | How often involved in: <Chat on line> (e.g., <Whatsapp>, <Messenger>) | 1~5 | 4.431 (1.060) | 4.632 (0.802) | 2.640 (1.249) |
| 16 | ST176Q06IA | How often involved in: Taking part in online group discussions or forums | 1~5 | 2.599 (1.188) | 2.495 (1.012) | 2.640 (1.249) |
| *Classroom-level factors* | | | | | | |
| 4 | ST158Q05HA_2 | Taught at school: How to use the short description below the links in the list of results of a search | 1~2 | — | — | — |
| 5 | ST154Q01HA | <this academic year>, how many pages was the longest piece of text you had to read for your <test language lessons>? | 1~6 | 3.493 (1.498) | 4.341 (1.252) | 3.165 (1.462) |

(Continued)

| Rank | Key factor | Description | Value scale | Overall M (SD) | M (SD) of high-performing students | M (SD) of low-performing students |
|---|---|---|---|---|---|---|
| 7 | ST158Q04HA_2 | Taught at school: To understand the consequences of making information publicly available online on <Facebook©>, <Instagram©>, etc. | 1~2 | — | — | — |
| 8 | ST158Q05HA_1 | Taught at school: How to use the short description below the links in the list of results of a search | 1~2 | — | — | — |
| 10 | DISCLIMA | Disciplinary climate in test language lessons | ~2.7124~2.3017 | ~0.103 (1.101) | 0.226 (1.019) | ~0.234 (1.105) |
| 11 | DIRINS | Teacher-directed instruction | ~2.9425~1.8202 | 0.076 (1.010) | ~0.092 (0.834) | 0.144 (1.065) |
| 19 | ADAPTIVITY | Adaptation of instruction | ~2.2652~2.0073 | ~0.019 (1.006) | 0.168 (0.965) | ~0.094 (1.012) |
| *School-level factors* | | | | | | |
| 6 | SC061Q01TA | Extent to which student learning is hindered by: Student truancy | 1~4 | 2.390 (0.8250) | 2.105(0.771) | 2.505 (0.818) |
| 9 | CREACTIV | Creative extra-curricular activities (Sum) | 0~3 | 1.801 (1.062) | 2.110 (1.000) | 1.678 (1.061) |
| 15 | PROATCE | Index proportion of all teachers fully certified | 0~1 | 0.841(0.319) | 0.905(0.254) | 0.815(0.338) |
| 17 | PROAT5AB | Index proportion of all teachers ISCED LEVEL 5A Bachelor | 0~1 | 0.661 (0.369) | 0.628 (0.386) | 0.674 (0.361) |
| 18 | SC001Q01TA | Which of the following definitions best describes the community in which your school is located? | 1~5 | 3.116(1.128) | 3.383(1.062) | 3.010(1.135) |
| 20 | SC037Q08TA_3 | Quality assurance at school: Teacher mentoring | 1~3 | — | — | — |

# References

Chen, J., Zhang, Y., Wei, Y., & HU, J. (2021). Discrimination of the contextual features of top performers in scientific literacy using a machine learning approach. *Research in Science Education, 51*(suppl. 1), 129–158. https://doi.org/10.1007/s11165-019-9835-y

Gorostiaga, A., & Rojo-Álvarez, J. (2016). On the use of conventional and statistical-learning techniques for the analysis of PISA results in Spain. *Neurocomputing, 171*, 625–637. https://doi.org/10.1016/j.neucom.2015.07.001

# 5
# DISCUSSION

After concrete steps of feature selection, classifier development, and performance evaluation, factors of three levels intertwined with each other, synergistically exerting effects on the final classification results. The identification of the top 20 features that synergistically differentiate the two groups empirically supports the protective and risk factors for students' digital performances in three levels of the dynamic model of educational effectiveness (namely, the school, classroom, and student levels). On the other hand, in addition to paying attention to the factors that affect students' reading literacy, we should also pay attention to the relationship between the influencing factors, to better "suit the remedy to the case". Therefore, the key findings are discussed.

## 5.1 The synergistic effects of the 20 key factors

The novel machine learning methods used in this analysis produced the optimal feature set that collectively shapes students' digital reading outcomes. In addition, the dynamic model of educational effectiveness was incorporated into a specific discipline, namely, the context of reading education and research, as some previously neglected factors were identified. These factors synergistically form a learning environment, indicating the necessity of building a learning context for young digital readers from different levels. Generally, students' individual characteristics play a great role in influencing students' reading performance, but teacher- and school-level factors also play a reconciliation role. There are differences in the influence modes of each layer of factors, which is worth further discussion.

In the context of fast-paced life and learning, high-quality digital reading resources, portable mobile reading devices and a convenient information-based reading environment make digital reading a new normal of reading and have a great impact on traditional reading. However, when readers are not fully prepared for digital reading, the improvement of reading ability is not easy to obtain. Individual factors with self-efficacy, reading motivation, and reading participation as the core are related to reading. This is a key predictor for exploring the relationship between digital readers and digital reading). The results show that the concerted efforts made by the students themselves, the teachers, the schools and the countries could contribute to the development of students' digital reading literacy.

## 5.2 The effects of the student-level factors

The ranking of the student-level factors is provided below in Table 5.1 for ease of reference. Individual level factors are the premise to improve readers' digital reading skills. Interaction with digital text is an important step for readers to understand the reading content and construct the meaning of the text. At the same time, when digital readers can actively participate in reading activities, the two core components of information literacy can also significantly improve reading ability.

Unsurprisingly, whether students like reading or not (JOYREAD) was found to be the strongest predictor of top-performing digital readers. Students' perception of reading competence (SCREADCOMP) and students' perception of reading difficulty (SCREADDIFF) are also found significant, which echoes with a plenty of previous findings on the strong effect of reading interests and self-efficacy on students' reading performance (e.g., HU et al., 2021; 2016; Susperreguy et al., 2018). Therefore, it is reasonable to posit that the interplay of various contextual factors shapes students' reading self-efficacy, which in turn contributes to digital reading performance.

Taking the uniqueness of digital reading into consideration, students' frequencies of taking part in online group discussions or forums (ST176Q06IA) and of searching for information online to learn about a specific topic (ST176Q05IA) are also of importance. These two activities are "information-searching activities"

**TABLE 5.1** The ranking of the student-level factors

| Rank | Key Factor | Description |
| --- | --- | --- |
| 1 | JOYREAD | Joy/Like reading |
| 2 | BSMJ | Students expected occupational status |
| 3 | SCREADCOMP | Self-concept of reading: perception of competence |
| 12 | SCREADDIFF | Self-concept of reading: perception of difficulty |
| 13 | GFOFAIL | General fear of failure |
| 14 | ST176Q02IA | How often involved in: <Chat on line> (e.g., <Whatsapp>, <Messenger>) |

*Seven of the 20 key features are student-level factors, with the top three features all.*

and "social interaction activities" respectively, playing a distinguished role in students' digital reading literacy. The information-searching activities mean more exposure to the online text, more often, academic text, which could help the students be familiar with the format of digital reading. However, the social interaction activities were found to negatively predict digital reading performance, because these activities performed in a playful way could largely sacrifice studying time for academic purposes.

Our results also contribute to the ongoing discussion about the role of reading self-efficacy affecting digital reading literacy development by identifying the important factor of students' interest in ICT (INTICT), which answers the question that whether digital reading and print reading share the same motivational process. Studies have shown that students with more positive attitudes towards computers are likely to take part in computer-related activities more frequently and develop more advanced computer knowledge and skills (e.g., Christoph et al., 2015). Different from print reading, motivational components related to ICT use is thus an important part in promoting students' digital reading literacy (Naumann, 2015).

Students interests in reading are followed directly by students' expected occupational status (BSMJ), which was found as a strong indicator of students digital reading literacy. This result echoes with a dominant number of studies testing the predictive power of occupational expectations (Han, 2015; Sikora, 2019). Previous studies have found that students who have clear occupational expectations tend to spend more time reading their job-related books (OECD, 2019). Our study further supports the idea that students' digital reading abilities were associated with perceptions of careers. However, since the impacts of different dimensions of occupational expectations tend to differ, future research could also consider disentangling the impact of different dimensions of occupational expectations in fostering high performers in digital reading.

## 5.3 The effects of the classroom-level factors

The ranking of the classroom-level factors is provided below in Table 5.2 for the ease of reference.

Basically, classroom activities and instructions (i.e., seven out of the top 20 key factors) are considered significant in explaining educational outcomes (Kyriakides et al., 2019). As for what students do and learn during class, the length of the reading material and the skills and knowledge of digital reading are identified as strong factors. Longer reading materials provided in class add more difficulties to reading, thus cultivating students' capability of coping with complex contents and logic in the materials. Teachers show students how to use the short description below the links in the list of results of a search (ST158Q05HA), to understand the consequences of making information publicly available online on social platform (ST158Q04HA), and to detect whether the information is

TABLE 5.2 The ranking of the classroom-level factors

| Rank | Key Factor | Description |
|---|---|---|
| 4 | ST158Q05HA_2 | Taught at school: How to use the short description below the links in the list of results of a search |
| 5 | ST154Q01HA | How many pages was the longest piece of text you had to read for your <test language lessons>? |
| 7 | ST158Q04HA_2 | Taught at school: To understand the consequences of making information publicly available online on <Facebook©>, <Instagram©>, etc. |
| 8 | ST158Q05HA_1 | Taught at school: How to use the short description below the links in the list of results of a search |
| 10 | DISCLIMA | Disciplinary climate in test language lessons |
| 11 | DIRINS | Teacher-directed instruction |
| 19 | ADAPTIVITY | Adaptation of instruction |

subjective or biased (ST158Q06HA) could help build a solid knowledge base for students. Additionally, the impartation of network morals could assist the students in being more cautious and prudent in judging online information.

Teachers' adaptation of instruction (ADAPTIVITY) and teacher support in test language lessons (TEACHSUP) could be conducive factors to students' digital reading literacy, while teacher-directed instruction (DIRINS) could inhibit their performances. It is suggested that inquiry-based instruction is generally more effective than other teacher-directed expository methods of instruction and (2) the effectiveness of inquiry-based instruction mainly depends on the appropriateness of guidance (Alfieri et al., 2011; Furtak et al., 2012; Lazonder & Harmsen, 2016). The detailed and intricate relationship between teacher instruction and student performances should be further explored in a more sophisticated experiment.

Contrary to previous findings that emphasized the benefits of teacher feedback and teacher support in students' learning (Borup et al., 2015; Burns et al., 2019; Grigoryan, 2017), the current findings suggest that perceived feedback (PERFEED) is a high-ranking risk factor for students' digital reading performance. The impact of teacher feedback depends heavily on not only the quality of the feedback provided by teachers but also students' perceptions of them (Higgins et al., 2002). For one thing, considering that there are relational boundaries between students and teachers and that teachers view learning as the primary goal, instructors would prefer to provide practical suggestions, which may help students circumvent obstacles rather than build resilience (Ellis, 2004). For another, Gikandi et al. (2011) point out that the effects of teacher feedback rest heavily on students' perceptions of it, which adds difficulties to the interpretation of results.

Informed by the general learning theories that student learning is influenced by the surroundings (Vygotsky, 1978), an orderly classroom environment has been considered indispensable for student learning (Sortkær & Reimer, 2018). This study identified the importance of a supportive classroom disciplinary climate (DISCLIMA), which could contribute to better academic achievement. In addition, the provision of ICT resources at school is way not enough for the improvement of students' digital reading literacy. Only in a strictly-managed and ordered classroom equipped with digital devices could students explore their potential to the greatest extent. Teachers should strengthen online reading training, actively carry out reading practice activities, help students improve their digital reading efficiency and reading comprehension, and make them become autonomous learners. A higher level of reading is closely related to effective teaching guidance. Instructors should improve the quality of digital guidance on students' reading strategies to help them improve their digital reading skills.

While increasing the frequency of ICT use, teachers should systematically consider the improvement of information literacy from the relationship between information awareness, knowledge, and skills. Information literacy needs targeted education intervention, which should be combined with students' understanding of their own ICT knowledge and skills defects, to carry out targeted training and strengthening, and guide them to further master the effective use strategies of ICT learning tools (HU & Yu, 2021). At the same time, we should actively explore how to improve the effectiveness of ICT use to continuously accumulate methods and ways to improve deep-seated information literacy. In addition, it is an important content of current reading education to strengthen the information literacy education of the existing curriculum system and cultivate students' ability to collect and analyse information that matches the knowledge society.

## 5.4 The effects of the school-level factors

The ranking of the school-level factors is provided below in Table 5.3 for ease of reference. The general development of information technology has changed the way of obtaining information and the form of carrier. Digital reading resources and learning materials have become an indispensable part of school life. Digital reading is an available skill. Schools should help students acquire effective or efficient digital reading abilities.

Different from the previous research that focuses on the number of teachers exclusively, the current findings draw special attention to the qualification of teachers. More specifically, the proportion of fully certified science teachers (PROSTCE) and the proportion of all teachers with ISCED LEVEL 5A Master (PROAT5AM) ranked top among the school-level factors in predicting high performance and their low-performing counterparts in digital reading, emphasizing the importance of taking teachers' qualifications into consideration in

**TABLE 5.3** The ranking of the school-level factors

| Rank | Key Factor | Description |
|---|---|---|
| 6 | SC061Q01TA | Extent to which student learning is hindered by: Student truancy |
| 9 | CREACTIV | Creative extra-curricular activities (sum) |
| 15 | PROATCE | Index proportion of all teachers fully certified |
| 17 | PROAT5AB | Index proportion of all teachers ISCED LEVEL 5A Bachelor |
| 18 | SC001Q01TA | Which of the following definitions best describes the community in which your school is located? |
| 20 | SC037Q08TA_3 | Quality assurance at school: Teacher mentoring |

promoting students' digital reading literacy. In addition, the location of a school could also predict the high and low performers. Schools at developed locations boast access to emerging learning materials and other resources, which could build a better environment for digital readers. However, it should be noted that the equity of the school (i.e., soft environment) and disciplinary context are also very important, because students may face severe discrimination and negative behavior (SC061Q01TA) in schools with low effectiveness.

As for the extracurricular activities provided by schools, our study has shown that involvement in creative extra-curricular activities (CREACTIV), or participation in the debating club or debating activities (SC053Q13IA) and art club or art activities (SC053Q09TA) could conduce to the development of digital reading literacy. This could be explained by the following two reasons. First, the provision of reading-related activities could increase student motivation to read, which in turn may enhance their performances. Second, debating could help improve students' logical thinking and familiarize them with certain topics, while art could provoke students' development of the brain and help the students stay focused when studying. Our results thus further provide evidence and concluded that participation in extra-curricular activities had positive outcomes for adolescents in digital reading, echoing abundant previous studies (Feldman & Matjasko, 2005; Schreiber & Chambers, 2002). In addition, schools should provide students with a variety of reading materials and electronic reading conditions, create a good reading environment, and make them gain more reading fun and positive reading experience.

## References

Alfieri, L., Brooks, P. J., Aldrich, N. J., & Tenenbaum, H. R. (2011). Does discovery-based instruction enhance learning? *Journal of Educational Psychology*, *103*(1), 1–18. https://doi.org/10.1037/a0021017

Borup, J., West, R. E., & Thomas, R. (2015). The impact of text versus video communication on instructor feedback in blended courses. *Educational Technology Research and Development*, *63*(2), 161–184. https://doi.org/10.1007/s11423-015-9367-8

Burns, E. C., Martin, A. J., & Collie, R. J. (2019). Examining the yields of growth feedback from science teachers and students' intrinsic valuing of science: Implications for student-and school-level science achievement. *Journal of Research in Science Teaching*, Advanced online publication. https://doi.org/10.1002/tea.21546

Christoph, G., Goldhammer, F., Zylka, J., & Hartig, J. (2015). Adolescents' computer performance: The role of self-concept and motivational aspects. *Computers & Education, 81,* 1–12. https://doi.org/10.1016/j.compedu.2014.09.004

Ellis, K. (2004). The impact of perceived teacher confirmation on receiver apprehension, motivation, and learning. *Communication Education, 53,* 1–20. https://doi.org/10.1080/036345203200013574

Feldman, A. F., & Matjasko, J. L. (2005). The role of school-based extracurricular activities in adolescent development: A comprehensive review and future directions. *Review of Educational Research.* https://doi.org/10.3102/00346543075002159

Furtak, E. M., Seidel, T., Iverson, H., & Briggs, D. C. (2012). Experimental and quasi-experimental studies of inquiry-based science teaching: A meta-analysis. *Review of Educational Research, 82*(3), 300–329. https://doi.org/10.3102/0034654312457206

Gikandi, J. W., Morrow, D., & Davis, N. E. (2011). Online formative assessment in higher education: A review of the literature. *Computers & Education, 57*(4), 2333–2351. https://doi.org/10.1016/j.compedu.2011.06.004

Grigoryan, A. (2017). Feedback 2.0 in online writing instruction: Combining audiovisual and text-based commentary to enhance student revision and writing competency. *Journal of Computing in Higher Education, 29*(3), 451–476. https://doi.org/10.1007/s12528-017-9152-2

Han, S. W. (2015). Curriculum standardization, stratification, and students' STEM-related occupational expectations: Evidence from PISA 2006. *International Journal of Educational Research, 72,* 103–115. https://doi.org/10.1016/j.ijer.2015.04.012

Higgins, R., Hartley, P. & Skelton, A. (2002). The conscientious consumer: Reconsidering the role of assessment feedback in student learning. *Studies in Higher Education, 27*(1), 53–64. https://doi.org/10.1080/03075070120099368

HU, J., Dong, X. & Peng, Y (2021). Discovery of the key contextual factors relevant to the reading performance of elementary school students from 61 countries/regions: Insight from a machine learning-based approach. *Reading and Writing, 35*(1), 93–127. https://doi.org/10.1007/s11145-021-10176-z

Kyriakides, L., Creemers, B. P. M., & Charalambous, E. (2019). Searching for differential teacher and school effectiveness in terms of student socioeconomic status and gender: implications for promoting equity. *School Effectiveness and School Improvement, 30*(3), 286–308. https://doi.org/10.1080/09243453.2018.1511603

Lazonder, A. W., & Harmsen, R. (2016). Meta-analysis of inquiry-based learning: Effects of guidance. *Review of Educational Research, 86*(3), 681–718. https://doi.org/10.3102/0034654315627366

Naumann, J. (2015). A model of online reading engagement: Linking engagement, navigation, and performance in digital reading. *Computers in Human Behavior, 53,* 263–277. https://doi.org/10.1016/j.chb.2015.06.051

OECD. (2019). *PISA 2018 results (Volume I): What students know and can do.* Paris: OECD Publishing. https://doi.org/10.1787/5f07c754-en

Schreiber, J. B., & Chambers, E. A. (2002). After-school pursuits, ethnicity, and achievement for 8th- and 10th-grade students. *Journal of Educational Research, 96*(2), 90–100. https://doi.org/10.1080/00220670209598796

Sikora, J. (2019). Is it all about early occupational expectations? How the gender gap in two science domains reproduces itself at subsequent stages of education: Evidence from longitudinal PISA in Australia. *International Journal of Science Education, 41*(16), 1464–5289. https://doi.org/10.1080/09500693.2019.1676933

Sortkær, B., & Reimer, D. (2018). Classroom disciplinary climate of schools and gender-evidence from the Nordic countries. *School Effectiveness and School Improvement, 29*(4), 511–528. https://doi.org/10.1080/09243453.2018.1460382

Susperreguy, M. I., Davis-Kean, P. E., Duckworht, K., & Chen, M. (2018). Self-concept predicts academic achievement across levels of the achievement distribution: Domain specificity for math and reading. *Child Development, 89*, 2196–2214. https://doi.org/10.1111/cdev.12924

Vygotsky, L. S. (1978). *Mind in society: The development of higher psychological processes.* Cambridge, MA: Harvard University Press.

# 6
# CONCLUSION AND LIMITATION

## 6.1 Conclusion

According to the 18th National Reading Survey, in 2020, the comprehensive reading rate of various media of China's adult citizens continued to grow steadily, and the book reading rate and digital reading contact rate showed an upward trend. In addition, the amount of e-book reading per capita has increased compared with the previous year, so has the scale of in-depth readers, which has called for the urgent need to promote the quality of digital reading literacy. Generally, students' interests in reading, classroom ICT teaching, and school learning environment are found significant in predicting students' digital reading performance. This study has provided innovative results and constructive perspectives that could shed light on the overall enhancement of pedagogy and the improvement of digital learning environment.

Schooling and teaching is a moderator of students' family socioeconomic background, gender, and digital reading literacy, and can bridge the "digital divide" in students' reading literacy. Therefore, schools and teachers play an indispensable role in promoting digital reading literacy education for students in the information age. In general, schools can strengthen the cultivation of students' digital reading literacy in the following ways. First, attention should be paid to engaging digital texts in the classroom to strengthen students' ability to read multiple texts and dynamic texts. It is important to note that images, videos, and other elements of digital text can be used to stimulate students' interest in reading, but not for this sole purpose. Digital reading instruction is not just about increasing sensory stimulation, but about improving students' cognitive abilities in the reading process. Second, schools should emphasize students' assessment and reflection on texts to develop higher-order reading literacy. In digital reading, students' ability to assess and reflect on texts has become an important indicator

DOI: 10.4324/9781003351108-6

of whether they are good readers. These skills could be cultivated through reading instruction (e.g., "controversial reading" and "evidence-based reading". In this way, students develop a deeper understanding of what evidence is and how to use it to find and use it and become scientifically prudent readers.

Teachers are the practitioners of national campus informatization policy, the integrators of social digital resources, and the promoters and experiencers of digital teaching. Teachers should improve their own digital reading literacy, shoulder social responsibility, maintain continuous communication and exchange with students, promote the rational and efficient use of resources, guide students in digital reading, and at the same time do a good job of regulating and guiding digital reading, and regulating students' digital reading. In addition, teachers cooperate with each other to increase innovation and research on digital teaching and learning, and to manage and guide students in different subjects, regions, and grades in a humane way. Therefore, to promote the construction and development of education informatization in the smart era, it is necessary to enhance the connotation of digital education resources, create a campus culture of digital education resources application, and improve the self-efficacy of teachers' digital education resources to better drive students to digital reading.

Students themselves should first try to be familiar with the digital environment and have certain information literacy or relevant reading experience, all of which affect their digital reading effect. To enhance students' ability to adapt to and use digital reading, they should find a sense of affinity and belonging in the digital environment, so that they can psychologically accept digital reading and become interested in it to improve the efficiency of reading. In today's digital environment, students should take the initiative to learn the skills of digital use, actively adapt to the digital reading environment, make reasonable use of digital technology, and consciously improve their digital reading ability. In addition, there is a large amount of false information in the digital reading environment, students should have certain screening and judging abilities and network public morality, improve students' search literacy, searchability and search skills, and have more accurate positioning and grasp of information and reading materials. At the same time, they should enhance their reading literacy and be familiar with the mode of digital reading. Students should be familiar with the mode of digital reading and the rules of reading, so that they can accurately locate and grasp the information.

## 6.2 Research limitations

There are several limitations in our study which might be of implications for future studies.

First, although the sample size used in this study covers 38 countries, the data from PISA 2018, like all other large international assessments, are cross-sectional rather than long-term studies, and therefore have a limited basis for determining the causal relationship between environmental factors and digital reading literacy. Future research suggests further validation of these characteristics by looking at some long-term characteristics (e.g., the impact of preschool education) to form longitudinal data.

Second, according to the dynamic model of educational effectiveness, each effective factor should be a multidimensional construct that can be measured by frequency, focus, stage, quality, and differentiation. However, the design of the PISA questionnaire treats each effective factor as a unidimensional construct, which may lead to a certain degree of missing information. Therefore, multidimensional constructs of factors should be considered in future laboratory designs to enhance the accuracy and reliability of the test.

Finally, similar to most statistical learning methods, the machine learning method of support vector machines can find the best set of influencing factors, but it is difficult to clarify the interactions among the factors and cannot prove the causality. Future research can build on this study and continue to use methods such as path analysis and mediation analysis to further explore the influence paths among the factors, clarify the specific effects of the influences, and propose more detailed scientific guidance for improving students' digital reading literacy.

# APPENDIX

The detailed description of the original 146 variables/factors

# Appendix

| Variable | Description | Question No. | Question | Value Scale | Questionnaire |
|---|---|---|---|---|---|
| *Variables for defining high and low performers* | | | | | |
| PV1READ | Plausible Value 1 in Reading | | It represents the students' reading test performance. | 0~887.692 | STU |
| *Student-level factors* | | | | | |
| ST004D01T | Student (Standardized) Gender | | 1 = Female<br>2 = Male | 1~2 | STU |
| BSMJ | Students expected occupational status (SEI) | | What kind of job do you expect to have when you are ~30 years old? | 11.01~88.96 | STU |
| BEINGBULLIED | Student's experience of being bullied (WLE) | | PISA 2018 asked (ST038) students how often ("never or almost never", "a few times a year", "a few times a month", "once a week or more") during the 12 months prior to the PISA test they had the following experiences in school, including those that happen in social media: "Other students left me out of things on purpose"; "Other students made fun of me"; "I was threatened by other students"; "Other students took away or destroyed things that belong to me"; "I got hit or pushed around by other students"; and "Other students spread nasty rumours about me". The first three statements were combined to construct the index of exposure to bullying (BEINGBULLIED). | −0.7823~3.8591 | STU |
| ESCS | Index of economic, social and cultural status | | For the purpose of computing the PISA index of economic, social, and cultural status (ESCS), values for students with missing PARED, HISEI, or HOMEPOS were imputed with predicted values plus a random component based on a regression on the other two variables. If there were missing data on more than one of the three variables, ESCS was not computed and a missing value was assigned for ESCS. | −8.1734~4.2051 | STU |

| Variable | Description | Question No. | Question | Value Scale | Questionnaire |
|---|---|---|---|---|---|
| JOYREAD | Joy/Like reading (WLE) | | The index of enjoyment of reading (JOYREAD) was constructed based on a trend question (ST160) from PISA 2009 (ID in 2009: ST24) asking students whether they agree ("strongly agree", "agree", "disagree", "strongly disagree") with the following statements: "I read only if I have to"; "Reading is one of my favourite hobbies"; "I like talking about books with other people"; "For me, reading is a waste of time"; and "I read only to get information that I need". | −3.2096~4.0128 | STU |
| SCREADCOMP | Self-concept of reading: Perception of competence (WLE) | | PISA 2018 asked (ST161) students to report the extent to which they agree ("strongly disagree", "disagree", "agree", "strongly agree") with the following statements about their self-concept in reading: "I am a good reader"; "I am able to understand difficult texts"; and "I read fluently". These statements were combined to create the index of perceived competence in reading (SCREADCOMP). | −2.4403~1.9713 | STU |
| SCREADDIFF | Self-concept of reading: Perception of difficulty (WLE) | | PISA 2018 asked (ST161) students to report the extent to which they agree ("strongly disagree", "disagree", "agree", "strongly agree") with the following statements about their self-concept in reading: "I have always had difficulty with reading"; "I have to read a text several times before completely understanding it."; and "I find it difficult to answer questions about a text". These statements were combined to create the index of the perceived difficulty in reading (SCREADDIFF). | −1.8876~2.7752 | STU |

*(Continued)*

| Variable | Description | Question No. | Question | Value Scale | Questionnaire |
|---|---|---|---|---|---|
| PISADIFF | Perception of difficulty of the PISA test (WLE) | PISA 2018 asked (ST163) students to report the extent to which they agree ("strongly disagree", "disagree", "agree", "strongly agree") with the following statements about their perception of the difficulty of the PISA test: "There were many words I could not understand"; "Many texts were too difficult for me"; and "I was lost when I had to navigate between different pages". These statements were combined to create the index of perception of the difficulty of the PISA test (PISADIFF). | −1.272~3.0064 | STU |
| PERCOMP | Perception of competitiveness at school (WLE) | PISA 2018 asked (ST205) students how true ("not at all true", "slightly true", "very true", "extremely true") the following statements about their school are: "Students seem to value competition"; "It seems that students are competing with each other"; "Students seem to share the feeling that competing with each other is important"; and "Students feel that they are being compared with others". The first three statements were combined to create the index of student competition (PERCOMP). | −1.9892~2.0378 | STU |
| PERCOOP | Perception of cooperation at school (WLE) | PISA 2018 asked (ST206) students how true ("not at all true", "slightly true", "very true", "extremely true") the following statements about their school are: "Students seem to value co-operation"; "It seems that students are co-operating with each other"; "Students seem to share the feeling that co-operating with each other is important"; and "Students feel that they are encouraged to cooperate with others". The first three statements were combined to create the index of student cooperation (PERCOOP). | −2.1428~1.6762 | STU |

| Variable | Description | Question No. | Question | Value Scale | Questionnaire |
|---|---|---|---|---|---|
| ATTLNACT | Attitude towards school: learning activities (WLE) | | The index of the value of school (ATTLNACT) was constructed based on a trend question (ST036) asking students whether they agree ("strongly agree", "agree", "disagree", "strongly disagree") with the following statements: "Trying hard at school will help me get a good job"; "Trying hard at school will help me get into a good <college>"; and "Trying hard at school is important". | −2.5375~1.0844 | STU |
| COMPETE | Competitiveness (WLE) | | The index of attitudes towards competition (COMPETE) was constructed using students' responses to a new question (ST181) over the extent they "strongly agreed", "agreed", "disagreed" or "strongly disagreed" with the following statements: "I enjoy working in situations involving competition with others"; "It is important for me to perform better than other people on a task"; and "I try harder when I'm in competition with other people". | −2.345~2.0054 | STU |
| WORKMAST | Work mastery (WLE) | | PISA 2018 asked students (ST182) to report the extent to which they agree or disagree ("strongly disagree", "disagree", "agree", "strongly agree") with the following statements: "I find satisfaction in working as hard as I can"; "Once I start a task, I persist until it is finished"; "Part of the enjoyment I get from doing things is when I improve on my past performance"; and "If I am not good at something, I would rather keep struggling to master it than move on to something I may be good at". The first three statements were combined to create the index of motivation to master tasks (WORKMAST). | −2.7365~1.8164 | STU |

*(Continued)*

| Variable | Description | Question No. | Question | Value Scale | Questionnaire |
|---|---|---|---|---|---|
| GFOFAIL | General fear of failure (WLE) | Students in PISA 2018 were asked to report the extent to which they agree ("strongly disagree", "disagree", "agree", "strongly agree") with the following statements (ST183): "When I am failing, I worry about what others think of me"; "When I am failing, I am afraid that I might not have enough talent"; and "When I am failing, this makes me doubt my plans for the future". These statements were combined to create the index of fear of failure (GFOFAIL). | | −1.8939~1.8905 | STU |
| RESILIENCE | Resilience (WLE) | PISA 2018 asked (ST188) students to report the extent to which they agree ("strongly disagree", "disagree", "agree", "strongly agree") with the following statements about themselves: "I usually manage one way or another"; "I feel proud that I have accomplished things"; "I feel that I can handle many things at a time"; "My belief in myself gets me through hard times"; and "When I'm in a difficult situation, I can usually find my way out of it". These statements were combined to create the index of self-efficacy (RESILIENCE). | | −3.205~3.0953 | STU |
| MASTGOAL | Mastery goal orientation (WLE) | Students in PISA 2018 were asked (ST208) to respond how true ("not at all true of me", "slightly true of me", "moderately true of me", "very true of me", "extremely true of me") the following statements are for them: "My goal is to learn as much as possible"; "My goal is to completely master the material presented in my classes"; and "My goal is to understand the content of my classes as thoroughly as possible". These statements were combined to construct the index of learning goals (MASTGOAL). | | −2.5252~1.8524 | STU |

Appendix **187**

| Variable | Description | Question No. | Question | Value Scale | Questionnaire |
|---|---|---|---|---|---|
| BELONG | Subjective well-being: Sense of belonging to school (WLE) | | The index of sense of belonging (BELONG) was constructed using students' responses to a trend question about their sense of belonging to school. Students were asked whether they agree ("strongly agree", "agree", "disagree", "strongly disagree") with the following statements (ST034): "I feel like an outsider (or left out of things) at school"; "I make friends easily at school"; "I feel like I belong at school"; "I feel awkward and out of place in my school"; "Other students seem to like me"; and "I feel lonely at school". Three of these items were reversed-coded. | −3.8448~3.9838 | STU |
| INTICT | Interest in ICT (WLE) | — | | −3.0242~2.7721 | STU |
| COMPICT | Perceived ICT competence (WLE) | — | | −2.6188~2.5782 | STU |
| ST150Q01IA | During the last month, how often did you have to read for school? | | Texts that include diagrams or maps. 1 = Many times 2 = Two or three times 3 = Once 4 = Not at all | 1~4 | STU |
| ST150Q02IA | During the last month, how often did you have to read for school? | | Fiction (e.g., novels, short stories) 1 = Many times 2 = Two or three times 3 = Once 4 = Not at all | 1~4 | STU |
| ST150Q03IA | During the last month, how often did you have to read for school? | | Texts that include tables or graphs. 1 = Many times 2 = Two or three times 3 = Once 4 = Not at all | 1~4 | STU |

(*Continued*)

# Appendix

| Variable | Description | Question No. | Question | Value Scale | Questionnaire |
|---|---|---|---|---|---|
| ST150Q04HA | During the last month, how often did you have to read for school? | Digital texts including links | 1 = Many times<br>2 = Two or three times<br>3 = Once<br>4 = Not at all | 1~4 | STU |
| ST154Q01HA | <this academic year>, how many pages was the longest piece of text you had to read for your <test language lessons>? | ST154Q01HA | 1 = One page or less<br>2 = Between 2 and 10 pages<br>3 = Between 11 and 50 pages<br>4 = Between 51 and 100 pages<br>5 = Between 101 and 500 pages<br>6 = More than 500 pages | 1~6 | STU |
| ST176Q01IA | How often are you involved in the following reading activities? | Reading emails | 1 = I don't know what it is<br>2 = Never or almost never<br>3 = Several times a month<br>4 = Several times a week<br>5 = Several times a day | 1~5 | STU |
| ST176Q02IA | How often are you involved in the following reading activities? | <Chat on line> (e.g. <Whatsapp>, <Messenger>) | 1 = I don't know what it is<br>2 = Never or almost never<br>3 = Several times a month<br>4 = Several times a week<br>5 = Several times a day | 1~5 | STU |
| ST176Q03IA | How often are you involved in the following reading activities? | Reading online news | 1 = I don't know what it is<br>2 = Never or almost never<br>3 = Several times a month<br>4 = Several times a week<br>5 = Several times a day | 1~5 | STU |

| Variable | Description | Question No. | Question | Value Scale | Questionnaire |
|---|---|---|---|---|---|
| ST176Q05IA | How often are you involved in the following reading activities? | Searching information online to learn about a particular topic | 1 = I don't know what it is<br>2 = Never or almost never<br>3 = Several times a month<br>4 = Several times a week<br>5 = Several times a day | 1~5 | STU |
| ST176Q06IA | How often are you involved in the following reading activities? | Taking part in online group discussions or forums | 1 = I don't know what it is<br>2 = Never or almost never<br>3 = Several times a month<br>4 = Several times a week<br>5 = Several times a day | 1~5 | STU |
| ST176Q07IA | How often are you involved in the following reading activities? | Searching for practical information online (e.g. schedules, events, tips, recipes) | 1 = I don't know what it is<br>2 = Never or almost never<br>3 = Several times a month<br>4 = Several times a week<br>5 = Several times a day | 1~5 | STU |
| *Classroom-level factors* | | | | | |
| DISCLIMA | Disciplinary climate in test language lessons (WLE) | The index of disciplinary climate (DISCLIMA) was constructed using students' responses to a trend question about how often ("every lesson", "most lessons", "some lessons", "never or hardly ever") the following happened in their language-of-instruction lessons (ST097): "Students don't listen to what the teacher says"; "There is noise and disorder"; "The teacher has to wait a long time for students to quiet down"; "Students cannot work well"; and "Students don't start working for a long time after the lesson begins". Positive values on this scale mean that the student enjoyed a better disciplinary climate in language-of-instruction lessons than the average student across OECD countries. | | −2.7124~2.3017 | STU |

*(Continued)*

| Variable | Description | Question No. Question | Value Scale | Questionnaire |
|---|---|---|---|---|
| TEACHSUP | Teacher support in test language lessons (WLE) | The index of teacher support (TEACHSUP) was constructed using students' responses to a trend question (ST100) about how often ("every lesson", "most lessons", "some lessons", "never or hardly ever") the following things happen in their language-of-instruction lessons: "The teacher shows an interest in every student's learning"; "The teacher gives extra help when students need it"; "The teacher helps students with their learning"; and "The teacher continues teaching until the students understand". Positive values on this scale mean that students perceived their teacher to be more supportive than did the average student across OECD countries. | −2.7426~1.3411 | STU |
| DIRINS | Teacher-directed instruction (WLE) | The index of teacher-directed instruction (DIRINS) was constructed from students' reports on how often ("never or almost never", "some lessons", "many lessons", "every lesson or almost every lesson") the following happened in their language-of-instruction lessons (ST102): "The teacher sets clear goals for our learning"; "The teacher asks questions to check whether we have understood what was taught"; "At the beginning of a lesson, the teacher presents a short summary of the previous lesson"; and "The teacher tells us what we have to learn". Positive values on this scale mean that students perceived their teachers to use teacher-directed practices more frequently than did the average student across OECD countries. | −2.9425~1.8202 | STU |

| Variable | Description | Question No. | Question | Value Scale | Questionnaire |
|---|---|---|---|---|---|
| PERFEED | Perceived feedback (WLE) | | The index of teacher feedback (PERFEED) was constructed using students' responses to a trend question (ST104) about how often ("never or hardly ever", "some lessons", "most lessons", "every lesson") the following things happen in their language-of-instruction lessons: "The teacher gives me feedback on my strengths in this subject"; "The teacher tells me in which areas I can still improve"; and "The teacher tells me how I can improve my performance". Positive values on this scale mean that students perceived their teachers to provide feedback more frequently than did the average student across OECD countries. | −1.6391~2.0165 | STU |
| STIMREAD | Teacher's stimulation of reading engagement perceived by student (WLE) | | The index of teachers' stimulation of reading engagement (STIMREAD) was constructed partly based on questions (ST152) from PISA 2009 (ID in 2009: ST37) asking students how often («never or hardly ever", "some lessons", "most lessons", "every lesson") the following occur in their language-of-instruction lessons: "The teacher encourages students to express their opinion about a text"; "The teacher helps students relate the stories they read to their lives"; "The teacher shows students how the information in texts builds on what they already know"; and "The teacher poses questions that motivate students to participate actively". Positive values on this scale mean that the students perceived their teacher to provide greater stimulation than did the average student across OECD countries. | −2.3003~2.0871 | STU |

(*Continued*)

| Variable | Description | Question No. | Question | Value Scale | Questionnaire |
|---|---|---|---|---|---|
| ADAPTIVITY | Adaptation of instruction (WLE) | | The index of adaptive instruction (ADAPTIVITY) was constructed using students' responses to a new question developed for PISA 2018 (ST212). Students reported how often ("never or almost never", "some lessons", "many lessons", "every lesson or almost every lesson") the following things happened in language-of-instruction lessons: "The teacher adapts the lesson to my class's needs and knowledge"; "The teacher provides individual help when a student has difficulties understanding a topic or task"; and "The teacher changes the structure of the lesson on a topic that most students find difficult to understand". Positive values on this scale mean that students perceived their language-of-instruction teachers to be more adaptive than did the average student across OECD countries. | −2.2652~2.0073 | STU |
| TEACHINT | Perceived teacher's interest (WLE) | | PISA 2018 asked (ST213) students whether they agree ("strongly agree", "agree", "disagree", "strongly disagree") with the following statements about the two language-of-instruction lessons they attended prior to sitting the PISA test: "It was clear to me that the teacher liked teaching us"; "The enthusiasm of the teacher inspired me"; "It was clear that the teacher likes to deal with the topic of the lesson"; and "The teacher showed enjoyment in teaching". These statements were combined to create the index of teacher enthusiasm (TEACHINT). Positive values in this index mean that students perceived their language-of-instruction teachers to be more enthusiastic than did the average student across OECD countries. | −2.2707~1.8245 | STU |

Appendix **193**

| Variable | Description | Question No. | Question | Value Scale | Questionnaire |
|---|---|---|---|---|---|
| SC042Q01TA | What is your school's policy about this for students in <national modal grade for 15-year-olds>? | Students are grouped by ability into different classes. | 1 = For all subjects<br>2 = For some subjects<br>3 = Not for any subjects | 1~3 | SCH |
| SC042Q02TA | What is your school's policy about this for students in <national modal grade for 15-year-olds>? | Students are grouped by ability within their classes. | 1 = For all subjects<br>2 = For some subjects<br>3 = Not for any subjects | 1~3 | SCH |
| SC154Q01HA | School's use of assessments of students | To guide students' learning | 1 = Yes<br>2 = No | 1~2 | SCH |
| SC154Q02WA | School's use of assessments of students | To inform parents about their child's progress | 1 = Yes<br>2 = No | 1~2 | SCH |
| SC154Q03WA | School's use of assessments of students | To make decisions about students' retention or promotion | 1 = Yes<br>2 = No | 1~2 | SCH |
| SC154Q04WA | School's use of assessments of students | To group students for instructional purposes | 1 = Yes<br>2 = No | 1~2 | SCH |

(*Continued*)

| Variable | Description | Question No. | Question | Value Scale | Questionnaire |
|---|---|---|---|---|---|
| SC154Q05WA | School's use of assessments of students | To compare the school to <district or national> performance | 1 = Yes<br>2 = No | 1~2 | SCH |
| SC154Q06WA | School's use of assessments of students | To monitor the schools progress from year to year | 1 = Yes<br>2 = No | 1~2 | SCH |
| SC154Q07WA | School's use of assessments of students | To make judgments about teachers' effectiveness | 1 = Yes<br>2 = No | 1~2 | SCH |
| SC154Q08WA | School's use of assessments of students | To identify aspects of the instruction or the curriculum that could be improved | 1 = Yes<br>2 = No | 1~2 | SCH |
| SC154Q09HA | School's use of assessments of students | To adapt teaching to the students' needs | 1 = Yes<br>2 = No | 1~2 | SCH |
| SC154Q10WA | School's use of assessments of students | To compare the school with other schools | 1 = Yes<br>2 = No | 1~2 | SCH |
| SC154Q11HA | School's use of assessments of students | To award certificates to students | 1 = Yes<br>2 = No | 1~2 | SCH |
| SC061Q01TA | In your school, to what extent is the learning of students hindered by the following phenomena? | Student truancy | 1 = Not at all<br>2 = Very little<br>3 = To some extent<br>4 = A lot | 1~4 | SCH |

| Variable | Description | Question No. | Question | Value Scale | Questionnaire |
|---|---|---|---|---|---|
| SC061Q02TA | In your school, to what extent is the learning of students hindered by the following phenomena? | Students skipping classes | 1 = Not at all<br>2 = Very little<br>3 = To some extent<br>4 = A lot | 1~4 | SCH |
| SC061Q03TA | In your school, to what extent is the learning of students hindered by the following phenomena? | Students lacking respect for teachers | 1 = Not at all<br>2 = Very little<br>3 = To some extent<br>4 = A lot | 1~4 | SCH |
| SC061Q04TA | In your school, to what extent is the learning of students hindered by the following phenomena? | Student use of alcohol or illegal drugs | 1 = Not at all<br>2 = Very little<br>3 = To some extent<br>4 = A lot | 1~4 | SCH |

*(Continued)*

| Variable | Description | Question No. | Question | Value Scale | Questionnaire |
|---|---|---|---|---|---|
| SC061Q05TA | In your school, to what extent is the learning of students hindered by the following phenomena? | Students intimidating or bullying other students | 1 = Not at all<br>2 = Very little<br>3 = To some extent<br>4 = A lot | 1~4 | SCH |
| SC061Q11HA | In your school, to what extent is the learning of students hindered by the following phenomena? | Students not being attentive | 1 = Not at all<br>2 = Very little<br>3 = To some extent<br>4 = A lot | 1~4 | SCH |
| SC061Q06TA | In your school, to what extent is the learning of students hindered by the following phenomena? | Teachers not meeting individual students' needs | 1 = Not at all<br>2 = Very little<br>3 = To some extent<br>4 = A lot | 1~4 | SCH |
| SC061Q07TA | In your school, to what extent is the learning of students hindered by the following phenomena? | Teacher absenteeism | 1 = Not at all<br>2 = Very little<br>3 = To some extent<br>4 = A lot | 1~4 | SCH |

Appendix **197**

| Variable | Description | Question No. | Question | Value Scale | Questionnaire |
|---|---|---|---|---|---|
| SC061Q08TA | In your school, to what extent is the learning of students hindered by the following phenomena? | Staff resisting change | 1 = Not at all<br>2 = Very little<br>3 = To some extent<br>4 = A lot | 1~4 | SCH |
| SC061Q09TA | In your school, to what extent is the learning of students hindered by the following phenomena? | Teachers being too strict with students | 1 = Not at all<br>2 = Very little<br>3 = To some extent<br>4 = A lot | 1~4 | SCH |
| SC061Q10TA | In your school, to what extent is the learning of students hindered by the following phenomena? | Teachers not being well prepared for classes | 1 = Not at all<br>2 = Very little<br>3 = To some extent<br>4 = A lot | 1~4 | SCH |
| ST158Q01HA | At school, have you ever been taught the following things? | How to use keywords when using a search engine such as <Google>, <Yahoo>, etc. | 1 = Yes<br>2 = No | 1~2 | STU |

(*Continued*)

# 198 Appendix

| Variable | Description | Question No. | Question | Value Scale | Questionnaire |
|---|---|---|---|---|---|
| ST158Q02HA | At school, have you ever been taught the following things? | How to decide whether to trust information from the Internet | 1 = Yes<br>2 = No | 1~2 | STU |
| ST158Q03HA | At school, have you ever been taught the following things? | How to compare different web pages and decide what information is more relevant for your school work | 1 = Yes<br>2 = No | 1~2 | STU |
| ST158Q04HA | At school, have you ever been taught the following things? | To understand the consequences of making information publicly available online on <Facebook©>, <Instagram©>, etc. | 1 = Yes<br>2 = No | 1~2 | STU |
| ST158Q05HA | At school, have you ever been taught the following things? | How to use the short description below the links in the list of results of a search | 1 = Yes<br>2 = No | 1~2 | STU |
| ST158Q06HA | At school, have you ever been taught the following things? | How to detect whether the information is subjective or biased | 1 = Yes<br>2 = No | 1~2 | STU |
| ST158Q07HA | At school, have you ever been taught the following things? | How to detect phishing or spam emails | 1 = Yes<br>2 = No | 1~2 | STU |
| *School-level factors* | | | | | |
| ICTSCH | ICT available at school | – | | 0~10 | STU |

Appendix **199**

| Variable | Description | Question No. | Question | Value Scale | Questionnaire |
|---|---|---|---|---|---|
| SCHLTYPE | School Ownership | | Schools are classified as either public or private according to whether a private entity or a public agency has the ultimate power to make decisions concerning its affairs. As in previous PISA surveys, the index of school type (SCHLTYPE) has three categories: (1) public schools managed directly or indirectly by a public education authority, government agency, or governing board appointed by the government or elected by a public franchise; (2) government-dependent private schools, managed directly or indirectly by a non-government organization (e.g., a church, trade union, business or other private institution), which receive more than 50% of their total funding in a typical school year from government agencies (including departments, local, regional, state and national agencies); and (3) government independent private schools, controlled by a non-government organization, which receive less han 50% of their core funding from government agencies. | 1~3 | SCH |
| STRATIO | Student–Teacher ratio | | This variable is derived from SC018, SC002, which is obtained by dividing the total number of students (SC002) by the number of Teachers in total (SC018Q01TA). | 1~100 | SCH |
| SCHSIZE | School size (sum) | | The PISA 2009 index of school size (SCHLSIZE) contains the total enrolment at school based on the enrolment data provided by the school principal, summing the number of girls and boys at a school. | 1~13,400 | SCH |
| RATCMP1 | Number of available computers per student at modal grade | | This variable is derived SC004, which asks about the student-computer ratio in school. (e.g., Approximately how many data projectors are available in the school altogether) | 0~25 | SCH |

*(Continued)*

| Variable | Description | Question No. | Question | Value Scale | Questionnaire |
|---|---|---|---|---|---|
| RATCMP2 | Proportion of available computers that are connected to the Internet | | This variable is also derived from SC004, which focuses on students' access to the Internet (e.g., Approximately, how many of these computers are connected to the Internet/World Wide Web). | 0~1 | SCH |
| PROATCE | Index proportion of all teachers fully certified | | | 0~1 | SCH |
| PROAT5AB | Index proportion of all teachers ISCED LEVEL 5A Bachelor | | This variable is derived from SC018 which asks questions about the number of certain kinds of teachers in the school. PROAT5AB was obtained through SC018Q05NA and was calculated by dividing the number of teachers 'with an <ISCED Level 5A Bachelor degree> qualification' by the total number (SC018Q01TA) of teachers. | 0~1 | SCH |
| PROAT5AM | Index proportion of all teachers ISCED LEVEL 5A Master | | This variable is based on SC018, which is obtained by dividing the number of teachers with an ISCED Level 5A Master's degree qualification (SC018Q06NA) by the total number. | 0~1 | SCH |
| PROAT6 | Index proportion of all teachers ISCED LEVEL 6 | | This variable is derived from SC018, which is obtained by diving the number of teachers with an <ISCED Level 6> qualification (SC018Q07NA) by the total number. | 0~1 | SCH |

| Variable | Description | Question No. | Question | Value Scale | Questionnaire |
|---|---|---|---|---|---|
| CLSIZE | Class Size | 13 = 15 students or fewer<br>18 = 16–20 students<br>23 = 21–25 students<br>28 = 26–30 students<br>33 = 31–35 students<br>38 = 36–40 students<br>43 = 41–45 students<br>48 = 46–50 students<br>53 = More than 50 students | | 13~53 | SCH |
| CREACTIV | Creative extra-curricular activities (Sum) | | This variable is derived from SC053 which describes several extra-curricular activities such as 'Band, orchestra or choir', 'School yearbook, newspaper or magazine' and 'Art club or art activities' and school principals should check the activities they provide. CREACTIV is obtained by summing the activities that students take part in. | 0~3 | SCH |
| STAFFSHORT | Shortage of educational staff (WLE) | | This variable is also derived from SC017 and STAFFSHORT is obtained through SC017Q01NA, SC017Q02NA, SC017Q03NA, and SC017Q04NA, which focuses on issues related to educational staff. (e.g., 'A lack of teaching staff', 'Inadequate or poorly qualified teaching staff'.) | −2.5891~4.1125 | SCH |
| STUBEHA | Student behavior hindering learning (WLE) | — | | −4.3542~3.6274 | SCH |

(Continued)

| Variable | Description | Question No. | Question | Value Scale | Questionnaire |
|---|---|---|---|---|---|
| EDUSHORT | Shortage of educational material (WLE) | | As in PISA 2015 and 2012, PISA 2018 included an eight-item question about school resources, measuring school principals' perceptions of potential factors hindering instruction at school ("Is your school's capacity to provide instruction hindered by any of the following issues?"). The four response categories were "not at all", "very little", "to some extent", and "a lot". A similar question was used in previous cycles, but items were reduced and reworded for 2012 focusing on two derived variables. The index of staff shortage (STAFFSHORT) was derived from the four items: a lack of teaching staff; inadequate or poorly qualified teaching staff; a lack of assisting staff; inadequate or poorly qualified assisting staff. The index of shortage of educational material (EDUSHORT) was scaled using the following four items: a lack of educational material (e.g. textbooks, IT equipment, library, or laboratory material); inadequate or poor quality educational material (e.g. textbooks, IT equipment, library or laboratory material); a lack of physical infrastructure (e.g. building, grounds, heating/cooling, lighting and acoustic systems); inadequate or poor quality physical infrastructure (e.g. building, grounds, heating/cooling, lighting and acoustic systems). Positive values in these indices mean that principals viewed the amount and/ or quality of resources in their schools as an obstacle to providing instruction to a greater extent than the OECD average. | −1.9319~3.5229 | SCH |

| Variable | Description | Question No. | Question | Value Scale | Questionnaire |
|---|---|---|---|---|---|
| TEACHBEHA | Teacher behavior hindering learning (WLE) | The index of teacher behavior hindering learning (TEACHBEHA) was constructed using school principals' responses to a trend question (SC061) about the extent to which ("not at all", "very little", "to some extent", "a lot") they think that student learning in their schools is hindered by such factors as "Teachers not meeting individual students' needs"; "Teacher absenteeism"; "School staff resisting change"; "Teachers being too strict with students"; and "Teachers not being well prepared for classes". Positive values reflect principals' perceptions that these teacher-related behaviors hinder learning to a greater extent; negative values indicate that principals believed that these teacher-related behaviors hinder learning to a lesser extent, compared to the OECD average. Answers to this question were also used to measure the proportion of students in schools where instruction is hindered at least to some extent by teacher absenteeism, according to principals' reports | | −3.2392~3.8338 | SCH |
| SC001Q01TA | Which of the following definitions best describes the community in which your school is located? | 1 = A village, hamlet, or rural area (fewer than 3,000 people)<br>2 = A small town (3,000 to about 15,000 people)<br>3 = A town (15,000 to about 100,000 people)<br>4 = A city (100,000 to about 1,000,000 people)<br>5 = A large city (with over 1,000,000 people) | | 1~5 | SCH |

*(Continued)*

| Variable | Description | Question No. | Question | Value Scale | Questionnaire |
|---|---|---|---|---|---|
| SC155Q01HA | School's capacity using digital devices: The number of digital devices connected to the Internet is sufficient | 1 = Strongly disagree<br>2 = Disagree<br>3 = Agree<br>4 = Strongly agree | | 1~4 | SCH |
| SC155Q02HA | School's capacity using digital devices: The school's Internet bandwidth or speed is sufficient | 1 = Strongly disagree<br>2 = Disagree<br>3 = Agree<br>4 = Strongly agree | | 1~4 | SCH |
| SC155Q03HA | School's capacity using digital devices: The number of digital devices for instruction is sufficient | 1 = Strongly disagree<br>2 = Disagree<br>3 = Agree<br>4 = Strongly agree | | 1~4 | SCH |

Appendix **205**

| Variable | Description | Question No. | Question | Value Scale | Questionnaire |
|---|---|---|---|---|---|
| SC155Q04HA | School's capacity using digital devices: Digital devices are sufficiently powerful in terms of computing capacity | 1 = Strongly disagree<br>2 = Disagree<br>3 = Agree<br>4 = Strongly agree | | 1~4 | SCH |
| SC155Q05HA | School's capacity using digital devices: The availability of adequate software is sufficient | 1 = Strongly disagree<br>2 = Disagree<br>3 = Agree<br>4 = Strongly agree | | 1~4 | SCH |
| SC155Q06HA | School's capacity using digital devices: Teachers have the skills to integrate digital devices in instruction | 1 = Strongly disagree<br>2 = Disagree<br>3 = Agree<br>4 = Strongly agree | | 1~4 | SCH |

(*Continued*)

| Variable | Description | Question No. | Question | Value Scale | Questionnaire |
|---|---|---|---|---|---|
| SC155Q07HA | School's capacity using digital devices: Teachers have sufficient time to prepare lessons integrating digital devices | 1 = Strongly disagree<br>2 = Disagree<br>3 = Agree<br>4 = Strongly agree | | 1~4 | SCH |
| SC155Q08HA | School's capacity using digital devices: Effective professional resources for teachers to learn how to use digital devices | 1 = Strongly disagree<br>2 = Disagree<br>3 = Agree<br>4 = Strongly agree | | 1~4 | SCH |
| SC155Q09HA | School's capacity using digital devices: An effective online learning support platform is available | 1 = Strongly disagree<br>2 = Disagree<br>3 = Agree<br>4 = Strongly agree | | 1~4 | SCH |

| Variable | Description | Question No. | Question | Value Scale | Questionnaire |
|---|---|---|---|---|---|
| SC155Q10HA | School's capacity using digital devices: Teachers are provided with incentives to integrate digital devices into their teaching | 1 = Strongly disagree<br>2 = Disagree<br>3 = Agree<br>4 = Strongly agree | | 1~4 | SCH |
| SC155Q11HA | School's capacity using digital devices: The school has sufficient qualified technical assistant staff | 1 = Strongly disagree<br>2 = Disagree<br>3 = Agree<br>4 = Strongly agree | | 1~4 | SCH |
| SC156Q01HA | At school: Its own written statement about the use of digital devices | 1 = Yes<br>2 = No | | 1~2 | SCH |
| SC156Q02HA | At school: Its own written statement specifically about the use of digital devices for pedagogical purposes | 1 = Yes<br>2 = No | | 1~2 | SCH |

(*Continued*)

Appendix **207**

# 208 Appendix

| Variable | Description | Question No. | Question | Value Scale | Questionnaire |
|---|---|---|---|---|---|
| SC156Q03HA | At school: A programme to use digital devices for teaching and learning in specific subjects | 1 = Yes<br>2 = No | | 1~2 | SCH |
| SC156Q04HA | At school: Regular discussions with teaching staff about the use of digital devices for pedagogical purposes | 1 = Yes<br>2 = No | | 1~2 | SCH |
| SC156Q05HA | At school: A specific programme to prepare students for responsible Internet behavior | 1 = Yes<br>2 = No | | 1~2 | SCH |
| SC156Q06HA | At school: A specific policy about using Social Networks (<Facebook>, etc.) in teaching and learning | 1 = Yes<br>2 = No | | 1~2 | SCH |

| Variable | Description | Question No. | Question | Value Scale | Questionnaire |
|---|---|---|---|---|---|
| SC156Q07HA | At school: A specific programme to promote collaboration on the use of digital devices among teachers | 1 = Yes<br>2 = No | | 1~2 | SCH |
| SC156Q08HA | Scheduled time for teachers to meet to share, evaluate or develop instructional materials and approaches that employ digital devices | 1 = Yes<br>2 = No | | 1~2 | SCH |
| SC012Q01TA | Student admission to school: Student's record of academic performance (including placement tests) | 1 = Never<br>2 = Sometimes<br>3 = Always | | 1~3 | SCH |
| SC012Q02TA | Student admission to school: Recommendation of feeder schools | 1 = Never<br>2 = Sometimes<br>3 = Always | | 1~3 | SCH |

(*Continued*)

**210** Appendix

| Variable | Description | Question No. | Question | Value Scale | Questionnaire |
|---|---|---|---|---|---|
| SC012Q03TA | Student admission to school: Parents' endorsement of the instructional or religious philosophy of the school | 1 = Never<br>2 = Sometimes<br>3 = Always | | 1~3 | SCH |
| SC012Q04TA | Student admission to school: Whether the student requires or is interested in a special programme | 1 = Never<br>2 = Sometimes<br>3 = Always | | 1~3 | SCH |
| SC012Q05TA | Student admission to school: Preference given to family members of current or former students | 1 = Never<br>2 = Sometimes<br>3 = Always | | 1~3 | SCH |
| SC012Q06TA | Student admission to school: Residence in a particular area | 1 = Never<br>2 = Sometimes<br>3 = Always | | 1~3 | SCH |

Appendix **211**

| Variable | Description | Question No. | Question | Value Scale | Questionnaire |
|---|---|---|---|---|---|
| SC012Q07TA | Student admission to school: Other | 1 = Never<br>2 = Sometimes<br>3 = Always | | 1~3 | SCH |
| SC036Q01TA | Use of achievement data in school: Achievement data are posted publicly (e.g. in the media) | 1 = Yes<br>2 = No | | 1~3 | SCH |
| SC036Q02TA | Use of achievement data in school: Achievement data are tracked over time by an administrative authority | 1 = Yes<br>2 = No | | 1~3 | SCH |
| SC036Q03NA | Use of achievement data in school: Achievement data are provided directly to parents | 1 = Yes<br>2 = No | | 1~3 | SCH |
| SC037Q01TA | Quality assurance at school: Internal evaluation/Self-evaluation | 1 = Yes, this is mandatory, e.g. based on district or ministry policies<br>2 = Yes, based on school initiative<br>3 = No | | 1~3 | SCH |

(*Continued*)

| Variable | Description | Question No. | Question | Value Scale | Questionnaire |
|---|---|---|---|---|---|
| SC037Q02TA | Quality assurance at school: External evaluation | | 1 = Yes, this is mandatory, e.g. based on district or ministry policies<br>2 = Yes, based on school initiative<br>3 = No | 1~3 | SCH |
| SC037Q03TA | Quality assurance at school: Written specification of the school's curricular profile and educational goals | | 1 = Yes, this is mandatory, e.g. based on district or ministry policies<br>2 = Yes, based on school initiative<br>3 = No | 1~3 | SCH |
| SC037Q04TA | Quality assurance at school: Written specification of student performance standards | | 1 = Yes, this is mandatory, e.g. based on district or ministry policies<br>2 = Yes, based on school initiative<br>3 = No | 1~3 | SCH |
| SC037Q05NA | Quality assurance at school: Systematic recording of data such as teacher or student attendance and professional development | | 1 = Yes, this is mandatory, e.g. based on district or ministry policies<br>2 = Yes, based on school initiative<br>3 = No | 1~3 | SCH |

| Variable | Description | Question No. | Question | Value Scale | Questionnaire |
|---|---|---|---|---|---|
| SC037Q06NA | Quality assurance at school: Systematic recording of student test results and graduation rates | | 1 = Yes, this is mandatory, e.g. based on district or ministry policies<br>2 = Yes, based on school initiative<br>3 = No | 1~3 | SCH |
| SC037Q07TA | Quality assurance at school: Seeking written feedback from students (e.g. regarding lessons, teachers, or resources) | | 1 = Yes, this is mandatory, e.g. based on district or ministry policies<br>2 = Yes, based on school initiative<br>3 = No | 1~3 | SCH |
| SC037Q08TA | Quality assurance at school: Teacher mentoring | | 1 = Yes, this is mandatory, e.g. based on district or ministry policies<br>2 = Yes, based on school initiative<br>3 = No | 1~3 | SCH |
| SC037Q09TA | Quality assurance at school: Seeking written feedback from students (e.g. regarding lessons, teachers or resources) | | 1 = Yes, this is mandatory, e.g. based on district or ministry policies<br>2 = Yes, based on school initiative<br>3 = No | 1~3 | SCH |

(Continued)

| Variable | Description | Question No. | Question | Value Scale | Questionnaire |
|---|---|---|---|---|---|
| SC037Q10NA | Implementation of a standardized policy for reading subjects (i.e. school curriculum with shared instructional materials accompanied by staff development and training) | 1 = Yes, this is mandatory, e.g. based on district or ministry policies<br>2 = Yes, based on school initiative<br>3 = No | | 1~3 | SCH |
| SC053Q01TA | <This academic year>, activities offered to <national modal grade for 15-year-olds>: Band, orchestra, or choir | 1 = Yes<br>2 = No | | 1~2 | SCH |
| SC053Q02TA | <This academic year>, activities offered to <national modal grade for 15-year-olds>: School play or school musical | 1 = Yes<br>2 = No | | 1~2 | SCH |

| Variable | Description | Question No. | Question | Value Scale | Questionnaire |
|---|---|---|---|---|---|
| SC053Q03TA | <This academic year>, activities offered to <national modal grade for 15-year-olds>: School yearbook, newspaper or magazine | 1 = Yes<br>2 = No | | 1~2 | SCH |
| SC053Q04TA | <This academic year>, activities offered to <national modal grade for 15-year-olds>: Volunteering or service activities | 1 = Yes<br>2 = No | | 1~2 | SCH |
| SC053Q12IA | <This academic year>, activities offered to <national modal grade for 15-year-olds>: Book club | 1 = Yes<br>2 = No | | 1~2 | SCH |

*(Continued)*

| Variable | Description | Question No. | Question | Value Scale | Questionnaire |
|---|---|---|---|---|---|
| SC053Q13IA | <This academic year>, activities offered to <national modal grade for 15-year-olds>: Debating club or debating activities | 1 = Yes<br>2 = No | | 1~2 | SCH |
| SC053Q09TA | <This academic year>, activities offered to <national modal grade for 15-year-olds>: Art club or art activities | 1 = Yes<br>2 = No | | 1~2 | SCH |
| SC053Q10TA | <This academic year>, activities offered to <national modal grade for 15-year-olds>: Sporting team or sporting activities | 1 = Yes<br>2 = No | | 1~2 | SCH |

Appendix 217

| Variable | Description | Question No. | Question | Value Scale | Questionnaire |
|---|---|---|---|---|---|
| SC053Q14IA | <This academic year>, activities offered to <national modal grade for 15-year-olds>: Lectures and/or seminars (e.g. guest speakers such as writers or journalists) | 1 = Yes<br>2 = No | | 1~2 | SCH |
| SC053Q15IA | <This academic year>, activities offered to <national modal grade for 15-year-olds>: Collaboration with local libraries | 1 = Yes<br>2 = No | | 1~2 | SCH |
| SC053Q16IA | <This academic year>, activities offered to <national modal grade for 15-year-olds>: Collaboration with local newspapers | 1 = Yes<br>2 = No | | 1~2 | SCH |

(*Continued*)

| Variable | Description | Question No. | Question | Value Scale | Questionnaire |
|---|---|---|---|---|---|
| SC064Q01TA | During <the last academic year>, what proportion of students' parents participated in the following school related activities? | SC064Q01TA | Discussed their child's progress with a teacher on their own initiative | 0~100 | SCH |
| SC064Q02TA | During <the last academic year>, what proportion of students' parents participated in the following school related activities? | SC064Q02TA | Discussed their child's progress on the initiative of one of their child's teachers | 0~100 | SCH |
| SC064Q03TA | During <the last academic year>, what proportion of students' parents participated in the following school related activities? | SC064Q03TA | Proportion of parents: Participated in local school government (e.g. parent council or school management committee) | 0~100 | SCH |

| Variable | Description | Question No. | Question | Value Scale | Questionnaire |
|---|---|---|---|---|---|
| SC064Q04NA | During <the last academic year>, what proportion of students' parents participated in the following school related activities? | Proportion of parents: Volunteered in physical or extra-curricular activities (e.g. building maintenance, carpentry, gardening or yard work, school play, sports, field trip) | SC064Q04NA | 0~100 | SCH |
| SC052Q01NA | For 15-year-old students, school provides study help: Room(s) where the students can do their homework | 1 = Yes<br>2 = No | | 1~2 | SCH |
| SC052Q02NA | For 15-year-old students, school provides study help: Staff help with homework | 1 = Yes<br>2 = No | | 1~2 | SCH |
| SC052Q03HA | For 15-year-old students, school provides study help: Peer-to-peer tutoring | 1 = Yes<br>2 = No | | 1~2 | SCH |

Source: PISA 2018 dataset.

# INDEX

academic: attainment 105; failure 105; outcome 48, 51, 80; performance 7, 48, 49, 53, 55, 102, 141, 142, 144, 147, 160, 161, 209; resilient student 152; self-concept 142, 162
accuracy score 72
achievement: motivation 52; score 102
adaptive nature 9
adjusted mean 137
affective factor 50, 166
affirmative class 73
aggregated: meaning 76; variable 76, 85
aggregation bias 76, 79, 105
algorithm: parameter 73; selection 73
amplifier technology 14
analogy symbols 29
analytical challenge 78
animated image 30
annual publication 13
antecedent: condition 48; variable 116, 117, 131, 135
application range 99
arithmetic achievement data 83
artificial: intelligence 58, 158; neural network 63, 158, 161
assembled language 145
association rule mining 145
atomistic fallacy 85
attendance rate 59
attribute value 149, 157
aural language 18
autism spectrum disorder 76
autonomous learner 174

auxiliary portrait 4
awarded grade 87

balanced data 79, 83, 87, 100
Bayesian: approach 98; estimation method 93; estimate 83, 99, 150, 151; network 3, 62, 63
bibliographic catalog unit 24
big data analysis 43, 75
Big-Fish-Little-Pond effect 140, 162
binary classification 59, 60, 62, 65, 165
black box 75, 117
bootstrap: confidence interval 122, 123, 124, 125; sample 97, 124; technique 124
bootstrap-based reasoning 125
bootstrapped correction 97
bootstrapping method 93
browser version 28

Chi square test 94
China's adult citizen 178
Chinese learner paradox 102
career aspiration 142, 158, 161, 45
casewise deletion 149
categorical data 141
causal: analysis 139, 154; antecedent 115, 116, 130; chain 119, 131, 134, 143; connection 139; effect 112, 116, 117, 120, 126; impact 113; inference 143, 144
chronological order 143
class level data 99
classification: error rate 70; outcome 69; performance 73, 165, 55, 65

classroom practice 39
cognitive abilities 19, 102, 103, 156, 178
collaborative problem solving 34
confirmatory factor analysis (CFA) 112
communication technology 13, 159
competent reader 19, 21
components estimation 79
composition difference 141
computational approach 150
computer: assessment 9, 39; familiarity questionnaire 13; game 51, 57, 162
conceptual: diagram 116, 117, 127; model 138, 139
confidence interval 90, 97, 98, 119, 122, 123, 124, 125, 126, 136, 137, 156
configurational variable 84
confusion matrix 72
consequent variable 133
consistent: link 76; result 94
constructive perspective 178
contextual factor 45, 54, 56, 77, 78, 100, 155, 157, 171, 176
continuous: data 141, 146; mediation model 134; observation variable 106; variable 3, 113; writing 25
control variable 130
controversial reading 179
convenient information 170
conventional: CFA model 113; context 34; inference approach 119
convergence: bias 101; speed 150
correlation: analysis 3, 145, 149; coefficient 72, 78, 90, 119, 140, 149
count variable 146
country specific language ideologies 103
course: difficulty 62; evaluation 4; formats 36; difficulty 62
covariance: components 75, 79, 80, 82, 83, 89, 92, 100, 156; components estimation 79; components model 75, 156; literature 137; matrix 92, 96, 111; structure analysis 112; structure modeling 112
creative extra-curricular activities 168, 175
credibility goal 39
cross classification 86, 87
cross-level: effect 80, 81; hypotheses 85; interactions 78, 105
cross-national data 52
cross-sectional: HLM models 75; data 75, 79, 88
cross validation 69, 70, 71, 160, 166
crucial link 4
cumulative effect 133
curriculum system 174

customized vocabulary growth trajectory 82

data: analytical process 43; attribute 150; cleaning 5; collection 4, 9, 88, 110, 143, 149; distribution 69, 151, 70, 71; hierarchy 140; imputation 151, 152; integration 5, 147; mining 1, 2, 43, 44, 45, 46, 53, 54, 55, 56, 58, 145, 147, 149, 151, 155, 156, 157, 159, 161, 162, 163, 164; preprocessing 145; processing 4, 6, 64, 122, 147; quality 148; stratification 99; structure 75, 76, 77, 79, 86, 87, 101, 114
decision tree (DT) 58, 59
deep learning approach 75
delta method 123
demographic factors 79
dependable source 42
dependency problem 79
dependent variable 60, 86, 107, 115, 117, 118, 138, 139, 140, 142, 144, 154, 163
depression scale score 88
derived factor 113
descriptive: feature 68; variable 38
detecting agent 122
deterministic fashion 113
diachronic: data 144; research 99
diagnosis report 3
digital: age 31; communication 31; device 15, 30, 51, 174, 204, 205, 206, 207, 208, 209; document 27, 29; education resource 179; environment 179; format 31; gadget 31; guidance 57, 174; information 27, 29; learning 54, 178; material 13, 20, 32; reader 43, 54, 170, 171, 175; resource 48, 52, 56, 179; teaching 179; technology (technologies) 27, 28, 30, 31, 179, 27, 31, 46, 57; text 15, 16, 23, 24, 27, 28, 29, 30, 32, 42, 52, 56, 157, 171, 178, 188; world 24
digital reading: ability 54, 179; literacy 50, 51, 52, 155, 171, 172, 173, 174, 175, 178, 179, 180; performance 43, 49, 51, 52, 54, 56, 57, 141, 157, 166, 171, 172, 173, 178; score 105; skill 52, 171, 174
disaggregated case 85
disciplinary context 175
discourse communication 30
discrete: outcome 93; variable 3
discrimination ability 69
disjointed text 26
document: arrangement 29; collection 29; type 145

dominant official language 103
double nested structure 77
dual problem 67, 68
dummy coding 135
dynamic: chart 6; interaction 138; model 43, 49, 50, 55, 56, 147, 170, 180; visualization 6

e-books 28, 39
ecological correlation 85, 162
economic: analysis 148; approach 48; homogeneity 152; indicator 52, 53, 77; involvement 14; prosperity 103
EDM approaches 43, 53
EDM methods 3, 53
education: amelioration 2, 43; decision making 6; informatization 179; intervention 174; management 4, 5, 6; manager 2, 5; production model 48; resource 101, 142, 179; education system 5, 13, 39, 53
educational: accomplishment 86; achievement 14, 53; data mining (EDM) 1, 2; ecosystem 2; effectiveness research 48, 57; intelligent decision support 4; management system 4; objective 11; outcome 48, 77, 102, 104, 172; program 103
educational resource 5, 6, 104, 140; system 8, 14, 100, 104; variable 7, 8; visual management 4
effect size 104, 128
electronic text 15, 28, 29, 47
EM algorithm 79, 156
e-mail 23, 30, 31, 34
embedded content page 29
empirical: finding 30, 109; knowledge 143; representation 124; testing 117; validity 108
endogenous: factor 108; variable 108, 113, 118
ensemble: model 61; technique 61
environmental characteristics 49
equity dimension 52
equivalent effect 130
e-resources 52
error rate 63, 70
evaluation: outcome 73; procedure 8; process 36, 37; result 4, 71
exogenous variable 108, 113, 118
expectation maximization 150
experimental evaluation 71
explanatory variable 81, 84, 86, 107, 150, 151

explicit: link 20; variable 107
exploratory: factor analysis 113, 146; structural equation model 146
exponential growth 37
extensive reading 51, 57
external: factors 144, 147; signal 22
extracurricular activities 13, 166, 175, 176, 201
extreme: gradient boosting 61; value 61
eye motion 29

F1-score 72, 73
Fisher scoring algorithm 80
factor: analysis 106, 112, 113, 141, 146; indicator correspondence 113; model 106, 113
fair treatment 36
false: information 179; null hypothesis 121; negative 72; positive 72, 73, 123
family: background 7, 78, 79, 103; environment 12; factor 100, 101, 104; income 149, 160; planning program 82
feature: interaction 61; removal approach 69; selection 68, 69, 170; literacy advantage 102
financial literacy 8, 10
fit: degree 111; index 111, 154
fitted hyperplane 65
fitting degree 111
fixed: distance type 150; effect 83, 89, 94, 99, 100
fluency assessment project 40
forecast event 11
foreign language 39
formal education 18, 35
foundational skills 15
fragmented information presentation 27
French communities 80, 159
functional: relationship 139; use 16

Gauss Hermite quadrature 94
GEE method 96
gender: composition 141, 142; difference 100, 101, 102, 103, 141, 155, 160, 163; discrepancy 103; equity 103; gap 50, 101, 102, 177; norms 101, 102, 162; variable 144
generalizability theory 87
generalization ability 69, 75
generalization performance 61
generalized: estimating equations (GEE) 93, 155; least squares (GLS) 80
genuine: hypothesis 61; null hypothesis 121; positive 73, 165

global: capability assessment 10; capacity project 9; difficulties 12
GLS estimate 95, 96
gradient boosting technique 61
group characteristics 84, 90; effect 78, 79, 90, 91; level analysis 98; level change 96

handwritten character 64
happiness questionnaire 13
harmonic mean 73, 156
heritability studies 82
heterogeneous association 76
heuristic measurement model 110
hidden: cause 113; variable 112
hierarchical: characteristics 140; clustering model 150; data 77, 79, 86, 87, 90, 105, 114, 157; feature 141; framework 26
hierarchical linear modeling (HLM) 43, 74, 75, 84
HLM: analyses 75; model 75, 100; statistical theories 79
home: resource 49; setting 82
homogenous class 61
Hong Kong students 102, 159
household income 140, 149
human: capacities 14; creation 121
hybrid recommendation 3
hyperlink: text fragments 24; link 18, 29; page 30; reading 29
hypothesis: model 111; space 61; test 89, 93, 121; testing 89, 93, 121

ICT: infused instruction 52; learning tools 174; related factors 104; resources 51, 52, 166, 174
Information Development Index (IDI) 52
International Adult Literacy Survey (IALS) 15
International Science Literacy Association (ISLA) 12
intra-class correlation co efficient (ICC) value 140
Item Response Theory (IRT) 41
image formats 146
immigrant background 42
immigration status 141, 142
implementation constraint 34
imputation: algorithm 151; approach 150, 151; error 42; procedure 150
imputed value 151
incidental vocabulary learning 52
incremental: development 42; fit index 154
independent: assessment 22; data 69, 85; data set 69; factor 139, 154; observation 76; variable 117, 118, 138, 139, 140, 144

indicator: codes 135; variable 135
indirect: assessment 107; attributes 143; causal effect 112; component 134; influence 121, 122, 123, 127, 130, 131, 132, 134, 136; uncertainty 122
inference: generation 21; program 121
inferential: meaning 21; reasoning strategies 50
influential factor 54, 101
information: age 44, 46, 178; and communication technology (ICT) 13; awareness 174; collection 14; engineering 68; explosion 1; literacy 171; technology 14, 46, 55, 174
instant messaging service 23
instructional: behavior 48, 166; technique 102
institutional characteristics 8
insufficient resource 37
intelligent education management 4, 5
intentional reading activities 22
interactive capabilities 23
intercept variance 94
intermediary: analysis 115, 139, 140, 141, 142, 145; model 131, 135, 138
intermediate: analysis 119, 126, 139; component 117
international assessment 102, 103, 154, 179
interpolated values 150
intertextual aspects 19
intervention variables 116
intrinsic motivation 38
irregular pattern 61
irrelevant paragraph 20
irrelevant question 33
item difficulty 35
iterative: procedure 95; process 95

JAVA environment 145
job advertisement 27
job hunting 18
job market 17, 31
job requirement 73
job seeker 27
joint distribution 151
joint significance test 122

kernel approach 64
kernel functions 65
knowledge development 14
knowledge integration 77
knowledge management system 1
knowledge society 174

## Index

Lagrange: function 68; multiplier method 68
language: course 39; development researcher 82; exposure 77; expression 32; processing skill 32; use 82
language use 82
large-scale: assessment 34, 36, 42, 53, 56, 57; data analyses 54; educational assessments 151; educational dataset 53; evaluation 36; group survey 88
latent: category analysis 146; variable 105, 106, 107, 109, 112, 114, 139, 141, 142, 147
layer: SEM 114, 138; hierarchical data structure 87
layered: hierarchical structure 114; structure 138
learning: ability 3; efficiency 3, 6; environment 7, 8, 162, 170, 178; outcome 8, 49, 140; performance 1, 3, 58; process 3, 4, 6, 44, 74; resource 2, 3, 4, 5, 6; software 1, 3; status 3; strategies 1, 102; task 61; time 101
life satisfaction 8, 13
lifelong learning 16, 18, 100
likelihood: approach 151; function 94, 161; technique 151
linear: arrangement 28; mixed effects model 75, 161; regression model 98, 117, 118, 141, 155; relationship 98
linguistic studies 77
literacy: assessment 18, 23, 36, 37, 40; construction 40
literal: meaning 21; memory representation 20; masterpieces 34; text 31
log file 38, 45
logical: consistency 38; inference 149; progression 29
logistic regression 3, 53, 58, 163
longitudinal: data 75, 76, 82, 83, 87, 144, 146, 156, 157, 159, 162, 180; design 84; investigation 87; research 87

Macao student 101
Matthews correlation coefficient 72
machine intelligent judgment 4
machine learning algorithm 145, 147
machine learning method 43, 58, 60, 61, 74, 75, 146, 147, 159, 170, 180
machine learning technique 42, 71, 158
macroscopic variable 105
marginal distribution 150
marital status 80
market economy 152
mass global database 43
mass popularity 105

material quality 39
material resource 12
maternal education 82
maternal speech effect 94
mathematical equations 139
mathematical estimate 126
mathematics literacy 11, 102, 103
mathematics performance 53, 103
maximum competence 40
maximum distance 65
maximum margin decision boundary 64
maximum possible degree 41
mean imputation 150, 151
mean score discrepancy 103
mean value 69, 138, 150
measurement: accuracy 39; data 87; design 77; equation 106; error 106, 107, 113, 160; hypothesis 107; linkage 112; model 106, 109, 110, 112, 113; reliability 106; research 99
median value 98
mediated effect 120
mediating role 141, 142, 163
mediation: analysis 1, 58, 115, 116, 124, 126, 127, 135, 140, 141, 143, 144, 145, 157, 158, 160, 163, 180; claim 122; function 137; hypothesis 139; model 115, 116, 117, 118, 119, 126, 127, 128, 130, 131, 132, 133, 134, 135, 137, 139, 143, 161, 162, 163, 164; standard 122; variable 115, 116, 139
metacognitive awareness 100; learning strategies 102; strategies 51, 52, 163
metric perspective 53
minimum: number 165; sample size 108
mining technology 4
minority: applicant 81; candidate 81; language 103; sample 81
mixed effect 50, 75, 161
ML estimate 93, 94, 95, 96, 150
ML method 93, 94, 95, 97, 147
ML program 95
mobile: device 29, 52; digital device 30; phone 24, 52
mother education 82
motivational component 172
multicategorical antecedent variable 135, 137
multidimensional: construct 180; hyperplane 65
multilayer linear model 99
multilevel: analysis 55, 57, 84, 87, 88, 89, 95, 104, 114, 140, 158, 160, 162, 163; data 80, 85, 86, 96, 114, 146, 160; effect 49, 78; factor 49; structure 48, 77
multimodal data 49

Naive Bayesian model 62
national: ICT access 105; ICT development 104; campus informatization policy 179; cohort 79; economic growth 77, 82; gender difference 103; policies 53
National Council 10
navigation: device 25, 28; skill 51, 163; structure 23; tool 24, 25; equipment 32
nested data 75, 76, 77, 82, 98, 105, 114
neural network algorithm 6
nominal attribute 151
nontrivial relationship 1
normal: distribution 97, 98, 150; regression methodologies 81; regression technique 139; single level regression assumption 76
normality hypothesis 96
normative assumption 109
noticeable characteristic 29
null: hypothesis 85, 119, 120, 121, 123, 136; value 150
numbering system 28

Oaxaca Blinder method 103
object: properties 59; values 59
objective: current condition 148; function 61, 67
observation: group 109; independence 76
observational variable 142
occupational: expectation 172, 176, 177; status 166, 167, 171, 172, 182
OECD: countries 54, 97, 102, 152, 153, 189, 190, 191, 192; gender differences 103
official: estimate 110; language 103
online: classroom 6; group discussion 167, 171, 189; information 33, 45, 157, 173; mobile device 52; publication 24, 155, 162, 176; reader 31, 55; reading activities 141, 155; reading exercises 39
optimal factor set 165
orderly classroom environment 174
ordinary regression 139
organizational: information 26; structure 13, 26, 29, 114
outcome variable 83, 86, 99, 100, 107, 115, 117, 118, 130, 138, 139, 146

paired deletion 146
pair-wise deletion 152
panel interview studies 87
paper: distribution 10; document 18; evaluation 9
parallel multiple mediator model 131, 132, 135

parameter adjustment 73, 74
parent node 62
parental: investment 104; participation 104; pressure 53; support 104
partial standardization effect 129
path analysis 112, 180
pattern recognition 64, 65, 156
Pearson correlation 106
pedagogical interest 101
peer group 49
percentile: bootstrap confidence interval 125; position confidence interval 125
performance change 16; estimation 74; evaluation 73, 170; indicator 73, 165
personalized learning experience 1
phenomenological connection 126
PISA: assessment 33, 35, 56, 102; cognitive exam 18; cycle 12, 14, 36, 38, 39, 40; dataset 53; digital reading evaluation 30; reading framework 11, 13, 15, 42; reading literacy assessment 18, 36; reading studies 98, 100, 101; science assessment program 12
plausible value 41, 42, 149, 154, 182
policy: implication 140; orientation 140
population: difference 96; heterogeneity 84; mean probability 96; parameter 42, 93, 97
portable mobile reading device 170
post test 88
posterior distribution 97, 98, 151
pragmatic application 64
pre-dependent variable 115, 118, 138
precision score 72
prediction: equation 81; function 5; group 109
predictive: analysis 145; model 53, 59; power 172
preliminary: data result 4; data screening 5; result 4
pre-posttest design 88
pre-processing 147
preschool education 151
pre-test 88
principal: component 113; concept 21
print reading 51, 172
prior assessment 34
probabilistic approach 151
professional: advice 35; career 17; skills 30
proficiency level 42
program: knowledge 12; logic 6
programmable language 146
Progress in International Reading Literacy Study (PIRLS) 53
propagation mechanism 119

protein interaction prediction 61
prudent: approach 38; reader 179
psychological: aspect 89; characteristics 142
psychometric model 42
publishing date 33
punctuation norm 26
pupils digital reading result 105
pure statistical practice 112
putative: causal antecedent 130; causal association 126

quantitative: approach 49; assessment 119; estimation 119; synthesis 77
questionable instance 73
questionnaire assessment 19
questionnaire item 38, 39

R Core Team 146, 161
random: background 143; coefficients regression model 89, 91, 92; component 95, 182; deletion 150; difference 100; effects model 159, 163; effects structure 96; error 92, 98; forest (RF) 58, 60; intercept model 91, 93; regression coefficient 100; resampling 124, 125; sample 97, 98, 151; sample imputation 151; structure 96, 162; variation 99
rational debate 12
raw data 126
readability indicators 38
reading: literacy assessment 18, 23, 36, 37, 40; literacy framework 10, 13, 15, 38; material 11, 19, 50, 172, 175, 179; proficiency 40, 57, 105; project 10; strategies 15, 38, 39, 100, 101, 174; time 38
recall score 72
receiver operating characteristic 72
recognition heuristics 110
recommendation: letter quality 62; letters 33
recreational: digital reading 50; use 105
recruitment website 27
redundant data processing 122
reflective project 21
regression: coefficient 91, 94, 96, 136, 138; equation 92, 138, 139; heterogeneity 76; tree 53, 60, 155, 159; weight 134
regular: basis 13; interval 89; practice 17
regularization term 61
relational: boundaries 173; regression equation system 138
remarkable: flexibility 61; result 51
remedial class 144
replacement procedure 124

representation mechanism 136
research: contextual background 77; design 126, 143, 144, 163; equipment 88; estimation option 93; evidence 39, 101; limitation 43, 179; mechanism 116; topics 2
residual: analysis index 111; error 61, 114; term 107; variance 92, 100
resource database 4, 5
respectable statistical estimate 95
respondent household income 149
response original hint 34
restricted maximum likelihood 94
restricted number 25, 26
review process 8, 21
revised specification 14
rigorous: international study 8; worldwide program 8
Robinson effect 85
robust: estimate 83, 97, 100; standard error 96
route: analysis 112; diagram 117, 138, 139
rural: fertility rate 82; school 76

sample: categories 70; classification error 70; covariance distribution 108; data 71, 109, 111; distribution 123, 124, 126; interference 151; mean 137, 149; proportion 71; space 65, 66
sampling procedure 124, 125
satisfactory causal step criterion 122
school: average achievement 42; background 78, 104; characteristics 104; components 80; composition 103; curriculum goal 13; disciplinary climate 52; educational resource 104; effectiveness 49, 53, 55, 56, 57, 161, 176, 177; environment 35, 101, 103, 105; extracurricular activities 166; governance 103; impact 83; information resource 105; learning environment 178; level covariate 142; level difference 142; level factors 43, 52, 102, 168, 170, 174, 175, 198; level information 64; location 77, 80, 104, 142; performance 53, 140; questionnaire 64, 152, 154; resources 52, 103, 202; science education resource 142; size 77, 84, 199; type 52, 53, 80, 199; variables 80
science: accomplishment 104; learning activities 104; literacy 12, 102, 103, 154; performance 46, 101, 152, 163; research 143; score 141, 154; subject 39; teacher 174, 176
scientific: achievement 142; area 115; backgrounds 12; competence 12; interest

142; knowledge 12; literacy 12, 104, 155, 169; performance 142; thinking 12
search: engine 20, 31, 45, 197; skill 179
secondary: intermediary model 138; level 52; school program 17
sectional: data 75, 79, 88; experimental data 144
self: confidence 50; diagnosis 2; expectation 78; initiated analyses 126; regulating goals 22
SEM: analysis 142; computer programs 110, 114; computer tools 110; family 112; method 107; model diagram 108; model image 108; model picture 108; process 111; programs 120, 140
semantic: link 29; matching 33
sensitivity score 72
sensory stimulation 178
sentence parsing 37
sequence mediation 133
sequential: correlation 100; manner 61
service solution software 145
skewed prediction coefficient 81
slope variance 93
slow reading 37, 38
smart: campus 6; era 179; technique 87
smooth reading 19
social: activities 23; capital 49; circumstance 98; contact 30; interaction 51, 172; media 56, 105, 157, 182; networking program 31; reading activities 51; relationship 13; responsibility 179; science data analysis 98; science research 143; science 39, 143, 144, 154, 157, 98
socioeconomic: background 104, 178; factor 48; status 39, 42, 49, 55, 79, 163, 176
soft: environment 175; margin 64
software: packages 68, 80, 94, 120, 140; products 140
sorted distribution 124
sound manner 12
source information 20
spatial ability 32
special: attention 174; function 146
specificity score 72
specified: computation 149; goal 19; number 113
SR: model 112, 114; models 114
stable: attribute 144; categorization system 32
standard: cell 34; deviation 40, 41, 42, 84, 106, 128, 129; font size 24; reading assessment 33; single level intermediate

variable analysis 138; single level regression 76; statistical technique 107
statistic calculation 111
statistical: analysis 74, 78, 85, 115, 145, 146, 150; diagram 117, 119, 131, 132, 133, 134, 135, 137; estimation 99, 108; graph 117; method 98, 99, 116, 143, 146, 156; modeling software 146; procedure 150; significance 122; software package 120, 140; standpoint 61; technique 107, 112, 114, 155; verification 145
strategic: awareness 39; processes 37, 38; thinking 39; understanding 20; knowledge 39
stratified sampling 69, 70, 114
structural: complexity 107; design 38; element 15; equation model (SEM) 105; properties 112; regression model 112; variable 84
structured menu 30
student: academic achievement 77; outcome 48, 49, 55; performance 2, 3, 8, 10, 15, 40, 54, 173, 212
subjective emotion 5
successive tree 61
support vector machine (SVM) 43, 54, 64
supportive classroom disciplinary climate 174
surrounding environment 78
survey measure 16
survival analysis 145, 146, 157
SVM classifier 65; library 68; model 9, 43, 69, 72, 165, 166
SVM-recursive feature elimination (SVM-RFE) 43, 68
SVM-RFE-cross validation (SVM-RFE-CV) 69
synergistic effect 54, 55, 150, 170
system framework 4

tabulated association 126
tangible object 28
Taiwan University 68
target information 20
targeted training 174
task: goal 19; management 19, 22; related reading goals 22; requirements 20, 22, 40
teacher: effectiveness research 49; feedback 173, 191; instruction 173; support 164, 173, 190
technical: circumstance 16; level 6; literature 121
technological: artifact 12; restriction 49
temporal sequence 139

temporary attribute 144
ten-fold cross validation 70
test: design 9, 88; developer 19; error 70; item 53
theoretical analysis 143, 145
time: series analysis technology 3; variable random slope 100
top: level structure 30; performing digital readers 54, 171
topics related article 33
traditional: PISA reading unit 33; analysis 82; approach 83; comprehension item 34; data application 6; decision support system 5; electronic gadgets 27; independent PISA reading unit 33; linear model 82, 98; linear regression model 98; regression analysis method 99, 101
trained: model 71; reader 22
training: data 65, 66; error 69; model 71; process 74; sample 65, 66, 70, 72; set 61, 65, 69, 70, 71
transnational studies 77
treatment: effect estimate 77; implementation 77
tree algorithm 53
Turkish students mathematics scores 141

unambiguous student hierarchies 86
unavoidable restriction 99
unbalanced data 79, 83, 100
unbiased estimate 41, 42
uncertainty measure 122
unconditional: covariance 92; variance 92; variance covariance component 92
unidimensional construct 180
uniform distribution 97
unit specific: intercept 96; model 96
unstructured covariance matrix 96
unsupervised methods 58
untimely feedback 4

updated: framework 14, 23; version 16
urban school 76
utilization efficiency 6

vacation arrangements 31
valid estimates 83, 100
validation set 71
value imputation 150, 151
variable: deletion 149; type 146
variance: covariance component 82, 100, 83, 89, 92; covariance matrix 92; term 113
verification method 99
versatile: machine 65; regression model 75
video: game 27; resource 30
visible heterogeneity 146
visual: depiction 41; displays 18; information 4; texts 18
vital: component 20; skill 26
vocabulary: acquisition 82; development 82; growth 82, 158
volume organization 28

Waikato Environment 145
weak assumption 114
web: link 20; search result 34
weight proportional 151
weighted: average 105, 106; combination 81
widespread: agreement 122; usage 30; use 31
word: processing document 23; recognition 37
work satisfaction 8

XGBoost: classification 62, 63; classifier 61

yes/no question 59
young: digital reader 170; people 37

zero change 122

For Product Safety Concerns and Information please contact our EU
representative GPSR@taylorandfrancis.com
Taylor & Francis Verlag GmbH, Kaufingerstraße 24, 80331 München, Germany

www.ingramcontent.com/pod-product-compliance
Lightning Source LLC
Chambersburg PA
CBHW051355290426
44108CB00015B/2023